The Translator

E. TALBOT DONALDSON was Distinguished Professor of English Emeritus at Indiana University. His books include *Piers Plowman: The C-Text and Its Poets, Chaucer's Poetry: An Anthology for the Modern Reader, The Swan at the Well, Shakespeare Reading Chaucer,* and with George Kane, the definitive edition of *Piers Plowman: The B Version.* He was a founding editor of *The Norton Anthology of English Literature.*

The Editor

NICHOLAS HOWE is Director of the Center for Medieval and Renaissance Studies and Professor of English at The Ohio State University. He is the author of *The Old English Catalogue Poems: A Study in Poetic Form, Migration and Mythmaking in Anglo-Saxon England,* and of articles on medieval literature and travel writing.

W. W. NORTON & COMPANY, INC.
Also Publishes

THE NORTON ANTHOLOGY OF AFRICAN AMERICAN LITERATURE
edited by Henry Louis Gates Jr. and Nellie Y. McKay et al.

THE NORTON ANTHOLOGY OF AMERICAN LITERATURE
edited by Nina Baym et al.

THE NORTON ANTHOLOGY OF CONTEMPORARY FICTION
edited by R. V. Cassill and Joyce Carol Oates

THE NORTON ANTHOLOGY OF ENGLISH LITERATURE
edited by M. H. Abrams and Stephen Greenblatt et al.

THE NORTON ANTHOLOGY OF LITERATURE BY WOMEN
edited by Sandra M. Gilbert and Susan Gubar

THE NORTON ANTHOLOGY OF MODERN POETRY
edited by Richard Ellmann and Robert O'Clair

THE NORTON ANTHOLOGY OF POETRY
edited by Margaret Ferguson, Mary Jo Salter, and Jon Stallworthy

THE NORTON ANTHOLOGY OF SHORT FICTION
edited by R. V. Cassill and Richard Bausch

THE NORTON ANTHOLOGY OF THEORY AND CRITICISM
edited by Vincent B. Leitch et al.

THE NORTON ANTHOLOGY OF WORLD LITERATURE
edited by Sarah Lawall et al.

THE NORTON FACSIMILE OF THE FIRST FOLIO OF SHAKESPEARE
prepared by Charlton Hinman

THE NORTON INTRODUCTION TO LITERATURE
edited by Jerome Beaty, Alison Booth, J. Paul Hunter, and Kelly J. Mays

THE NORTON INTRODUCTION TO THE SHORT NOVEL
edited by Jerome Beaty

THE NORTON READER
edited by Linda H. Peterson, John C. Brereton, and Joan E. Hartman

THE NORTON SAMPLER
edited by Thomas Cooley

THE NORTON SHAKESPEARE, BASED ON THE OXFORD EDITION
edited by Stephen Greenblatt et al.

For a complete list of Norton Critical Editions, visit
www.wwnorton.com/college/english/nce.welcome.htm

A NORTON CRITICAL EDITION

BEOWULF
A PROSE TRANSLATION

BACKGROUNDS AND CONTEXTS
CRITICISM
SECOND EDITION

Translated by

E. TALBOT DONALDSON

LATE OF INDIANA UNIVERSITY

Edited by

NICHOLAS HOWE

THE OHIO STATE UNIVERSITY

W • W • NORTON & COMPANY • *New York* • *London*

The text of this book is composed in Electra with the display set in Bernhard Modern.
Composition by Publishing Synthesis Ltd., New York.
Book design by Antonina Krass.

Library of Congress Cataloging-in-Publication Data

Beowulf. English.
    Beowulf : a prose translation : contexts, criticism / translated by E. Talbot Donaldson ; edited by Nicholas Howe. – 2nd ed.
        p.   cm. — (A Norton critical edition)
        Includes bibliographical references.

    ISBN 0-393-97406-5 (pbk.)

    1. Epic poetry, English (Old)—History and criticism. 2. Epic poetry, English (Old)–Modernized versions. 3. Scandinavia—In literature. 4. Monsters in literature. 5. Dragons in literature. 6. Scandinavia-Poetry 7. Heroes in literature. 8. Monsters–Poetry. 9. Dragons—Poetry. 10. Heroes—Poetry. 11. Beowulf. 1. Donaldson, E. Talbot (Ethelbert Talbot), 1910–   II. Howe, Nicholas.   III. Title.

PR1583.D6 2001
829'.3 — dc21   2001030889

W. W. Norton & Company, Inc., 500 Fifth Avenue, New York, N.Y. 10110
                          www.wwnorton.com

W. W. Norton & Company Ltd., Castle House, 75/76 Wells Street, London W1T 3QT

                    3 4 5 6 7 8 9 0

Contents

Preface

Beowulf is the longest extant poem written in Old English or, as it is sometimes called, Anglo-Saxon. At 3,182 lines, *Beowulf* represents about 10 percent of the poetry that survives from the earliest stage of the English language, a period that lasted from about 600 to 1100 C.E. Some of the most basic facts we can know about any work of literature—who wrote it, and when, and where—elude us about *Beowulf*. Scholars have argued for generations about these matters, as is evident from some of the critical discussions included in this edition, but they have also agreed on the extraordinary qualities of the poem. For it is a remarkably vivid and powerful narrative of the hero Beowulf and the world he moves through as a slayer of monsters and ruler of his people.

The poem we call *Beowulf* survives in only one manuscript version, now housed in the British Library and known as Cotton Vitellius A.xv. The editions listed in the bibliography at the end of this volume have facsimile pages of the manuscript from which readers can gain some sense of how the poem appears in its original form, as they can from the reproduction on p. 55 below. Those familiar with beautiful illuminated manuscripts from the Anglo-Saxon period, such as the Lindisfarne Gospels, may well be surprised at how simple and unadorned the poem seems in Cotton Vitellius. Yet this manuscript is a very precious relic, for had it not survived through the centuries after it was written, which was most likely in the first quarter of the eleventh century, we would know nothing of *Beowulf*.

Cotton Vitellius A.xv. is one of four great manuscripts containing Old English poetry to survive. The others are known as the Exeter Book, after the city in southwestern England where it has long rested; the Vercelli Book, after the city in northern Italy where it was found in the nineteenth century; and the Junius Manuscript, after the Dutch scholar who edited its contents in 1654. Each of these four manuscripts dates to within a generation or so of the year 1000 C.E., and each is written chiefly in the dialect of Old English known as Late West Saxon. While we can roughly date the time when the poems were written down in these manuscripts, we cannot know with much confidence when any one of the poems was first composed. Some may go back hundreds of years to the seventh century, and some of them surely had their origin in the oral poetry of the Anglo-Saxons. Others seem likely to have been first com-

posed as written poems, even if they also display such features of oral
poetry as alliteration and formulaic diction.

The first complete edition of *Beowulf* appeared in 1815, and the first
translation into Modern English was published in 1837. The poem
was, for all intents and purposes, almost unknown between the end of
the Anglo-Saxon period and the early nineteenth century. Unlike other
medieval works, such as Geoffrey Chaucer's *Canterbury Tales*, *Beowulf*
was not read continuously over the centuries. Indeed, it has entered
the canon of English literature only in the last 150 years or so. Since
the first translation of the poem into English, there have been at least
sixty later versions, as well as renderings into many other modern
European languages. The translation presented in this edition, by the
late E. Talbot Donaldson, was first published in 1966. At least a dozen
others have appeared in the intervening years, including highly read-
able poetic versions by Seamus Heaney, R. M. Liuzza, and Kevin
Crossley-Holland, as well as the well-known novel by John Gardner
entitled *Grendel*. Those who find the poem compelling and moving
but who cannot read it in the original might want to explore it by com-
paring several different modern versions. If no single translation can
fully capture a poem as subtle as *Beowulf*, several different versions can,
when read together, give one something approaching the experience
of knowing the poem in the original.

Among the many available versions of *Beowulf*, the Donaldson trans-
lation has achieved a notable position and an enduring value within the
study of English literature. First done for the widely used *Norton
Anthology of English Literature*, it has been published separately and as
a Norton Critical Edition in 1975, edited by Joseph F. Tuso. During the
last third of the twentieth century, thousands—perhaps hundreds of
thousands—of readers first met *Beowulf* in the Donaldson version, and
they were well served by its faithful, accurate, and deeply informed prose
version of the original poem. No doubt some qualities of the poem must
inevitably be lost by any rendering into prose, but much can also be
gained. In the case of Donaldson's version, what is gained is a strong
sense of the poem's forward motion from the exploits of the young
Beowulf in Denmark to his long rule and death at home in Geatland.
Moreover, Donaldson was remarkably adept at capturing the verbal tex-
ture of the poem, especially its use of variation, in a type of Modern
English that was clearly that of the second half of the twentieth century.
He avoids the cuteness or pseudomedieval English that mars many older
translations of *Beowulf*.

A personal testimonial may help make my point about the abiding
value of Donaldson's work. I first read *Beowulf* as an undergraduate in the
early 1970s in a rather overblown poetic version that gave little sense of
the poem's subtlety. Only after reading Donaldson's translation did I
understand that *Beowulf* was a sophisticated poem and not at all the work

of a primitive bard of the Dark Ages. From reading Donaldson's transla-
tion, I turned to studying Old English and have been teaching it to stu-
dents for more than twenty years. Through these years, Donaldson's ver-
sion has remained for me the prose translation of choice, the one that I
recommend to students, colleagues, friends, and strangers when asked to
suggest a readable and literal rendition of *Beowulf.*

As *Beowulf* has yielded a wide variety of translations over the years, so
it has given rise to a staggering amount of scholarship and criticism. The
various bibliographies cited at the end of this volume will allow readers
to gain a sense of how much has been written on the poem over the last
two centuries. In preparing this new Norton Critical Edition of *Beowulf,*
I have set certain terms for choosing critical articles. I have included
only complete pieces, whether first published as articles or as chapters
in books, so that readers can gain a full understanding of each critic's
interpretation of *Beowulf.* They thus will not need to fill in the gaps that
inevitably come with any abridgment or excerpting, no matter how skill-
fully done, of a critical piece. I have also limited the selection to studies
published since 1980 so that readers can be exposed to the current con-
versation in the field about *Beowulf.* But it should be stressed that much
work of enduring value on *Beowulf* was published before 1980. Some of
these studies are cited in the bibliography. More specifically, readers
interested in earlier monuments of *Beowulf* scholarship would do well to
read through previous collections of critical readings prepared by
Donald K. Fry, Lewis E. Nicholson, Harold Bloom, R. D. Fulk, and
Peter S. Baker (as listed in the bibliography). If there were one early crit-
ical work on *Beowulf* that most scholars would cite as essential, it would
unquestionably be J. R. R. Tolkien's "*Beowulf*: The Monsters and the
Critics," first published in 1936 and frequently reprinted. Readers who
know Tolkien as a fiction writer will not be entirely surprised by this
essay, for it displays his expertise as an Anglo-Saxonist.

The critical essays collected in this volume offer a wide range of ways to
read *Beowulf.* Fred C. Robinson demonstrates how careful attention to
the poet's use of apposition, the artful arrangement of synonymous words
or phrases, helps to carry the large thematic concerns of the poem. The
retrospective quality of the poem, the fact that it looks back to an earlier
time in the history of the Germanic tribes, is explored subtly by Roberta
Frank in her discussion of the poet's sense of history. The diverse ways in
which *Beowulf* does cultural work by depicting forms of social communi-
ty and folkloric belief systems are treated by John D. Niles through the
concept of what he terms "social praxis." In a more psychological reading
of the poem, Michael Lapidge focuses on how it creates and sustains the
element of terror that is, at least in part, responsible for its immediate
appeal as a work of literature. In this study, Lapidge also introduces the
reader to Scandinavian poetry that can be seen as culturally analogous to
Beowulf. In another wide-ranging study, Joyce Hill traces representations

of women in *Beowulf* and other Old English poems in order to debunk stereotypes about them and, yet more important, to suggest how they are to be understood within a larger cultural context. Helen Bennett continues the examination of women and their representation in *Beowulf* by concentrating on a brief and highly puzzling passage. Through this study, the reader will gain a better sense of the difficulties presented by the damaged manuscript of the poem as well as some of the fruitful ways in which contemporary feminist theory may be used to read *Beowulf*. In the final essay, I turn to the problematic issue of dating *Beowulf* and its consequences for how we interpret the poem.

In order to assist readers, I have supplied annotations for technical terms and historical figures that may require explanation. I have also supplied translations of Old English and Latin passages where necessary; these translations appear in square brackets following the passages. I have used the translation by E. Talbot Donaldson for passages of a line or longer from *Beowulf*. A list of abbreviations used throughout this volume for titles of periodicals and dictionaries as well as for linguistic terms appears on pages xv–xvi. Readers should be aware that all line references to *Beowulf* follow the same sequence, so they can locate passages quoted or cited in the critical essays by consulting the running heads given with the translation.

Preparing this volume for publication has pleasantly reminded me that scholarship is a collaborative event. Let me therefore acknowledge with gratitude the encouragement offered to me by the late Joseph F. Tuso, the editor of the first Norton Critical Edition of *Beowulf*, and Carol Bemis of W. W. Norton, who guided my work with patience and discretion. In selecting the critical essays to be used for this edition, I had the great good fortune to have had the advice of Thomas A. Bredehoft, Roberta Frank, Stacy S. Klein, Katherine O'Brien O'Keeffe, Fred C. Robinson, and Alice Sheppard. Thanks are due as well to Timothy J. Lundgren, Robin J. Norris, Dana Oswald, and Cynthia Wittman Zollinger for continually reminding me of how exciting and subtle is this poem we call *Beowulf*. Robert Davis helped me collect materials for this edition and also spent hours with me discussing the articles to be included. I owe him thanks for his care and dedication. For his appointment as my research assistant, I express my gratitude to the English Department at The Ohio State University and its chair, James Phelan.

My deepest debt is to the many students with whom I have read *Beowulf* over the years. Their love for the poem has been sustaining to me as a teacher and scholar, as have their hard questions about it. To them I dedicate this critical edition of *Beowulf*.

The Translation[†]

The chief purpose of this translation is to try to preserve for the reader what the translator takes to be the most striking characteristic of the style of the original: extraordinary richness of rhetorical elaboration alternating with—often combined with—the barest simplicity of statement. The effect of this, impressive though it is, is difficult to analyze; perhaps the principal thing it accomplishes is to keep us constantly aware that while the aspirations of the people concerned are high-heroic, the people themselves are merely people—men with almost all the limitations (Beowulf's great physical strength is an exception) of ordinary mortals. That is, men may rise to the heroism of the rhetorical style, but they are nevertheless always the human beings of the plain style. In order to try to reproduce this effect, it has seemed best to translate as literally as possible, confining oneself to the linguistic and intellectual structure of the original. It is perfectly true that a literal translation such as this is bound to result in a style of modern English prose that was never seen before on land or sea and is not apt to be again—a good example of what Ben Jonson would surely call "no language." But no received English style that I know, modern or archaic, sounds anything like *Beowulf*: there seems to be no accepted alternate to a literal rendering.

For a good many years prose translators of *Beowulf* chose to use a "heroic" style which at least sounded archaic, for it borrowed liberally from Milton, Pope, Shakespeare, and the King James Bible, as well as from later imitators of these. A good many serviceable translations were thus produced, but in general the homogeneousness of their style necessarily proved false to the original by elevating even its simplest statements into highly adorned ones: the hero can perform the commonest actions—like sitting down—only by means of an elaborate periphrasis. More recent translators have eschewed the artificiality of such style and have rendered the poem into what is called "modern colloquial English." This has resulted in bringing out very effectively the starker side of the poem, its understatements and its directness, but has also given the unfortunate impression that the heavily rhetorical side is

† From *Beowulf*, a new prose translation by E. Talbot Donaldson, pp. xii–xv by E. T. Donaldson. Revised for this edition in 1975. Copyright © 1966 by W. W. Norton & Company, Inc. Reprinted by permission of the publisher.

excrescent and unnecessary: heaped-up epithets are reduced, like fractions to be simplified, to one or two terms, the "whale-road" is resolved into what it surely is, the sea, and "þæt wæs god cyning" becomes, colloquially but rather donnishly, "He was an excellent king." Decorum expects translators to maintain a consistent point of view through their style, but the *Beowulf* poet (along with most great poets) forges a complex style that simultaneously discloses differing aspects of the same situation; lacking his vision and his language (not to mention his talent), we tend to emphasize one aspect at the expense of the other.

One sentence will illustrate the kind of difficulty the translator of *Beowulf* constantly encounters. It occurs during the hero's fight with Grendel's mother in her underwater hall. The sword Hrunting has failed him; he has grappled with the monster-woman and thrown her to the floor; then he himself stumbles and falls. At this point the poet says, "Ofsæt þa þone selegyst": "Then she sat upon the hall-guest." This is a reasonable action, for she is much bigger than he, and is preparing to stab him. Yet if one is using a consistently heroic style, the simple verb "sat"—especially in juxtaposition with the seemingly "epic" epithet "hall-guest"—will simply not do; in order to preserve the translator's and the hero's dignity, Grendel's mother must throw, hurl, fling, or otherwise precipitate herself upon her adversary. If, on the other hand, one is using the colloquial style, then "hall-guest" is an embarrassment, and one is apt to go through the (perfectly correct) semantic process of *hall-guest = hall-visitor* or *hall-stranger = visitor* or *stranger in the hall = intruder*. And "intruder" is in many ways quite satisfactory, but it lacks whatever potential for quick, grim humor the expression "hall-guest" has. Surely something specious has been added if Grendel's mother acts more dramatically than just sitting upon Beowulf, and something good has been lost if he becomes other than a hall-guest.

An honest translator must confess that while he has tried to avoid the defects of his predecessors, he has probably introduced defects of which they were free. My resolute avoidance of such terms as bill, buckler, and byrnie undoubtedly gives the impression that the poet's vocabulary was limited in words for sword, shield, and mailshirt: actually it was so rich that bill, buckler, and byrnie lend only paltry, stopgap aid, and I have thought it better to make the poet monotonous than quaint. At times I have been guiltily aware that an Old English word might be more exactly translated by a polysyllabic Latinate synonym than by the word's modern English monosyllabic descendant which I have preferred, but one is so often absolutely compelled to use Latinisms that I have tried to avoid them whenever there was the slightest possibility of doing so. With words whose potential translations range from the colorless to the highly colored—such as "man: warrior: hero"—I have generally preferred the more modest of the alternates, though it might be argued that I have thus behaved anti-heroically. I am not sure that my feeling that *thou* and *thee* are inappropriate in a modern translation may not be idiosyncratic, but it has at least enabled me to evade such monstrosities as "thou achievedest." I am sorry we have lost the interjection "lo" from modern English: it is enormously useful, and hard to get around for Old English *hwæt*, though I have got around it when I could. While my translation is not intended to be in purely "natural" English, I have avoided unnatural expressions unless they performed some function in rendering the Old English style.

I cannot boast that I have been able to resolve with entire honesty every dilemma presented by the original. Like most translators, I have put in proper names in some places where the poet used only pronouns, have occasionally changed difficult constructions to easy ones, and have altered word order—and thus the poet's emphasis—in sentences where to preserve the literal would be to obscure the sense. I have also occasionally introduced glosses into the text. For instance, after the Danes and Geats have journeyed from Heorot to Grendel's mere and have found it boiling with blood—and Aeschere's head upon the shore—the poet says, "Again and again the horn sang its urgent war-song. The whole troop sat down." Seen from a realistic point of view, there is nothing surprising about this: the warriors have had a hard trip, and nothing is, for the moment, to be gained by remaining standing. Yet even one who believes that heroic warriors need not always be in furious motion experiences a sense of anticlimax here, and I have wilfully added a gloss: "The whole troop sat down to rest." A problem of a different sort, to be solved only by suppression of sense, occurs in the Danish coast-guard's speech to the arriving Geats. After marveling at their boldness and warlike appearance, he says to them (literally): "Hear my simple thought: haste is best to make known whence your comings are." The thought is, indeed, simple enough, but the expression is highly elaborate, a plain question put in a most formal way that shows at once respect for and defiance of the Geatish warriors. I know of no way to render such shades of meaning in modern English, and my translation makes of the coast-guard a plainer, blunter man than the poet probably conceived. In general I hope, however, that I have not played false too often, and that the reader unfamiliar with Old English may derive from this translation some real sense of the poem's extraordinary qualities. I have eschewed verse in the same hope, for I am persuaded that only a prose translation, made with no other end in mind than fidelity to the original, can bring out the distinctive qualities of the work. To make it a modern poem is, inevitably, to make it a different poem. The author of one of the best verse translations of *Beowulf* emphasizes that "a creative re-creation [i.e., a poetic translation] is a creation"; no two creative artists can create the same thing. If, on the other hand, a verse translation does not try to be a poem in its own right, then it can only be versification, a literal rendering constantly distracted from literalism by the need to versify, as a more creative translation is constantly distracted from literalism by the translator's creativity. Rather than try to create a new and lesser poem for the reader, it seems better to offer him in prose the literal materials from which he can re-create the poem.

I should like to thank Miss Mary Carruthers for her great help in checking the translation, correcting errors, and suggesting improvements. To several of my friends who are enormously learned in Old English I am also much indebted for their patient kindness in answering my sometimes naïve questions, but since they did not see the manuscript, I shall not embarrass them by naming them. Two colleagues who did see the manuscript—William Wiatt of Indiana and Albert H. Marckwardt of Princeton—offered most helpful suggestions; I am grateful, both for those that I used and those that I didn't. I tried not to consult other translations during the course of my own work (except in the case of several venerable cruxes), but I was familiar with several of them—especially Clark Hall's—before I began, and I know that they often helped me when I was not aware of their doing so. The translation is based on F. Klaeber's third edition of the poem (1950); in general, the emendations suggested by J. C. Pope, *The Rhythm of Beowulf,* second edition (1966), have been adopted.

E. TALBOT DONALDSON

Abbreviations

The following abbreviations for linguistic terms are used throughout this volume. Words marked with an asterisk (*) in the critical essays are hypothetical or reconstructed forms and are not attested in surviving texts.

eWS	Early West Saxon
ME	Middle English
ModE	Modern English
MS	Manuscript (plural: MSS)
OE	Old English
OHG	Old High German
ON	Old Norse

The following abbreviations for journal and book titles are used throughout this volume.

ASE	*Anglo-Saxon England*
BTD	Bosworth and Toller, *An Anglo-Saxon Dictionary* (3 vols.)
CL	*Comparative Literature*
CSEL	Corpus Scriptorum Ecclesiasticorum Latinorum
DAEM	*Deutsches Archiv für Erforschung des Mittelalters*
EETS	Early English Text Society
ES	*English Studies*
EStn	*Englische Studien*
JEGP	*Journal of English and Germanic Philology*
MGH	Monumenta Germaniae Historica
MHRA Bulletin	*Modern Humanities Research Association Bulletin*
MLN	*Modern Languages Notes*
MP	*Modern Philology*
NED	*New English Dictionary* (now called the *Oxford English Dictionary*)
NM	*Neuphilologische Mitteilungen*
PBA	*Proceedings of the British Academy*
PL	*Patrologiae Cursus Completus, Series Latina*
PMLA	*Publications of the Modern Language Association*
RES	*Review of English Studies*

SBVS   *Saga Book of the Viking Society of Northern*
                  Research
SP   *Studies in Philology*
TRHS   *Transactions of the Royal Historical Society*
TSLL   *Texas Studies in Language and Literature*

The Text of
BEOWULF

Beowulf

[*Prologue: The Earlier History of the Danes*]

Yes, we have heard of the glory of the Spear-Danes' kings in the old days—how the princes of that people did brave deeds.

Often Scyld Scefing[1] took mead-benches away from enemy bands, from many tribes, terrified their nobles—after the time that he was first found helpless.[2] He lived to find comfort for that, became great under the skies, prospered in honors until every one of those who lived about him, across the whale-road,[3] had to obey him, pay him tribute. That was a good king.

Afterwards a son was born to him, a young boy in his house, whom God sent to comfort the people: He had seen the sore need they had suffered during the long time they lacked a king. Therefore the Lord of Life, the Ruler of Heaven, gave him honor in the world: Beow[4] was famous, the glory of the son of Scyld spread widely in the Northlands. In this way a young man ought by his good deeds, by giving splendid gifts while still in his father's house, to make sure that later in life beloved companions will stand by him, that people will serve him when war comes. Through deeds that bring praise, a man shall prosper in every country.

Then at the fated time Scyld the courageous went away into the protection of the Lord. His dear companions carried him down to the sea-currents, just as he himself had bidden them do when, as protector of the Scyldings,[5] he had ruled them with his words—long had the beloved prince governed the land. There in the harbor stood the ring-prowed ship, ice-covered and ready to sail, a prince's vessel. Then they laid down the ruler they had loved, the ring-giver,[6] in the hollow of the ship, the glorious man beside the mast. There was brought great store of treasure, wealth from lands far away. I have not heard of a ship more splendidly

---

1. The meaning is probably "son of Sceaf," although Scyld's origins are mysterious.
2. As is made clear shortly below, Scyld arrived in Denmark as a child alone in a ship loaded with treasures.
3. A kenning, or metaphoric epithet, for the sea.
4. Although the manuscript reads "Beowulf," most scholars now agree that it should read "Beow." Beow was the grandfather of the Danish king Hrothgar.
5. I.e., the Danes ("descendants of Scyld").
6. A traditional epithet for a generous king or lord in Old English poetry.

furnished with war-weapons and battle-dress, swords and mail-shirts. On his breast lay a great many treasures that should voyage with him far out into the sea's possession. They provided him with no lesser gifts, treasure of the people, than those had done who at his beginning first sent him forth on the waves, a child alone. Then also they set a golden standard high over his head, let the water take him, gave him to the sea. Sad was their spirit, mournful their mind. Men cannot truthfully say who received that cargo, neither counselors in the hall nor warriors under the skies.

(I.)[7] Then in the cities was Beow of the Scyldings, beloved king of the people, long famous among nations (his father had gone elsewhere, the king from his land), until later great Healfdene was born to him. As long as he lived, old and fierce in battle, he upheld the glorious Scyldings. To him all told were four children born into the world, to the leader of the armies: Heorogar and Hrothgar and the good Halga. I have heard tell that [. . . was On]ela's queen,[8] beloved bed-companion of the Battle-Scylfing.

[Beowulf and Grendel]

[The Hall Heorot is Attacked by Grendel]

Then Hrothgar was given success in warfare, glory in battle, so that his retainers gladly obeyed him and their company grew into a great band of warriors. It came to his mind that he would command men to construct a hall, a mead-building large[r] than the children of men had ever heard of, and therein he would give to young and old all that God had given him, except for common land and men's bodies.[9] Then I have heard that the work was laid upon many nations, wide through this middle-earth,[1] that they should adorn the folk-hall. In time it came to pass—quickly, as men count it—that it was finished, the largest of hall-dwellings. He gave it the name of Heorot,[2] he who ruled wide with his words. He did not forget his promise: at the feast he gave out rings, treasure. The hall stood tall, high and wide-gabled: it would wait for the fierce flames of vengeful fire;[3] the time was not yet at hand for

---

7. The numbering of sections is that of the manuscript, which makes, however, no provision for Section XXX.
8. The text is faulty, so that the name of Healfdene's daughter has been lost; her husband, Onela, was a Swedish (Scylfing) king.
9. Or "men's lives." Apparently slaves, along with public land, were not in the king's power to give away.
1. In traditional Germanic cosmology, "middle-earth" is the region inhabited by human beings.
2. I.e., "Hart."
3. The destruction by fire of Heorot occurred at a later time than that of the poem's action, probably during the otherwise unsuccessful attack of the Heatho-Bard Ingeld on his father-in-law, Hrothgar, mentioned in the next clause.

sword-hate between son-in-law and father-in-law to awaken after murderous rage.

Then the fierce spirit[4] painfully endured hardship for a time, he who dwelt in the darkness, for every day he heard loud mirth in the hall; there was the sound of the harp, the clear song of the scop.[5] There he spoke who could relate the beginning of men far back in time, said that the Almighty made earth, a bright field fair in the water that surrounds it, set up in triumph the lights of the sun and the moon to lighten landdwellers, and adorned the surfaces of the earth with branches and leaves, created also life for each of the kinds that move and breathe.—Thus these warriors lived in joy, blessed, until one began to do evil deeds, a hellish enemy. The grim spirit was called Grendel, known as a rover of the borders, one who held the moors, fen and fastness. Unhappy creature, he lived for a time in the home of the monsters' race, after God had condemned them as kin of Cain. The Eternal Lord avenged the murder in which he slew Abel. Cain had no pleasure in that feud, but He banished him far from mankind, the Ruler, for that misdeed. From him sprang all bad breeds, trolls and elves and monsters—likewise the giants who for a long time strove with God: He paid them their reward for that.

(II.) Then, after night came, Grendel went to survey the tall house— how, after their beer-drinking, the Ring-Danes had disposed themselves in it. Then he found therein a band of nobles asleep after the feast: they felt no sorrow, no misery of men. The creature of evil, grim and fierce, was quickly ready, savage and cruel, and seized from their rest thirty thanes. From there he turned to go back to his home, proud of his plunder, sought his dwelling with that store of slaughter.

Then in the first light of dawning day Grendel's war-strength was revealed to men: then after the feast weeping arose, great cry in the morning. The famous king, hero of old days, sat joyless; the mighty one suffered, felt sorrow for his thanes, when they saw the track of the foe, of the cursed spirit: that hardship was too strong, too loathsome and longlasting. Nor was there a longer interval, but after one night Grendel again did greater slaughter—and had no remorse for it—vengeful acts and wicked: he was too intent on them. Thereafter it was easy to find the man who sought rest for himself elsewhere, farther away, a bed among the outlying buildings—after it was made clear to him, told by clear proof, the hatred of him who now controlled the hall.[6] Whoever escaped the foe held himself afterwards farther off and more safely. Thus Grendel held sway and fought against right, one against all, until the best of houses stood empty. It was a long time, the length of twelve winters, that the lord of the Scyldings suffered grief, all woes, great sorrows.

variation

litotes

---

4. I.e., Grendel.
5. The "scop" was the Anglo-Saxon minstrel, who recited poetic stories to the accompaniment of a harp.
6. I.e., Grendel.

Therefore, sadly in songs, it became well-known to the children of men that Grendel had fought a long time with Hrothgar, for many half-years maintained mortal spite, feud, and enmity—constant war. He wanted no peace with any of the men of the Danish host, would not withdraw his deadly rancor, or pay compensation: no counselor there had any reason to expect splendid repayment at the hands of the slayer.[7] For the monster was relentless, the dark death-shadow, against warriors old and young, lay in wait and ambushed them. In the perpetual darkness he held to the misty moors: men do not know where hell-demons direct their footsteps.

Thus many crimes the enemy of mankind committed, the terrible walker-alone, cruel injuries one after another. In the dark nights he dwelt in Heorot, the richly adorned hall. He might not approach the throne, [receive] treasure, because of the Lord; He had no love for him.[8]

This was great misery to the lord of the Scyldings, a breaking of spirit. Many a noble sat often in council, sought a plan, what would be best for strong-hearted men to do against the awful attacks. At times they vowed sacrifices at heathen temples, with their words prayed that the soul-slayer[9] would give help for the distress of the people. Such was their custom, the hope of heathens; in their spirits they thought of Hell, they knew not the Ruler, the Judge of Deeds, they recognized not the Lord God, nor indeed did they know how to praise the Protector of Heaven, the glorious King. Woe is him who in terrible trouble must thrust his soul into the fire's embrace, hope for no comfort, not expect change. Well is the man who after his death-day may seek the Lord and find peace in the embrace of the Father.

[The Coming of Beowulf to Heorot]

(III.) So in the cares of his times the son of Healfdene constantly brooded, nor might the wise warrior set aside his woe. Too harsh, hateful, and long-lasting was the hardship that had come upon the people, distress dire and inexorable, worst of night-horrors.

A thane of Hygelac,[1] a good man among the Geats, heard in his homeland of Grendel's deeds: of mankind he was the strongest of might in the time of this life, noble and great. He bade that a good ship be made ready for him, said he would seek the war-king over the swan's road,[2] the famous prince, since he had need of men. Very little did wise

---

7. According to old Germanic law, a slayer could achieve peace with his victim's kinsmen only by paying them *wergild*, i.e., compensation for the life of the slain man.
8. Behind this obscure passage seems to lie the idea that Grendel, unlike Hrothgar's thanes, could not approach the throne to receive gifts from the king, having been condemned by God as an outlaw.
9. I.e., the Devil. Despite the following assertion that the Danes were heathen, their king, Hrothgar, speaks consistently as a Christian.
1. I.e., Beowulf the Great, whose king was Hygelac.
2. A kenning or truncated metaphor; the "swan's road" is the sea.

men blame him for that adventure, though he was dear to them; they urged the brave one on, examined the omens. From the folk of the Geats the good man had chosen warriors of the bravest that he could find; one of fifteen he led the way, the warrior sought the wooden ship, the sea-skilled one the land's edge. The time had come: the ship was on the waves, the boat under the cliff. The warriors eagerly climbed on the prow—the sea-currents eddied, sea against sand; men bore bright weapons into the ship's bosom, splendid armor. Men pushed the well-braced ship from shore, warriors on a well-wished voyage. Then over the sea-waves, blown by the wind, the foam-necked boat traveled, most like a bird, until at good time on the second day the curved prow had come to where the seafarers could see land, the sea-cliffs shine, towering hills, great headlands. Then was the sea crossed, the journey at end. Then quickly the men of the Geats climbed upon the shore, moored the wooden ship; mail-shirts rattled, dress for battle. They thanked God that the wave-way had been easy for them.

Then from the wall the Scyldings' guard who should watch over the sea-cliffs saw bright shields borne over the gangway, armor ready for battle; strong desire stirred him in mind to learn what the men were. He went riding on his horse to the shore, thane of Hrothgar, forcefully brandished a great spear in his hands, with formal words questioned them: "What are you, bearers of armor, dressed in mail-coats, who thus have come bringing a tall ship over the sea-road, over the water to this place? Lo, for a long time I have been guard of the coast, held watch by the sea so that no foe with a force of ships might work harm on the Danes' land: never have shield-bearers more openly undertaken to come ashore here; nor did you know for sure of a word of leave from our warriors, consent from my kinsmen. I have never seen a mightier warrior on earth than is one of you, a man in battle-dress. That is no retainer made to seem good by his weapons—unless his appearance belies him, his unequalled form. Now I must learn your lineage before you go any farther from here, spies on the Danes' land. Now you far-dwellers, sea-voyagers, hear what I think: you must straightway say where you have come from."

(IV.) To him replied the leader, the chief of the band unlocked his word-hoard: "We are men of the Geatish nation and Hygelac's hearth-companions. My father was well-known among the tribes, a noble leader named Ecgtheow. He lived many winters before he went on his way, an old man, from men's dwellings. Every wise man wide over the earth readily remembers him. Through friendly heart we have come to seek your lord, the son of Healfdene, protector of the people. Be good to us and tell us what to do: we have a great errand to the famous one, the king of the Danes. And I too do not think that anything ought to be kept secret: you know whether it is so, as we have indeed heard, that among the Scyldings I know not what foe, what dark doer of hateful deeds in the black nights, shows in terrible manner strange malice, injury and slaughter. In openness of heart I may teach Hrothgar remedy for that, how he, wise and good, shall overpower the foe—if change is ever to come to him, relief from evil's distress—and how his surging cares may be made to cool. Or else ever after he will suffer tribulations, constraint, while the best of houses remains there on its high place."

The guard spoke from where he sat on his horse, brave officer: "A sharp-witted shield-warrior who thinks well must be able to judge each of the two things, words and works. I understand this: that here is a troop friendly to the Scyldings' king. Go forward, bearing weapons and war-gear. I will show you the way; I shall also bid my fellow-thanes honorably to hold your boat against all enemies, your new-tarred ship on the sand, until again over the sea-streams it bears its beloved men to the Geatish shore, the wooden vessel with curved prow. May it be granted by fate that one who behaves so bravely pass whole through the battle-storm."

Then they set off. The boat lay fixed, rested on the rope, the deep-bosomed ship, fast at anchor. Boar-images[3] shone over cheek-guards gold-adorned, gleaming and fire-hardened—the war-minded boar held guard over fierce men. The warriors hastened, marched together until they might see the timbered hall, stately and shining with gold; for earth-dwellers under the skies that was the most famous of buildings in which the mighty one waited—its light gleamed over many lands. The battle-brave guide pointed out to them the shining house of the brave ones so that they might go straight to it. Warrior-like he turned his horse, then spoke words: "It is time for me to go back. The All-Wielding Father in His grace keep you safe in your undertakings. I shall go back to the sea to keep watch against hostile hosts."

(V.) The road was stone-paved, the path showed the way to the men in ranks. War-corselet shone, hard and hand-wrought, bright iron rings sang on their armor when they first came walking to the hall in their grim gear. Sea-weary they set down their broad shields, marvelously strong protections, against the wall of the building. Then they sat down on the bench—mail-shirts, warrior's clothing, rang out. Spears stood together, seamen's weapons, ash steel-gray at the top. The armed band was worthy of its weapons.

Then a proud-spirited man[4] asked the warriors there about their lineage: "Where do you bring those gold-covered shields from, gray mail-shirts and visored helmets, this multitude of battle-shafts? I am Hrothgar's herald and officer. I have not seen strangers—so many men—more bold. I think that it is for daring—not for refuge, but for greatness of heart—that you have sought Hrothgar." The man known for his courage replied to him; the proud man of the Geats, hardy under helmet, spoke words in return: "We are Hygelac's table-companions.

---

3. Carved images of boars (sometimes represented as clothed like human warriors) were placed on helmets in the belief that they would protect the wearer in battle.
4. Identified below as Wulfgar.

Beowulf is my name. I will tell my errand to Healfdene's son, the great prince your lord, if, good as he is, he will grant that we might address him." Wulfgar spoke—he was a man of the Wendels, his bold spirit known to many, his valor and wisdom: "I will ask the lord of the Danes about this, the Scyldings' king, the ring-giver, just as you request—will ask the glorious ruler about your voyage, and will quickly make known to you the answer the good man thinks best to give me."

He returned at once to where Hrothgar sat, old and hoary, with his company of earls. The man known for his valor went forward till he stood squarely before the Danes' king: he knew the custom of tried retainers. Wulfgar spoke to his lord and friend: "Here have journeyed men of the Geats, come far over the sea's expanse. The warriors call their chief Beowulf. They ask that they, my prince, might exchange words with you. Do not refuse them your answer, gracious Hrothgar. From their war-gear they seem worthy of earls' esteem. Strong indeed is the chief who has led the warriors here."

(VI.) Hrothgar spoke, protector of the Scyldings: "I knew him when he was a boy. His father was called Ecgtheow: Hrethel of the Geats[5] gave him his only daughter for for his home. Now has his hardy offspring come here, sought a fast friend. Then, too, seafarers who took gifts there to please the Geats used to say that he has in his handgrip the strength of thirty men, a man famous in battle. Holy God of His grace has sent him to us West-Danes, as I hope, against the terror of Grendel. I shall offer the good man treasures for his daring. Now make haste, bid them come in together to see my company of kinsmen. In your speech say to them also that they are welcome to the Danish people."

Then Wulfgar went to the hall's door, gave the message from within: "The lord of the East-Danes, my victorious prince, has bidden me say to you that he knows your noble ancestry, and that you brave-hearted men are welcome to him over the sea-swells. Now you may come in your war-dress, under your battle helmets, to see Hrothgar. Let your war-shields, your wooden spears, await here the outcome of the talk."

Then the mighty one rose, many a warrior about him, a company of strong thanes. Some waited there, kept watch over the weapons as the brave one bade them. Together they hastened, as the warrior directed them, under Heorot's roof. The war-leader, hardy under helmet, advanced till he stood on the hearth. Beowulf spoke, his mail-shirt glistened, armor-net woven by the blacksmith's skill: "Hail, Hrothgar! I am kinsman and thane of Hygelac. In my youth I have set about many brave deeds. The affair of Grendel was made known to me on my native soil: sea-travelers say that this hall, best of buildings, stands empty and useless to all warriors after the evening-light becomes hidden beneath the cover of the sky. Therefore my people, the best wise earls, advised me thus,

5. Hrethel was the father of Hygelac and Beowulf's grandfather and guardian.

lord Hrothgar, that I should seek you because they know what my
strength can accomplish. They themselves looked on when, bloody from
my foes, I came from the fight where I had bound five, destroyed a fam-
ily of giants, and at night in the waves slain water-monsters, suffered
great pain, avenged an affliction of the Weather-Geats on those who had
asked for trouble—ground enemies to bits. And now alone I shall settle
affairs with Grendel, the monster, the demon. Therefore, lord of the
Bright-Danes, protector of the Scyldings, I will make a request of you,
refuge of warriors, fair friend of nations, that you refuse me not, now that
I have come so far, that alone with my company of earls, this band of
hardy men, I may cleanse Heorot. I have also heard say that the monster
in his recklessness cares not for weapons. Therefore, so that my liege
lord[6] Hygelac may be glad of me in his heart, I scorn to bear sword or
broad shield, yellow wood, to the battle, but with my grasp I shall grap-
ple with the enemy and fight for life, foe against foe. The one whom
death takes can trust the Lord's judgment. I think that if he may accom-
plish it, unafraid he will feed on the folk of the Geats in the war-hall as
he as often done on the flower of men. You will not need to hide my
head[7] if death takes me, for he will have me blood-smeared; he will bear
away my bloody flesh meaning to savor it, he will eat ruthlessly, the walk-
er alone, will stain his retreat in the moor; no longer will you need trou-
ble yourself to take care of my body. If battle takes me, send to Hygelac
the best of war-clothes that protects my breast, finest of mail-shirts. It is
a legacy of Hrethel, the work of Weland.[8] Fate always goes as it must."

(VII.) Hrothgar spoke, protector of the Scyldings: "For deeds done, my
friend Beowulf, and for past favors you have sought us. A fight of your
father's brought on the greatest of feuds. With his own hands he became
the slayer of Heatholaf among the Wylfings. After that the country of the
Weather-Geats might not keep him, for fear of war. From there he
sought the folk of the South-Danes, the Honor-Scyldings, over the sea-
swell. At that time I was first ruling the Danish people and, still in my
youth, held the wide kingdom, hoard-city of heroes. Heorogar had died
then, gone from life, my older brother, son of Healfdene—he was better
than I. Afterwards I paid blood-money to end the feud; over the sea's
back I sent to the Wylfings old treasures; he[9] swore oaths to me.

"It is a sorrow to me in spirit to say to any man what Grendel has
brought me with his hatred—humiliation in Heorot, terrible violence.
My hall-troop, warrior-band, has shrunk; fate has swept them away into
Grendel's horror. (God may easily put an end to the wild ravager's
deeds!) Full often over the ale-cups warriors made bold with beer have

6. The chieftain to whom a retainer swears allegiance and from whom he receives reward and
   protection.
7. I.e., "bury my body."
8. The blacksmith of the Norse gods.
9. Ecgtheow, whose feud with the Wylfings Hrothgar had settled.

boasted that they would await with grim swords Grendel's attack in the beer-hall. Then in the morning this mead-hall was a hall shining with blood, when the day lightened, all the bench-floor blood-wet, a gore-hall. I had fewer faithful men, beloved retainers, for death had destroyed them. Now sit down to the feast and unbind your thoughts, your famous victories, as heart inclines."

[The Feast at Heorot]

Then was a bench cleared in the beer-hall for the men of the Geats all together. Then the stout-hearted ones went to sit down, proud in their might. A thane did his work who bore in his hands an embellished ale-cup, poured the bright drink. At times a scop sang, clear-voiced in Heorot. There was joy of brave men, no little company of Danes and Weather-Geats.

(VIII.) Unferth spoke, son of Ecglaf, who sat at the feet of the king of the Scyldings, unbound words of contention—to him was Beowulf's undertaking, the brave seafarer, a great vexation, for he would not allow that any other man of middle-earth should ever achieve more glory under the heavens than himself: "Are you that Beowulf who contended with Breca, competed in swimming on the broad sea, where for pride you explored the water, and for foolish boast ventured your lives in the deep? Nor might any man, friend nor enemy, keep you from the perilous venture of swimming in the sea. There you embraced the sea-streams with your arms, measured the sea-ways, flung forward your hands, glided over the ocean; the sea boiled with waves, with winter's swell. Seven nights you toiled in the water's power. He overcame you at swimming, had more strength. Then in the morning the sea bore him up among the Heathoraemas; from there he sought his own home, dear to his people, the land of the Brondings, the fair stronghold, where he had folk, castle, and treasures. All his boast against you the son of Beanstan carried out in deed. Therefore I expect the worse results for you—though you have prevailed everywhere in battles, in grim war—if you dare wait near Grendel a night-long space."

Beowulf spoke, the son of Ecgtheow: "Well, my friend Unferth, drunk with beer you have spoken a great many things about Breca—told about his adventures. I maintain the truth that I had more strength in the sea, hardship on the waves, than any other man. Like boys we agreed together and boasted—we were both in our first youth—that we would risk our lives in the salt sea, and that we did even so. We had naked swords, strong in our hands, when we went swimming; we thought to guard ourselves against whale-fishes. He could not swim at all far from me in the flood-waves, be quicker in the water, nor would I move away from him. Thus we were together on the sea for the time of five nights until the flood drove us apart, the swelling sea, coldest of weathers, darkening night, and the north wind battle-grim turned against us: rough were the waves. The anger of the sea-fishes was roused. Then my body-mail, hard and hand-linked, gave me help against my foes; the woven war-garment, gold-adorned, covered my breast. A fierce cruel attacker dragged me to the bottom, held me grim in his grasp, but it was granted me to reach the monster with my sword-point, my battle-blade. The war-stroke destroyed the mighty sea-beast—through my hand.

(IX.) "Thus often loathsome assailants pressed me hard. I served them with my good sword, as the right was. They had no joy at all of the feast, the malice-workers, that they should eat me, sit around a banquet near the sea-bottom. But in the morning, sword-wounded they lay on the shore, left behind by the waves, put to sleep by the blade, so that thereafter they would never hinder the passage of sea-voyagers over the deep water. Light came from the east, bright signal of God, the sea became still so that I might see the headlands, the windy walls of the sea. Fate often saves an undoomed man when his courage is good. In any case it befell me that I slew with my sword nine sea-monsters. I have not heard tell of a harder fight by night under heaven's arch, nor of a man more hard-pressed in the sea-streams. Yet I came out of the enemies' grasp alive, weary of my adventure. Then the sea bore me onto the lands of the Finns, the flood with its current, the surging waters.

"I have not heard say of you any such hard matching of might, such sword-terror. Breca never yet in the games of war—neither he nor you—achieved so bold a deed with bright swords (I do not much boast of it), though you became your brothers' slayer, your close kin; for that you will suffer punishment in hell, even though your wit is keen. I tell you truly, son of Ecglaf, that Grendel, awful monster, would never have performed so many terrible deeds against your chief, humiliation in Heorot, if your spirit, your heart, were so fierce in fight as you claim. But he has noticed that he need not much fear the hostility, not much dread the terrible sword-storm of your people, the Victory-Scyldings. He exacts forced levy, shows mercy to none of the Danish people; but he is glad, kills, carves for feasting, expects no fight from the Spear-Danes. But I shall show him soon now the strength and courage of the Geats, their warfare. Afterwards he will walk who may, glad to the mead, when the morning light of another day, the bright-clothed sun, shines from the south on the children of men."

Then was the giver of treasure in gladness, gray-haired and battle-brave. The lord of the Bright-Danes could count on help. The folk's guardian had heard from Beowulf a fast-resolved thought.

There was laughter of warriors, voices rang pleasant, words were cheerful. Wealhtheow came forth, Hrothgar's queen, mindful of customs, gold-adorned, greeted the men in the hall; and the noble woman offered the cup first to the keeper of the land of the East-Danes, bade him be glad at the beer-drinking, beloved of the people. In joy he partook of feast and hall-cup, king famous for victories. Then the woman of the Helmings went about to each one of the retainers, young and old, offered them the costly cup, until the time came that she brought the mead-bowl to Beowulf, the ring-adorned queen, mature of mind. Sure of speech she greeted the man of the Geats, thanked God that her wish was fulfilled, that she might trust in some man for help against deadly deeds. He took the cup, the warrior fierce in battle, from Wealhtheow, and then spoke, one ready for fight—Beowulf spoke, the son of Ecgtheow: "I resolved, when I set out on the sea, sat down in the sea-boat with my band of men, that I should altogether fulfill the will of your people or else fall in slaughter, fast in the foe's grasp. I shall achieve a deed of manly courage or else have lived to see in this mead-hall my ending day." These words were well-pleasing to the woman, the boast of the Geat. Gold-adorned, the noble folk-queen went to sit by her lord.

Then there were again as at first strong words spoken in the hall, the people in gladness, the sound of a victorious folk, until, in a little while, the son of Healfdene wished to seek his evening rest. He knew of the battle in the high hall that had been plotted by the monster, plotted from the time that they might see the light of the sun until the night, growing dark over all things, the shadowy shapes of darkness, should come gliding, black under the clouds. The company all arose. Then they saluted each other, Hrothgar and Beowulf, and Hrothgar wished him good luck, control of the wine-hall, and spoke these words: "Never before, since I could raise hand and shield, have I entrusted to any man the great hall of the Danes, except now to you. Hold now and guard the best of houses: remember your fame, show your great courage, keep watch against the fierce foe. You will not lack what you wish if you survive that deed of valor."

[The Fight with Grendel]

(X.) Then Hrothgar went out of the hall with his company of warriors, the protector of the Scyldings. The war-chief would seek the bed of Wealhtheow the queen. The King of Glory—as men had learned—had appointed a hall-guard against Grendel; he had a special mission to the prince of the Danes: he kept watch against monsters.

And the man of the Geats had sure trust in his great might, the favor of the Ruler. Then he took off his shirt of armor, the helmet from his head, handed his embellished sword, best of irons, to an attendant, bade him keep guard over his war-gear. Then the good warrior spoke some boast-words before he went to his bed, Beowulf of the Geats: "I claim myself no poorer in war-strength, war works, than Grendel claims himself. Therefore I will not put him to sleep with a sword, so take away his life, though surely I might. He knows no good tools with which he might strike against me, cut my shield in pieces, though he is strong in fight.

But we shall forgo the sword in the night—if he dare seek war without weapon—and then may wise God, Holy Lord, assign glory on whichever hand seems good to Him."

The battle-brave one laid himself down, the pillow received the earl's head, and about him many a brave seaman lay down to hall-rest. None of them thought that he would ever again seek from there his dear home, people or town where he had been brought up; for they knew that bloody death had carried off far too many men in the wine-hall, folk of the Danes. But the Lord granted to weave for them good fortune in war, for the folk of the Weather-Geats, comfort and help that they should quite overcome their foe through the might of one man, through his sole strength: the truth has been made known that mighty God has always ruled mankind.

There came gliding in the black night the walker in darkness. The warriors slept who should hold the horned house—all but one. It was known to men that when the Ruler did not wish it the hostile creature might not drag them away beneath the shadows. But he, lying awake for the fierce foe, with heart swollen in anger awaited the outcome of the fight.

(XI.) Then from the moor under the mist-hills Grendel came walking, wearing God's anger. The foul ravager thought to catch some one of mankind there in the high hall. Under the clouds he moved until he could see most clearly the wine-hall, treasure-house of men, shining with gold. That was not the first time that he had sought Hrothgar's home. Never before or since in his life-days did he find harder luck, hardier hall-thanes. The creature deprived of joy came walking to the hall. Quickly the door gave way, fastened with fire-forged bands, when he touched it with his hands. Driven by evil desire, swollen with rage, he tore it open, the hall's mouth. After that the foe at once stepped onto the shining floor, advanced angrily. From his eyes came a light not fair, most like a flame. He saw many men in the hall, a band of kinsmen all asleep together, a company of war-men. Then his heart laughed: dreadful monster, he thought that before the day came he would divide the life from the body of every one of them, for there had come to him a hope of full-feasting. It was not his fate that when that night was over he should feast on more of mankind.

The kinsman of Hygelac, mighty man, watched how the evil-doer would make his quick onslaught. Nor did the monster mean to delay it, but, starting his work, he suddenly seized a sleeping man, tore at him ravenously, bit into his bone-locks, drank the blood from his veins, swallowed huge morsels; quickly he had eaten all of the lifeless one, feet and hands. He stepped closer, then felt with his arm for the brave-hearted man on the bed, reached out towards him, the foe with his hand; at once in fierce response Beowulf seized it and sat up, leaning on his own arm. Straightway the fosterer of crimes knew that he had not encountered on

middle-earth, anywhere in this world, a harder hand-grip from another
man. In mind he became frightened, in his spirit: not for that might he
escape the sooner. His heart was eager to get away, he would flee to his
hiding-place, seek his rabble of devils. What he met there was not such
as he had ever before met in the days of his life. Then the kinsman of
Hygelac, the good man, thought of his evening's speech, stood upright
and laid firm hold on him: his fingers cracked. The giant was pulling
away, the earl stepped forward. The notorious one thought to move far-
ther away, wherever he could, and flee his way from there to his fen-
retreat; he knew his fingers' power to be in a hateful grip. That was a
painful journey that the loathsome despoiler had made to Heorot. The
retainers' hall rang with the noise—terrible drink[1] for all the Danes, the
house-dwellers, every brave man, the earls. Both were enraged, fury-
filled, the two who meant to control the hall. The building resounded.
Then was it much wonder that the wine-hall withstood them joined in
fierce fight, that it did not fall to the ground, the fair earth-dwelling; but
it was so firmly made fast with iron bands, both inside and outside,
joined by skillful smith-craft. There started from the floor—as I have
heard say—many a mead-bench, gold-adorned, when the furious ones
fought. No wise men of the Scyldings ever before thought that any men
in any manner might break it down, splendid with bright horns, have
skill to destroy it, unless flame should embrace it, swallow it in fire.
Noise rose up, sound strange enough. Horrible fear came upon the
North-Danes, upon every one of those who heard the weeping from the
wall, God's enemy sing his terrible song, song without triumph—the
hell-slave bewail his pain. There held him fast he who of men was
strongest of might in the days of this life.

(XII.) Not for anything would the protector of warriors let the mur-
derous guest go off alive: he did not consider his life-days of use to any
of the nations. There more than enough of Beowulf's earls drew swords,
old heirlooms, wished to protect the life of their dear lord, famous
prince, however they might. They did not know when they entered the
fight, hardy-spirited warriors, and when they thought to hew him on every
side, to seek his soul, that not any of the best of irons on earth, no war-
sword, would touch the evil-doer: for with a charm he had made victory-
weapons useless, every sword-edge. His departure to death from the time
of this life was to be wretched; and the alien spirit was to travel far off
into the power of fiends. Then he who before had brought trouble of
heart to mankind, committed many crimes—he was at war with God—
found that his body would do him no good, for the great-hearted kins-
man of Hygelac had him by the hand. Each was hateful to the other
alive. The awful monster had lived to feel pain in his body, a huge

---

1. The metaphor reflects the idea that the chief purpose of a hall such as Heorot was as a place
   for men to feast in.

wound in his shoulder was exposed, his sinews sprang apart, his bone-
locks broke. Glory in battle was given to Beowulf. Grendel must flee
from there, mortally sick, seek his joyless home in the fen-slopes. He
knew the more surely that his life's end had come, the full number of his
days. For all the Danes was their wish fulfilled after the bloody fight.
Thus he who had lately come from far off, wise and stout-hearted, had
purged Heorot, saved Hrothgar's house from affliction. He rejoiced in
his night's work, a deed to make famous his courage. The man of the
Geats had fulfilled his boast to the East-Danes; so too he had remedied
all the grief, the malice-caused sorrow that they had endured before, and
had had to suffer from harsh necessity, no small distress. That was clear-
ly proved when the battle-brave man set the hand up under the curved
roof—the arm and the shoulder: there all together was Grendel's grasp.

[Celebration at Heorot]

(XIII.) Then in the morning, as I have heard, there was many a war-
rior about the gift-hall. Folk-chiefs came from far and near over the
wide-stretching ways to look on the wonder, the footprints of the foe.
Nor did his going from life seem sad to any of the men who saw the
tracks of the one without glory—how, weary-hearted, overcome with
injuries, he moved on his way from there to the mere[2] of the water-
monsters with life-failing footsteps, death-doomed and in flight. There
the water was boiling with blood, the horrid surge of waves swirling, all
mixed with hot gore, sword-blood. Doomed to die he had hidden, then,
bereft of joys, had laid down his life in his fen-refuge, his heathen soul:
there hell took him.

From there old retainers—and many a young man, too—turned back
in their glad journey to ride from the mere, high-spirited on horseback,
warriors on steeds. There was Beowulf's fame spoken of; many a man
said—and not only once—that, south nor north, between the seas, over
the wide earth, no other man under the sky's expanse was better of those
who bear shields, more worthy of ruling. Yet they found no fault with
their own dear lord, gracious Hrothgar, for he was a good king. At times
battle-famed men let their brown horses gallop, let them race where the
paths seemed fair, known for their excellence. At times a thane of the
king, a man skilled at telling adventures, songs stored in his memory,
who could recall many of the stories of the old days, wrought a new tale
in well-joined words; this man undertook with his art to recite in turn
Beowulf's exploit, and skillfully to tell an apt tale, to lend words to it.

He spoke everything that he had heard tell of Sigemund's valorous
deeds, many a strange thing, the strife of Waels's son,[3] his far journeys,
feuds, and crimes, of which the children of men knew nothing—except

2. Lake.
3. Waels was Sigemund's father.

for Fitela with him, to whom he would tell everything, the uncle to his nephew, for they were always friends in need in every fight. Many were the tribes of giants that they had laid low with their swords. For Sigemund there sprang up after his death-day no little glory—after he, hardy in war, had killed the dragon, keeper of the treasure-hoard: under the hoary stone the prince's son had ventured alone, a daring deed, nor was Fitela with him. Yet it turned out well for him, so that his sword went through the gleaming worm and stood fixed in the wall, splendid weapon: the dragon lay dead of the murdering stroke. Through his courage the great warrior had brought it about that he might at his own wish enjoy the ring-hoard. He loaded the sea-boat, bore into the ship's bosom the bright treasure, offspring of Waels. The hot dragon melted.

He was adventurer most famous, far and wide through the nations, for deeds of courage—he had prospered from that before, the protector of warriors—after the war-making of Heremod had come to an end, his strength and his courage.[4] Among the Jutes Heremod came into the power of his enemies, was betrayed, quickly dispatched. Surging sorrows had oppressed him too long: he had become a great care to his people, to all his princes; for many a wise man in former times had bewailed the journey of the fierce-hearted one—people who had counted on him as a relief from affliction—that that king's son should prosper, take the rank of his father, keep guard over the folk, the treasure and stronghold, the kingdom of heroes, the home of the Scyldings. The kinsman of Hygelac became dearer to his friends, to all mankind: crime took possession of Heremod.

Sometimes racing their horses they passed over the sand-covered ways. By then the morning light was far advanced, hastening on. Many a stout-hearted warrior went to the high hall to see the strange wonder. The king himself walked forth from the women's apartment, the guardian of the ring-hoards, secure in his fame, known for his excellence, with much company; and his queen with him passed over the path to the mead-hall with a troop of attendant women.

(XIV.) Hrothgar spoke—he had gone to the hall, taken his stand on the steps, looked at the high roof shining with gold, and at Grendel's hand: "For this sight may thanks be made quickly to the Almighty: I endured much from the foe, many griefs from Grendel: God may always work wonder upon wonder, the Guardian of Heaven. It was not long ago that I did not expect ever to live to see relief from any of my woes—when the best of houses stood shining with blood, stained with slaughter, a far-reaching woe for each of my counselors, for every one, since none thought he could ever defend the people's stronghold from its enemies, from demons and evil spirits. Now through the Lord's might a warrior

4. Heremod was an unsuccessful king of the Danes, one who began brilliantly but became cruel and avaricious, ultimately having to take refuge among the Jutes, who put him to death. His reputation was thus overshadowed by that of Sigemund.

has accomplished the deed that all of us with our skill could not per-
form. Yes, she may say, whatever woman brought forth this son among
mankind—if she still lives—that the God of Old was kind to her in her
child-bearing. Now, Beowulf, best of men, in my heart I will love you as
a son: keep well this new kinship. To you will there be no lack of the
good things of the world that I have in my possession. Full often I have
made reward for less, done honor with gifts to a lesser warrior, weaker in
fighting. With your deeds you yourself have made sure that your glory
will be ever alive. May the Almighty reward you with good—as just now
he has done."

Beowulf spoke, the son of Ecgtheow: "With much good will we have
achieved this work of courage, that fight, have ventured boldly against
the strength of the unknown one. I should have wished rather that you
might have seen him, your enemy brought low among your furnishings.
I thought quickly to bind him on his deathbed with hard grasp, so that
because of my hand-grip he should lie struggling for life—unless his
body should escape. I could not stop his going, since the Lord did not
wish it, nor did I hold him firmly enough for that, my life-enemy: he was
too strong, the foe in his going. Yet to save his life he has left his hand
behind to show that he was here—his arm and shoulder; nor by that has
the wretched creature bought any comfort; none the longer will the
loathsome ravager live, hard-pressed by his crimes, for a wound has
clutched him hard in its strong grip, in deadly bonds. There, like a man
outlawed for guilt, he shall await the great judgment, how the bright
Lord will decree for him."

Then was the warrior more silent in boasting speech of warlike deeds,
the son of Ecglaf,[5] after the nobles had looked at the hand, now high on
the roof through the strength of a man, the foe's fingers. The end of each
one, each of the nail-places, was most like steel; the hand-spurs of the
heathen warrior were monstrous spikes. Everyone said that no hard
thing would hurt him, no iron good from old times would harm the
bloody battle-hand of the monster.

(XV.) Then was it ordered that Heorot be within quickly adorned by
hands. Many there were, both men and women, who made ready the
wine-hall, the guest-building. The hangings on the walls shone with
gold, many a wondrous sight for each man who looks on such things.
That bright building was much damaged, though made fast within by
iron bonds, and its door-hinges sprung; the roof alone came through
unharmed when the monster, outlawed for his crimes, turned in flight,
in despair of his life. That is not easy to flee from—let him try it who
will—but driven by need one must seek the place prepared for earth-
dwellers, soul-bearers, the sons of men, the place where, after its feast-
ing, one's body will sleep fast in its deathbed.

---

5. I.e., Unferth, who had taunted Beowulf the night before.

Then had the proper time come that Healfdene's son should go to the hall; the king himself would share in the feast. I have never heard that a people in a larger company bore themselves better about their treasure-giver. Men who were known for courage sat at the benches, rejoiced in the feast. Their kinsmen, stout-hearted Hrothgar and Hrothulf, partook fairly of many a mead-cup in the high hall. Heorot within was filled with friends: the Scylding-people had not then known treason's web.[6]

Then the son of Healfdene gave Beowulf a golden standard to reward his victory—a decorated battle-banner—a helmet and mail-shirt: many saw the glorious, costly sword borne before the warrior. Beowulf drank of the cup in the mead-hall. He had no need to be ashamed before fighting men of those rich gifts. I have not heard of many men who gave four precious, gold-adorned things to another on the ale-bench in a more friendly way. The rim around the helmet's crown had a head-protection, wound of wire, so that no battle-hard sharp sword might badly hurt him when the shield-warrior should go against his foe. Then the people's protector commanded eight horses with golden bridles to be led into the hall, within the walls. The saddle of one of them stood shining with hand-ornaments, adorned with jewels: that had been the war-seat of the high king when the son of Healfdene would join sword-play: never did the warfare of the wide-known one fail when men died in battle. And then the prince of Ing's friend[7] yielded possession of both, horses and weapons, to Beowulf: he bade him use them well. So generously the famous prince, guardian of the hoard, repaid the warrior's battle-deeds with horses and treasure that no man will ever find fault with them—not he that will speak truth according to what is right.

(XVI.) Then further the lord gave treasure to each of the men on the mead-bench who had made the sea-voyage with Beowulf, gave heirlooms; and he commanded that gold be paid for the one whom in his malice Grendel had killed—as he would have killed more if wise God and the man's courage had not forestalled that fate. The Lord guided all the race of men then, as he does now. Yet is discernment everywhere best, forethought of mind. Many a thing dear and loath he shall live to see who here in the days of trouble long makes use of the world.

There was song and music together before Healfdene's battle-leader, the wooden harp touched, tale oft told, when Hrothgar's scop should speak hall-pastime among the mead-benches . . . [of] Finn's retainers when the sudden disaster fell upon them. . . .[8]

---

6. A reference to the later history of the Danes, when after Hrothgar's death, his nephew Hrothulf apparently drove his son and successor Hrethric from the throne.
7. Ing was a legendary Danish king, and his "friends" are the Danes.
8. The lines introducing the scop's song seem faulty. The story itself is recounted in a highly allusive way, and many of its details are obscure, though some help is offered by an independent version of the story given in a fragmentary Old English lay called *The Fight at Finnsburg*.

Hnaef + Hildeburch siblings

Hildeburch married to Finn as peace pledge

The hero of the Half-Danes, Hnaef of the Scyldings, was fated to fall on Frisian battlefield. And no need had Hildeburh[9] to praise the good faith of the Jutes: blameless she was deprived of her dear ones at the shield-play, of son and brother; wounded by spears they fell to their fate. That was a mournful woman. Not without cause did Hoc's daughter lament the decree of destiny when morning came and she might see, under the sky, the slaughter of kinsmen—where before she had the greatest of world's joy. The fight took away all Finn's thanes except for only a few, so that he could in no way continue the battle on the field against Hengest, nor protect the survivors by fighting against the prince's thane. But they offered them peace-terms,[1] that they should clear another building for them, hall and high seat, that they might have control of half of it with the sons of the Jutes; and at givings of treasure the son of Folcwalda[2] should honor the Danes each day, should give Hengest's company rings, such gold-plated treasure as that with which he would cheer the Frisians' kin in the high hall. Then on both sides they confirmed the fast peace-compact. Finn declared to Hengest, with oaths deep-sworn, unfeigned, that he would hold those who were left from the battle in honor in accordance with the judgment of his counselors, so that by words or by works no man should break the treaty nor because of malice should ever mention that, princeless, the Danes followed the slayer of their own ring-giver, since necessity forced them. If with rash speech any of the Frisians should insist upon calling to mind the cause of murderous hate, then the sword's edge should settle it.

The funeral pyre was made ready and gold brought up from the hoard. The best of the warriors of the War-Scyldings[3] was ready on the pyre. At the fire it was easy to see many a blood-stained battle-shirt, boar-image all golden—iron-hard swine—many a noble destroyed by wounds: more than one had died in battle. Then Hildeburh bade give her own son to the flames on Hnaef's pyre, burn his blood vessels, put him in the fire at the shoulder of his uncle. The woman mourned, sang her lament. The warrior took his place.[4] The greatest of death-fires wound to the skies, roared before the barrow. Heads melted as blood

---

9. Hildeburh, daughter of the former Danish king Hoc and sister of the ruling Danish king Hnaef, was married to Finn, king of the Jutes (Frisians). Hnaef with a party of Danes made what was presumably a friendly visit to Hildeburh and Finn at their home Finnsburg, but during a feast a quarrel broke out between the Jutes and the Danes (since the scop's sympathies are with the Danes, he ascribes the cause to the bad faith of the Jutes), and in the ensuing fight Hnaef and his nephew, the son of Finn and Hildeburh, were killed, along with many other Danes and Jutes.

1. It is not clear who proposed the peace terms, but in view of the teller's Danish sympathies, it was probably the Jutes that sought the uneasy truce from Hengest, who became the Danes' leader after Hnaef's death. The truce imposed upon Hengest and the Danes the intolerance condition of having to dwell in peace with the Jutish king who was responsible for the death of their own king.

2. I.e., Finn.

3. I.e., Hnaef.

4. The line is obscure, but it perhaps means that the body of Hildeburh's son was placed on the pyre.

sprang out—wounds opened wide, hate-bites of the body. Fire swal-
lowed them—greediest of spirits—all of those whom war had taken away
from both peoples: their strength had departed.

(XVII.) Then warriors went to seek their dwellings, bereft of friends,
to behold Friesland, their homes and high city.[5] Yet Hengest stayed on
with Finn for a winter darkened with the thought of slaughter, all deso-
late. He thought of his land, though he might not drive his ring-prowed
ship over the water—the sea boiled with storms, strove with the wind,
winter locked the waves in ice-bonds—until another year came to men's
dwellings, just as it does still, glorious bright weather always watching for
its time. Then winter was gone, earth's lap fair, the exile was eager to go,
the guest from the dwelling: [yet] more he thought of revenge for his
wrongs than of the sea-journey—if he might bring about a fight where
he could take account of the sons of the Jutes with his iron. So he made
no refusal of the world's custom when the son of Hunlaf[6] placed on his
lap Battle-Bright, best of swords: its edges were known to the Jutes. Thus
also to war-minded Finn in his turn cruel sword-evil came in his own
home, after Guthlaf and Oslaf complained of the grim attack, the injury
after the sea-journey, assigned blame for their lot of woes: breast might
not contain the restless heart. Then was the hall reddened from foes'
bodies, and thus Finn slain, the king in his company, and the queen
taken. The warriors of the Scyldings bore to ship all the hall-furnishings
of the land's king, whatever of necklaces, skillfully wrought treasures,
they might find at Finn's home. They brought the noble woman on the
sea-journey to the Danes, led her to her people. *all Hildeburh's family killed = goes home to Danes*

The lay was sung to the end, the song of the scop. Joy mounted again,
bench-noise brightened, cup-bearers poured wine from wonderful ves-
sels. Then Wealhtheow came forth to walk under gold crown to where *Hrothgar*
the good men sat, nephew and uncle: their friendship was then still *+ Hrothulf*
unbroken, each true to the other.[7] There too Unferth the spokesman sat
at the feet of the prince of the Scyldings: each of them trusted his spirit,
that he had much courage, though he was not honorable to his kinsmen
at sword-play. Then the woman of the Scyldings spoke:

"Take this cup my noble lord, giver of treasure. Be glad, gold-friend of
warriors, and speak to the Geats with mild words, as a man ought to do.
Be gracious to the Geats, mindful of gifts [which][8] you now have from
near and far. They have told me that you would have the warrior for your

5. This seems to refer to the few survivors on the Jutish side.
6. The text is open to various interpretations. The one adopted here assumes that the Dane
   Hunlaf, brother of Guthlaf and Oslaf, had been killed in the fight, and that ultimately Hunlaf's
   son demanded vengeance by the symbolical act of placing his father's sword in Hengest's lap,
   while at the same time Guthlaf and Oslaf reminded Hengest of the Jutes' treachery. It is not
   clear whether the subsequent fight in which Finn was killed was waged by the Danish survivors
   alone, or whether the party first went back to Denmark and then returned to Finnsburg with
   reinforcements.
7. See section XV, note 6, above.
8. The text seems corrupt.

son. Heorot is purged, the bright ring-hall. Enjoy while you may many
rewards, and leave to your kinsmen folk and kingdom when you must go
forth to look on the Ruler's decree. I know my gracious Hrothulf, that he
will hold the young warriors in honor if you, friend of the Scyldings,
leave the world before him. I think he will repay our sons with good if
he remembers all the favors we did to his pleasure and honor when he
was a child."

Then she turned to the bench where her sons were, Hrethric and
Hrothmund, and the sons of the warriors, young men together. There sat
the good man Beowulf of the Geats beside the two brothers.

(XVIII.) The cup was borne to him and welcome offered in friendly
words to him, and twisted gold courteously bestowed on him, two arm-
ornaments, a mail-shirt and rings, the largest of necklaces of those that I
have heard spoken of on earth. I have heard of no better hoard-treasure
under the heavens since Hama carried away to his bright city the neck-
lace of the Brosings,[9] chain and rich setting: he fled the treacherous
hatred of Eormenric, got eternal favor. This ring Hygelac of the Geats,[1]
grandson of Swerting, had on his last venture, when beneath his battle-
banner he defended his treasure, protected the spoils of war: fate took
him when for pride he sought trouble, feud with the Frisians. Over the
cup of the waves the mighty prince wore that treasure, precious stone.
He fell beneath his shield; the body of the king came into the grasp of
the Franks, his breast-armor and the neck-ring together. Lesser warriors
plundered the fallen after the war-harvest: people of the Geats held the
place of corpses.

The hall was filled with noise. Wealhtheow spoke, before the compa-
ny she said to him: "Wear this ring, beloved Beowulf, young man, with
good luck, and make use of this mail-shirt from the people's treasure,
and prosper well; make yourself known with your might, and be kind of
counsel to these boys: I shall remember to reward you for that. You have
brought it about that, far and near, for a long time all men shall praise
you, as wide as the sea surrounds the shores, home of the winds. While
you live, prince, be prosperous. I wish you well of your treasure. Much
favored one, be kind of deeds to my son. Here is each earl true to other,
mild of heart, loyal to his lord; the thanes are at one, the people obedi-
ent, the retainers cheered with drink do as I bid."

Then she walked to her seat. There was the best of feasts, men drank
wine. They did not know the fate, the grim decree made long before, as
it came to pass to many of the earls after evening had come and
Hrothgar had gone to his chambers, the noble one to his rest. A great

---

9. The Brisings' (Brosings') necklace had been worn by the goddess Freya. Nothing more is
known of this story of Hama, who seems to have stolen the necklace from the famous Gothic
king Eormenric.
1. Beowulf is later said to have presented the necklace to Hygelac's queen, Hygd, though here
Hygelac is said to have been wearing it on his ill-fated expedition against the Franks and
Frisians, into whose hands it fell at his death.

number of men remained in the hall, just as they had often done before. They cleared the benches from the floor. It was spread over with beds and pillows. One of the beer-drinkers, ripe and fated to die, lay down to his hall-rest. They set at their heads their battle-shields, bright wood; there on the bench it was easy to see above each man his helmet that towered in battle, his ringed mail-shirt, his great spear-wood. It was their custom to be always ready for war whether at home or in the field, in any case at any time that need should befall their liege lord: that was a good nation.

[Grendel's Mother's Attack]

(XIX.) Then they sank to sleep. One paid sorely for his evening rest, just as had often befallen them when Grendel guarded the gold-hall, wrought wrong until the end came, death after misdeeds. It came to be seen, wide-known to men, that after the bitter battle an avenger still lived for an evil space: Grendel's mother, woman, monster-wife, was mindful of her misery, she who had to dwell in the terrible water, the cold currents, after Cain became sword-slayer of his only brother, his own father's son. Then Cain went as an outlaw to flee the cheerful life of men, marked for his murder, held to the wasteland. From him sprang many a devil sent by fate. Grendel was one of them, hateful outcast who at Heorot found a waking man waiting his warfare. There the monster had laid hold upon him, but he was mindful of the great strength, the large gift God had given him, and relied on the Almighty for favor, comfort and help. By that he overcame the foe, subdued the hell-spirit. Then he went off wretched, bereft of joy, to seek his dying-place, enemy of mankind. And his mother, still greedy and gallows-grim, would go on a sorrowful venture, avenge her son's death.

Then she came to Heorot where the Ring-Danes slept throughout the hall. Then change came quickly to the earls there, when Grendel's mother made her way in. The attack was the less terrible by just so much as is the strength of women, the war-terror of a wife, less than an armed man's when a hard blade, forge-hammered, a sword shining with blood, good of its edges, cuts the stout boar on a helmet opposite. Then in the hall was hard-edged sword raised from the seat, many a broad shield lifted firmly in hand: none thought of helmet, of wide mail-shirt, when the terror seized him. She was in haste, would be gone out from there, protect her life after she was discovered. Swiftly she had taken fast hold on one of the nobles, then she went to the fen. He was one of the men between the seas most beloved of Hrothgar in the rank of retainer, a noble shield-warrior whom she destroyed at his rest, a man of great repute. Beowulf was not there, for earlier, after the treasure-giving, another lodging had been appointed for the renowned Geat. Outcry arose in Heorot: she had taken, in its gore, the famed hand. Care was

renewed, come again on the dwelling. That was not a good bargain, that
on both sides they had to pay with the lives of friends.

Then was the old king, the hoary warrior, of bitter mind when he
learned that his chief thane was lifeless, his dearest man dead. Quickly
Beowulf was fetched to the bed-chamber, man happy in victory. At day-
break together with his earls he went, the noble champion himself with
his retainers, to where the wise one was, waiting to know whether after
tidings of woe the All-Wielder would ever bring about change for him.
The worthy warrior walked over the floor with his retainers—hall-wood
resounded—that he might address words to the wise prince of Ing's
friends, asked if the night had been pleasant according to his desires.

(XX.) Hrothgar spoke, protector of the Scyldings: "Ask not about plea-
sure. Sorrow is renewed to the people of the Danes: Aeschere is dead,
Yrmenlaf's elder brother, my speaker of wisdom and my bearer of coun-
sel, my shoulder-companion when we used to defend our heads in bat-
tle, when troops clashed, beat on boar-images. Whatever an earl should
be, a man good from old times, such was Aeschere. Now a wandering
murderous spirit has slain him with its hands in Heorot. I do not know
by what way the awful creature, glorying in its prey, has made its retreat,
gladdened by its feast. She has avenged the feud—that last night you
killed Grendel with hard hand-grips, savagely, because too long he had
diminished and destroyed my people. He fell in the fight, his life forfeit-
ed, and now the other has come, a mighty worker of wrong, would
avenge her kinsman, and has carried far her revenge—as many a thane
may think who weeps in his spirit for his treasure-giver, bitter sorrow in
heart. Now the hand lies lifeless that was strong in support of all your
desires.

"I have heard landsmen, my people, hall-counselors, say this, that
they have seen two such huge walkers in the wasteland holding to the
moors, alien spirits. One of them, so far as they could clearly discern,
was the likeness of a woman. The other wretched shape trod the tracks
of exile in the form of a man, except that he was bigger than any other
man. Land-dwellers in the old days named him Grendel. They know of
no father, whether in earlier times any was begotten for them among the
dark spirits. They hold to the secret land, the wolf-slopes, the windy
headlands, the dangerous fen-paths where the mountain stream goes
down under the darkness of the hills, the flood under the earth. It is not
far from here, measured in miles, that the mere stands; over it hang frost-
covered woods, trees fast of root close over the water. There each night
may be seen fire on the flood, a fearful wonder. Of the sons of men there
lives none, old of wisdom, who knows the bottom. Though the heath-
stalker, the strong-horned hart, harassed by hounds makes for the forest
after long flight, rather will he give his life, his being, on the bank than
save his head by entering. That is no pleasant place. From it the surging
waves rise up black to the heavens when the wind stirs up awful storms,

until the air becomes gloomy, the skies weep. Now once again is the
cure in you alone. You do not yet know the land, the perilous place,
where you might find the seldom-seen creature: seek if you dare. I will
give you wealth for the feud, old treasure, as I did before, twisted gold—
if you come away."

(XXI.) Beowulf spoke, the son of Ecgtheow: "Sorrow not, wise warrior.
It is better for a man to avenge his friend than much mourn. Each of us
must await his end of the world's life. Let him who may get glory before
death: that is best for the warrior after he has gone from life. Arise,
guardian of the kingdom, let us go at once to look on the track of
Grendel's kin. I promise you this: she will not be lost under cover, not
in the earth's bosom nor in the mountain woods nor at the bottom of the
sea, go where she will. This day have patience in every woe—as I expect
you to."

Then the old man leapt up, thanked God, the mighty Lord, that the
man had so spoken. Then was a horse bridled for Hrothgar, a curly-
maned mount. The wise king moved in state; the band of shield-bearers
marched on foot. The tracks were seen wide over the wood-paths where
she had gone on the ground, made her way forward over the dark moor,
borne lifeless the best of retainers of those who watched over their home
with Hrothgar. The son of noble forebears[2] moved over the steep rocky
slopes, narrow paths where only one could go at a time, an unfamiliar
trail, steep hills, many a lair of water-monsters. He went before with a
few wise men to spy out the country, until suddenly he found mountain
trees leaning out over hoary stone, a joyless wood: water lay beneath,
bloody and troubled. It was pain of heart for all the Danes to suffer, for
the friends of the Scyldings, for many a thane, grief to each earl when
on the cliff over the water they came upon Aeschere's head. The flood
boiled with blood—the men looked upon it—with hot gore. Again and
again the horn sang its urgent war-song. The whole troop sat down to
rest. Then they saw on the water many a snake-shape, strong sea-serpents
exploring the mere, and water-monsters lying on the slopes of the shore
such as those that in the morning often attend a perilous journey on the
paths of the sea, serpents and wild beasts.

These fell away from the shore, fierce and rage-swollen: they had
heard the bright sound, the war-horn sing. One of them a man of the
Geats with his bow cut off from his life, his water-warring, after the hard
war-arrow stuck in his heart: he was weaker in swimming the lake when
death took him. Straightway he was hard beset on the waves with barbed
boar-spears, strongly surrounded, pulled up on the shore, strange spawn
of the waves. The men looked on the terrible alien thing.

Beowulf put on his warrior's dress, had no fear for his life. His war-
shirt, hand-fashioned, broad and well-worked, was to explore the mere:

2. I.e., Hrothgar.

it knew how to cover his body-cave so that foe's grip might not harm his heart, or grasp of angry enemy his life. But the bright helmet guarded his head, one which was to stir up the lake-bottom, seek out the troubled water—made rich with gold, surrounded with splendid bands, as the weapon-smith had made it in far-off days, fashioned it wonderfully, set it about with boar-images so that thereafter no sword or battle-blade might bite into it. And of his strong supports that was not the least which Hrothgar's spokesman[3] lent to his need: Hrunting was the name of the hilted sword; it was one of the oldest of ancient treasures; its edge was iron, decorated with poison-stripes, hardened with battle-sweat. Never had it failed in war any man of those who grasped it in their hands, who dared enter on dangerous enterprises, onto the common meeting place of foes: this was not the first time that it should do work of courage. Surely the son of Ecglaf, great of strength, did not have in mind what, drunk with wine, he had spoken, when he lent that weapon to a better sword-fighter. He did not himself dare to risk his life under the warring waves, to engage his courage: there he lost his glory, his name for valor. It was not so with the other when he had armed himself for battle.

[Beowulf Attacks Grendel's Mother]

(XXII.) Beowulf spoke, the son of Ecgtheow: "Think now, renowned son of Healfdene, wise king, now that I am ready for the venture, gold-friend of warriors, of what we said before, that, if at your need I should go from life, you would always be in a father's place for me when I am gone: be guardian of my young retainers, my companions, if battle should take me. The treasure you gave me, beloved Hrothgar, send to Hygelac. The lord of the Geats may know from the gold, the son of Hrethel may see when he looks on that wealth, that I found a ring-giver good in his gifts, enjoyed him while I might. And let Unferth have the old heirloom, the wide-known man my splendid-waved sword, hard-edged: with Hrunting I shall get glory, or death will take me."

After these words the man of the Weather-Geats turned away boldly, would wait for no answer: the surging water took the warrior. Then was it a part of a day before he might see the bottom's floor. Straightway that which had held the flood's tract a hundred half-years, ravenous for prey, grim and greedy, saw that some man from above was exploring the dwelling of monsters. Then she groped toward him, took the warrior in her awful grip. Yet not the more for that did she hurt his hale body within: his ring-armor shielded him about on the outside so that she could not pierce the war-dress, the linked body-mail, with hateful fingers. Then as she came to the bottom the sea-wolf bore the ring-prince to her house so that—no matter how brave he was—he might not wield

---

3. I.e., Unferth.

weapons; but many monsters attacked him in the water, many a sea-beast tore at his mail-shirt with war-tusks, strange creatures afflicted him. Then the earl saw that he was in some hostile hall where no water harmed him at all, and the flood's onrush might not touch him because of the hall-roof. He saw firelight, a clear blaze shine bright.

Then the good man saw the accursed dweller in the deep, the mighty mere-woman. He gave a great thrust to his sword—his hand did not withhold the stroke—so that the etched blade sang at her head a fierce war-song. Then the stranger found that the battle-lightning would not bite, harm her life, but the edge failed the prince in his need: many a hand-battle had it endured before, often sheared helmet, war-coat of man fated to die: this was the first time for the rare treasure that its glory had failed.

But still he was resolute, not slow of his courage, mindful of fame, the kinsman of Hygelac. Then, angry warrior, he threw away the sword, wavy-patterned, bound with ornaments, so that it lay on the ground, hard and steel-edged: he trusted in his strength, his mighty hand-grip. So ought a man to do when he thinks to get long-lasting praise in battle: he cares not for his life. Then he seized by the hair Grendel's mother—the man of the War-Geats did not shrink from the fight. Battle-hardened, now swollen with rage, he pulled his deadly foe so that she fell to the floor. Quickly in her turn she repaid him his gift with her grim claws and clutched at him: then weary-hearted, the strongest of warriors, of foot-soldiers, stumbled so that he fell. Then she sat upon the hall-guest and drew her knife, broad and bright-edged. She would avenge her child, her only son. The woven breast-armor lay on his shoulder: that protected his life, withstood entry of point or of edge. Then the son of Ecgtheow would have fared amiss under the wide ground, the champion of the Geats, if the battle-shirt had not brought help, the hard war-net—and holy God brought about victory in war; the wise Lord, Ruler of the Heavens, decided it with right, easily, when Beowulf had stood up again.

(XXIII.) Then he saw among the armor a victory-blessed blade, an old sword made by the giants, strong of its edges, glory of warriors: it was the best of weapons, except that it was larger than any other man might bear to war-sport, good and adorned, the work of giants. He seized the linked hilt, he who fought for the Scyldings, savage and slaughter-bent, drew the patterned blade; desperate of life, he struck angrily so that it bit her hard on the neck, broke the bone-rings. The blade went through all the doomed body. She fell to the floor, the sword was sweating, the man rejoiced in his work.

The blaze brightened, light shone within, just as from the sky heaven's candle shines clear. He looked about the building; then he moved along the wall, raised his weapon hard by the hilt, Hygelac's thane, angry and resolute: the edge was not useless to the warrior, for he would quickly repay Grendel for the many attacks he had made on the West-

Danes—many more than the one time when he slew in their sleep fif-teen hearth-companions of Hrothgar, devoured men of the Danish peo-ple while they slept, and another such number bore away, a hateful prey. He had paid him his reward for that, the fierce champion, for there he saw Grendel, weary of war, lying at rest, lifeless with the wounds he had got in the fight at Heorot. The body bounded wide[4] when it suffered the blow after death, the hard sword-swing; and thus he cut off his head.

At once the wise men who were watching the water with Hrothgar saw that the surging waves were troubled, the lake stained with blood. Gray-haired, old, they spoke together of the good warrior, that they did not again expect of the chief that he would come victorious to seek their great king; for many agreed on it, that the sea-wolf had destroyed him.

Then came the ninth hour of the day. The brave Scyldings left the hill. The gold-friend of warriors went back to his home. The strangers sat sick at heart and stared at the mere. They wished—and did not expect—that they would see their beloved lord himself.

Then the blade began to waste away from the battle-sweat, the war-sword into battle-icicles. That was a wondrous thing, that it should all melt, most like the ice when the Father loosens the frost's fetters, undoes the water-bonds—He Who has power over seasons and times: He is the true Ruler. Beowulf did not take from the dwelling, the man of the Weather-Geats, more treasures—though he saw many there—but only the head and the hilt, bright with jewels. The sword itself had already melted, its patterned blade burned away: the blood was too hot for it, the spirit that had died there too poisonous. Quickly he was swimming, he who had lived to see the fall of his foes; he plunged up through the water. The currents were all cleansed, the great tracts of the water, when the dire spirit left her life-days and this loaned world.

Then the protector of seafarers came toward the land, swimming stout-hearted; he had joy of his sea-booty, the great burden he had with him. They went to meet him, thanked God, the strong band of thanes, rejoiced in their chief that they might see him again sound. Then the helmet and war-shirt of the mighty one were quickly loosened. The lake drowsed, the water beneath the skies, stained with blood. They went forth on the foot-tracks, glad in their hearts, measured the path back, the known ways, men bold as kings. They bore the head from the mere's cliff, toilsomely for each of the great-hearted ones: four of them had trou-ble in carrying Grendel's head on spear-shafts to the gold-hall—until at last they came striding to the hall, fourteen bold warriors of the Geats; their lord, high-spirited, walked in their company over the fields to the mead-hall.

Then the chief of the thanes, man daring in deeds, enriched by new glory, warrior dear to battle, came in to greet Hrothgar. Then Grendel's

4. A reference to the violent force with which Beowulf decapitates the dead Grendel.

head was dragged by the hair over the floor to where men drank, a terrible thing to the earls and the woman with them, an awful sight: the men looked upon it.

[Further Celebration at Heorot]

(XXIV). Beowulf spoke, the son of Ecgtheow: "Yes, we have brought you this sea-booty, son of Healfdene, man of the Scyldings, gladly, as evidence of glory—what you look on here. Not easily did I come through it with my life, the war under water, not without trouble carried out the task. The fight would have been ended straightway if God had not guarded me. With Hrunting I might not do anything in the fight, though that is a good weapon. But the Wielder of Men granted me that I should see hanging on the wall a fair, ancient great-sword— most often He has guided the man without friends—that I should wield the weapon. Then in the fight when the time became right for me I hewed the house-guardians. Then that war-sword, wavy-patterned, burnt away as their blood sprang forth, hottest of battle-sweats. I have brought the hilt away from the foes. I have avenged the evil deeds, the slaughter of Danes, as it was right to do. I promise you that you may sleep in Heorot without care with your band of retainers, and that for none of the thanes of your people, old or young, need you have fear, prince of the Scyldings—for no life-injury to your men on that account, as you did before."

Then the golden hilt was given into the hand of the old man, the hoary war-chief—the ancient work of giants. There came into the possession of the prince of the Danes, after the fall of devils, the work of wonder-smiths. And when the hostile-hearted creature, God's enemy, guilty of murder, gave up this world, and his mother too, it passed into the control of the best of worldly kings between the seas, of those who gave treasure in the Northlands.

Hrothgar spoke—he looked on the hilt, the old heirloom, on which was written the origin of ancient strife, when the flood, rushing water, slew the race of giants—they suffered terribly: that was a people alien to the Everlasting Lord. The Ruler made them a last payment through water's welling. On the sword-guard of bright gold there was also rightly marked through rune-staves, set down and told, for whom that sword, best of irons, had first been made, its hilt twisted and ornamented with snakes. Then the wise man spoke, the son of Healfdene—all were silent: "Lo, this may one say who works truth and right for the folk, recalls all things far distant, an old guardian of the land: that this earl was born the better man. Glory is raised up over the far ways—your glory over every people, Beowulf my friend. All of it, all your strength, you govern steadily in the wisdom of your heart. I shall fulfill my friendship to you, just as

we spoke before. You shall become a comfort, whole and long-lasting, to
your people, a help to warriors.

"So was not Heremod to the sons of Ecgwela, the Honor-Scyldings.
He grew great not for their joy, but for their slaughter, for the destruction
of Danish people. With swollen heart he killed his table-companions,
shoulder-comrades, until he turned away from the joys of men, alone,
notorious king, although mighty God had raised him in power, in the
joys of strength, had set him up over all men. Yet in his breast his heart's
thought grew blood-thirsty: no rings did he give to the Danes for glory.
He lived joyless to suffer the pain of that strife, the long-lasting harm of
the people. Teach yourself by him, be mindful of munificence. Old of
winters, I tell this tale for you.[5]

"It is a wonder to say how in His great spirit mighty God gives wisdom
to mankind, land and earlship—He possesses power over all things. At
times He lets the thought of a man of high lineage move in delight, gives
him joy of earth in his homeland, a stronghold of men to rule over,
makes regions of the world so subject to him, wide kingdoms, that in his
unwisdom he may not himself have mind of his end. He lives in plenty;
illness and age in no way grieve him, neither does dread care darken his
heart, nor does enmity bare sword-hate, for the whole world turns to his
will—he knows nothing worse—(XXV.) until his portion of pride
increases and flourishes within him; then the watcher sleeps, the soul's
guardian; that sleep is too sound, bound in its own cares, and the slayer
most near whose bow shoots treacherously. Then is he hit in the heart,
beneath his armor, with the bitter arrow—he cannot protect himself—
with the crooked dark commands of the accursed spirit. What he has
long held seems to him too little, angry-hearted he covets, no plated
rings does he give in men's honor, and then he forgets and regards not
his destiny because of what God, Wielder of Heaven, has given him
before, his portion of glories. In the end it happens in turn that the
loaned body weakens, falls doomed; another takes the earl's ancient trea-
sure, one who recklessly gives precious gifts, does not fearfully guard
them.

"Keep yourself against that wickedness, beloved Beowulf, best of men,
and choose better—eternal gains. Have no care for pride, great warrior.
Now for a time there is glory in your might: yet soon it shall be that sick-
ness or sword will diminish your strength, or fire's fangs, or flood's surge,
or sword's swing, or spear's flight, or appalling age; brightness of eyes will
fail and grow dark; then it shall be that death will overcome you, warrior.

"Thus I ruled the Ring-Danes for a hundred half-years under the
skies, and protected them in war with spear and sword against many
nations over middle-earth, so that I counted no one as my adversary

5. Heremod is the type of evil ruler who hoards rather than gives treasure to his followers.
Hrothgar intends Heremod to be understood as a negative exemplar for Beowulf.

underneath the sky's expanse. Well, disproof of that came to me in my own land, grief after my joys, when Grendel, ancient adversary, came to invade my home. Great sorrow of heart I have always suffered for his per- secution. Thanks be to the Ruler, the Eternal Lord, that after old strife I have come to see in my lifetime, with my own eyes, his blood-stained head. Go now to your seat, have joy of the glad feast, made famous in battle. Many of our treasures will be shared when morning comes."

The Geat was glad at heart, went at once to seek his seat as the wise one bade. Then was a feast fairly served again, for a second time, just as before, for those famed for courage, sitting about the hall.

Night's cover lowered, dark over the warriors. The retainers all arose. The gray-haired one would seek his bed, the old Scylding. It pleased the Geat, the brave shield-warrior, immensely that he should have rest. Straightway a hall-thane led the way on for the weary one, come from far country, and showed every courtesy to the thane's need, such as in those days seafarers might expect as their due.

Then the great-hearted one rested; the hall stood high, vaulted and gold-adorned; the guest slept within until the black raven, blithe- hearted, announced heaven's joy. Then the bright light came passing over the shadows. The warriors hastened, the nobles were eager to set out again for their people. Bold of spirit, the visitor would seek his ship far thence.

Then the hardy one bade that Hrunting be brought to the son of Ecglaf,[6] that he take back his sword, precious iron. He spoke thanks for that loan, said that he accounted it a good war-friend, strong in bat- tle; in his words he found no fault at all with the sword's edge: he was a thoughtful man. And then they were eager to depart, the warriors ready in their armor. The prince who had earned honor of the Danes went to the high seat where the other was: the man dear to war greet- ed Hrothgar.

[Beowulf Returns Home]

(XXVI.) Beowulf spoke, the son of Ecgtheow: "Now we sea-travelers come from afar wish to say that we desire to seek Hygelac. Here we have been entertained splendidly according to our desire: you have dealt well with us. If on earth I might in any way earn more of your heart's love, prince of warriors, than I have done before with warlike deeds, I should be ready at once. If beyond the sea's expanse I hear that men dwelling near threaten you with terrors, as those who hated you did before, I shall bring you a thousand thanes, warriors to your aid. I know of Hygelac, lord of the Geats, though he is young as a guardian of the people, that he will further me with words and works so that I may do you honor and

6. I.e., Unferth.

bring spears to help you, strong support where you have need of men. If Hrethric, king's son, decides to come to the court of the Geats, he can find many friends there; far countries are well sought by him who is himself strong."

Hrothgar spoke to him in answer: "The All-Knowing Lord sent those words into your mind: I have not heard a man of so young age speak more wisely. You are great of strength, mature of mind, wise of words. I think it likely if the spear, sword-grim war, takes the son of Hrethel, sickness or weapon your prince, the people's ruler, and you have your life, that the Sea-Geats will not have a better to choose as their king, as guardian of their treasure, if you wish to hold the kingdom of your kinsmen. So well your heart's temper has long pleased me, beloved Beowulf. You have brought it about that peace shall be shared by the peoples, the folk of the Geats and the Spear-Danes, and enmity shall sleep, acts of malice which they practiced before; and there shall be, as long as I rule the wide kingdom, sharing of treasures, many a man shall greet his fellow with good gifts over the seabird's baths; the ring-prowed ship will bring gifts and tokens of friendship over the sea. I know your people, blameless in every respect, set firm after the old way both as to foe and to friend."

Then the protector of earls, the kinsman of Healfdene, gave him there in the hall twelve precious things; he bade him with these gifts seek his own dear people in safety, quickly come back. Then the king noble of race, the prince of the Scyldings, kissed the best of thanes and took him by his neck: tears fell from the gray-haired one. He had two thoughts of the future, the old and wise man, one more strongly than the other— that they would not see each other again, bold men at council. The man was so dear to him that he might not restrain his breast's welling, for fixed in his heartstrings a deep-felt longing for the beloved man burned in his blood. Away from him Beowulf, warrior glorious with gold, walked over the grassy ground, proud of his treasure. The sea-goer awaited its owner, riding at anchor. Then on the journey the gift of Hrothgar was oft-praised: that was a king blameless in all things until age took from him the joys of his strength—old age that has often harmed many.

(XXVII.) There came to the flood the band of brave-hearted ones, of young men. They wore mail-coats, locked limb-shirts. The guard of the coast saw the coming of the earls, just as he had done before. He did not greet the guests with taunts from the cliff's top, but rode to meet them, said that the return of the warriors in bright armor in their ship would be welcome to the people of the Weather-Geats. There on the sand the broad seaboat was loaded with armor, the ring-prowed ship with horses and rich things. The mast stood high over Hrothgar's hoard-gifts. He gave the boat-guard a sword wound with gold, so that thereafter on the mead-bench he was held the worthier for the treasure, the heirloom. The boat moved out to furrow the deep water, left the land of the Danes. Then on the mast a sea-cloth, a sail, was made fast by a rope. The boat's beams creaked: wind did not keep the sea-floater from its way over the waves. The sea-goer moved, foamy-necked floated forth over the swell, the ship with bound prow over the sea-currents until they might see the cliffs of the Geats, the well-known headlands. The ship pressed ahead, borne by the wind, stood still at the land. Quickly the harbor-guard was at the sea-side, he who had gazed for a long time far out over the currents, eager to see the beloved men. He[7] moored the deep ship in the sand, fast by its anchor ropes, lest the force of the waves should drive away the fair wooden vessel. Then he bade that the prince's wealth be borne ashore, armor and plated gold. It was not far for them to seek the giver of treasure, Hygelac son of Hrethel, where he dwelt at home near the sea-wall, himself with his retainers.

The building was splendid, its king most valiant, set high in the hall, Hygd[8] most youthful, wise and well-taught, though she had lived within the castle walls few winters, daughter of Haereth. For she was not niggardly, nor too sparing of gifts to the men of the Geats, of treasures. Modthryth,[9] good folk-queen, did dreadful deeds [in her youth]: no bold one among her retainers dared venture—except her great lord—to set his eyes on her in daylight, but [if he did] he should reckon deadly bonds prepared for him, arresting hands: that straightway after his seizure the sword awaited him, that the patterned blade must settle it, make known its death-evil. Such is no queenly custom for a woman to practice, though she is peerless—that one who weaves peace[1] should take away the life of a beloved man after pretended injury. However the kinsman of Hemming stopped that:[2] ale-drinkers gave another account, said that she did less harm to the people, fewer injuries, after she was given, gold-adorned, to the young warrior, the beloved noble, when by her father's teaching she sought Offa's hall in a voyage over the pale sea. There on the throne she was afterwards famous for generosity, while living made use of her life, held high love toward the lord of warriors, [who was] of all mankind the best, as I have heard, between the seas of the races of men. Since Offa was a man brave of wars and gifts, wide-honored, he held his native land in wisdom. From him sprang Eomer to the help of warriors, kinsman of Hemming, grandson of Garmund, strong in battle.[3]

7. Beowulf.
8. Hygd is Hygelac's young queen. The suddenness of her introduction here is perhaps due to a faulty text.
9. A transitional passage introducing the contrast between Hygd's good behavior and Modthryth's bad behavior as young women of royal blood seems to have been lost. Modthryth's practice of having those who looked into her face put to death may reflect the folk-motif of the princess whose unsuccessful suitors are executed, though the text does not say that Modthryth's victims were suitors. Modthryth's "great lord" was probably her father.
1. Daughters of kings were frequently given in marriage to the king of a hostile nation in order to bring about peace; hence Modthryth may be called "one who weaves peace."
2. Offa, a fourth-century continental Angle king, forebear of the famous English king, Offa of Mercia; who Hemming was—besides being a kin of Offa's—is unknown.
3. By praising Offa the Angle; his father, Garmund; and son, Eomer—heroes familiar to his audience—the poet reflects glory on the eighth-century English Offa.

(XXVIII.) Then the hardy one came walking with his troop over the sand on the sea-plain, the wide shores. The world-candle shone, the sun moved quickly from the south. They made their way, strode swiftly to where they heard that the protector of earls, the slayer of Ongentheow,[4] the good young war-king, was dispensing rings in the stronghold. The coming of Beowulf was straightway made known to Hygelac, that there in his home the defender of warriors, his comrade in battle, came walking alive to the court, sound from the battle-play. Quickly the way within was made clear for the foot-guests, as the mighty one bade.

Then he sat down with him, he who had come safe through the fight, kinsman with kinsman, after he had greeted his liege lord with formal speech, loyal, with vigorous words. Haereth's daughter moved through the hall-building with mead-cups, cared lovingly for the people, bore the cup of strong drink to the hands of the warriors. Hygelac began fairly to question his companion in the high hall, curiosity pressed him, what the adventures of the Sea-Geats had been. "How did you fare on your journey, beloved Beowulf, when you suddenly resolved to seek distant combat over the salt water, battle in Heorot? Did you at all help the wide-known woes of Hrothgar, the famous prince? Because of you I burned with seething sorrows, care of heart—had no trust in the venture of my beloved man. I entreated you long that you should in no way approach the murderous spirit, should let the South-Danes themselves settle the war with Grendel. I say thanks to God that I may see you sound."

Beowulf spoke, the son of Ecgtheow: "To many among men it is not hidden, lord Hygelac, the great encounter—what a fight we had, Grendel and I, in the place where he made many sorrows for the Victory-Scyldings, constant misery. All that I avenged, so that none of Grendel's kin over the earth need boast of that clash at night—whoever lives longest of the loathsome kind, wrapped in malice. There I went forth to the ring-hall to greet Hrothgar. At once the famous son of Healfdene, when he knew my purpose, gave me a seat with his own sons. The company was in joy: I have not seen in the time of my life under heaven's arch more mead-mirth of hall-sitters. At times the famous queen, peace-pledge of the people, went through all the hall, cheered the young men; often she would give a man a ring-band before she went to her seat. At times Hrothgar's daughter bore the ale-cup to the retainers, to the earls throughout the hall. I heard hall-sitters name her Freawaru when she offered the studded cup to warriors. Young and gold-adorned, she is promised to the fair son of Froda.[5] That has seemed good to the lord of the Scyldings, the guardian of the kingdom, and he believes of this plan that he may, with this woman, settle their portion of

---

4. Ongentheow was a Scylfing (Swedish) king, whose story is fully told below, sections XL and XLI. In fact Hygelac was not his slayer, but is called so because he led the attack on the Scylfings in which Ongentheow was killed.
5. I.e., Ingeld, who succeeded his father as king of the Heath-Bards. *peace treaty*

deadly feuds, of quarrels.[6] Yet most often after the fall of a prince in any nation the deadly spear rests but a little while, even though the bride is good.

"It may displease the lord of the Heatho-Bards and each thane of that people when he goes in the hall with the woman, [that while] the noble sons of the Danes, her retainers, [are] feasted,[7] the heirlooms of their ancestors will be shining on them[8]—the hard and wave-adorned treasure of the Heatho-Bards, [which was theirs] so long as they might wield those weapons, (XXIX.) until they led to the shield-play, to destruction, their dear companions and their own lives. Then at the beer he[9] who sees the treasure, an old ash-warrior who remembers it all, the spear-death of warriors—grim is his heart—begins, sad of mind, to tempt a young fighter in the thoughts of his spirit, to awaken war-evil, and speaks this word:

"'Can you, my friend, recognize that sword, the rare iron-blade, that your father, beloved man, bore to battle his last time in armor, where the Danes slew him, the fierce Scyldings, got possession of the battle-field, when Withergeld[1] lay dead, after the fall of warriors? Now here some son of his murderers walks in the hall, proud of the weapon, boasts of the murder, and wears the treasure that you should rightly possess.' So he will provoke and remind at every chance with wounding words until that moment comes that the woman's thane,[2] forfeiting life, shall lie dead, blood-smeared from the sword-bite, for his father's deeds. The other escapes with his life, knows the land well. Then on both sides the oath of the earls will be broken; then deadly hate will well up in Ingeld, and his wife-love after the surging of sorrows will become cooler. Therefore I do not think the loyalty of the Heatho-Bards, their part in the alliance with the Danes, to be without deceit—do not think their friendship fast.

"I shall speak still more of Grendel, that you may readily know, giver of treasure, what the hand-fight of warriors came to in the end. After heaven's jewel had glided over the earth, the angry spirit came, awful in the evening, to visit us where, unharmed, we watched over the hall. There the fight was fatal to Hondscioh, deadly to one who was doomed. He was dead first of all, armed warrior. Grendel came to devour him, good young retainer, swallowed all the body of the beloved man. Yet not for this would the bloody-toothed slayer, bent on destruction, go from the gold-hall empty-handed; but, strong of might, he made trial of me,

---

6. I.e., the feud between the Danes and Heatho-Bards.
7. The text is faulty here.
8. I.e., the weapons and armor which had once belonged to the Heatho-Bards and were captured by the Danes will be worn by the Danish attendants of Hrothgar's daughter, Freawaru, when she goes to the Heatho-Bards to marry king Ingeld.
9. I.e., some old Heatho-Bard warrior.
1. Apparently a leader of the Heatho-Bards in their unsuccessful war with the Danes.
2. I.e., the Danish attendant of Freawaru who is wearing the sword of his Heatho-Bard attacker's father.

grasped me with eager hand. His glove[3] hung huge and wonderful, made fast with cunning clasps: it had been made all with craft, with devil's devices and dragon's skins. The fell doer of evils would put me therein, guiltless, one of many. He might not do so after I had stood up in anger. It is too long to tell how I repaid the people's foe his due for every crime. My prince, there with my deeds I did honor to your people. He slipped away, for a little while had use of life's joy. Yet his right hand remained as his spoor in Heorot, and he went from there abject, mournful of heart sank to the mere's bottom.

"The lord of the Scyldings repaid me for that bloody combat with much plated gold, many treasures, after morning came and we sat down to the feast. There was song and mirth. The old Scylding, who has learned many things, spoke of times far-off. At times a brave one in battle touched the glad wood, the harp's joy; at times he told tales, true and sad; at times he related strange stories according to right custom; at times, again, the great-hearted king, bound with age, the old warrior, would begin to speak of his youth, his battle-strength. His heart welled within when, old and wise, he thought of his many winters. Thus we took pleasure there the livelong day until another night came to men.

"Then in her turn Grendel's mother swiftly made ready to take revenge for his injuries, made a sorrowful journey. Death had taken her son, war-hate of the Weather-Geats. The direful woman avenged her son, fiercely killed a warrior: there the life of Aeschere departed, a wise old counselor. And when morning came the folk of the Danes might not burn him, death-weary, in the fire, nor place him on the pyre, beloved man: she had borne his body away in fiend's embrace beneath the mountain stream. That was the bitterest of Hrothgar's sorrows, of those that had long come upon the people's prince. Then the king, sore-hearted, implored me by your life[4] that I should do a man's work in the tumult of the waters, venture my life, finish a glorious deed. He promised me reward. Then I found the guardian of the deep pool, the grim horror, as is now known wide. For a time there we were locked hand in hand. Then the flood boiled with blood, and in the war-hall I cut off the head of Grendel's mother with a mighty sword. Not without trouble I came from there with my life. I was not fated to die then, but the protector of earls again gave me many treasures, the son of Healfdene.

(XXXI.) "Thus the king of that people lived with good customs. I had lost none of the rewards, the meed of my might, but he gave me treasures, the son of Healfdene, at my own choice. I will bring these to you, great king, show my good will. On your kindnesses all still depends: I have few close kinsmen besides you, Hygelac."

---

3. Apparently a large glove that could be used as a pouch.
4. I.e., "in your name."

Then he bade bring in the boar-banner—the head-sign—the helmet towering in battle, the gray battle-shirt, the splendid sword—afterwards spoke words: "Hrothgar, wise king, gave me this armor; in his words he bade that I should first tell you about his gift: he said that king Heorogar,[5] lord of the Scyldings, had had it for a long time; not for that would he give it, the breast-armor, to his son, bold Heoroweard, though he was loyal to him. Use it all well!"

I have heard that four horses, swift and alike, followed that treasure, fallow as apples. He gave him the gift of both horses and treasure. So ought kinsmen do, not weave malice-nets for each other with secret craft, prepare death for comrades. To Hygelac his nephew was most true in hard fights, and each one mindful of helping the other. I have heard that he gave Hygd the neck-ring, the wonderfully wrought treasure, that Wealhtheow had given him—gave to the king's daughter as well three horses, supple and saddle-bright. After the gift of the necklace, her breast was adorned with it.

Thus Beowulf showed himself brave, a man known in battles, of good deeds, bore himself according to discretion. Drunk, he slew no hearth-companions. His heart was not savage, but he held the great gift that God had given him, the most strength of all mankind, like one brave in battle. He had long been despised,[6] so that the sons of the Geats did not reckon him brave, nor would the lord of the Weather-Geats do him much gift-honor on the mead-bench. They strongly suspected that he was slack, a young man unbold. Change came to the famous man for each of his troubles.

Then the protector of earls bade fetch in the heirloom of Hrethel,[7] king famed in battle, adorned with gold. There was not then among the Geats a better treasure in sword's kind. He laid that in Beowulf's lap, and gave him seven thousand [hides of land], a hall, and a throne. To both of them alike land had been left in the nation, home and native soil: to the other more especially wide was the realm, to him who was higher in rank.

[Beowulf and the Dragon]

Afterwards it happened, in later days, in the crashes of battle, when Hygelac lay dead and war-swords came to slay Heardred[8] behind the shield-cover, when the Battle-Scylfings, hard fighters, sought him among his victorious nation, attacked bitterly the nephew of Hereric— then the broad kingdom came into Beowulf's hand. He held it well fifty

5. Hrothgar's elder brother, whom Hrothgar succeeded as king.
6. Beowulf's poor reputation as a young man is mentioned only here.
7. Hygelac's father.
8. Hygelac's son, Heardred, who succeeded Hygelac as king, was killed by the Swedes (Heatho-Scylfings) in his own land, as is explained more fully below, section XXXIII. His uncle Hereric was perhaps Hygd's brother.

winters—he was a wise king, an old guardian of the land—until in the
dark nights a certain one, a dragon, began to hold sway, which on the
high heath kept watch over a hoard, a steep stone-barrow. Beneath lay a
path unknown to men. By this there went inside a certain man [who
made his way near to the heathen hoard; his hand took a cup, large, a
shining treasure. The dragon did not afterwards conceal it though in his
sleep he was tricked by the craft of the thief. That the people discovered,
the neighboring folk—that he was swollen with rage].[9]

(XXXII.) Not of his own accord did he who had sorely harmed him[1]
break into the worm's hoard, not by his own desire, but for hard con-
straint; the slave of some son of men fled hostile blows, lacking a shelter,
and came there, a man guilty of wrong-doing. As soon as he saw him,[2]
great horror arose in the stranger; [yet the wretched fugitive escaped the
terrible worm . . . When the sudden shock came upon him, he car-
ried off a precious cup.][3] There were many such ancient treasures in the
earth-house, as in the old days some one of mankind had prudently hid-
den there the huge legacy of a noble race, rare treasures. Death had
taken them all in earlier times, and the only one of the nation of people
who still survived, who walked there longest, a guardian mourning his
friends, supposed the same of himself as of them—that he might little
while enjoy the long-got treasure. A barrow stood all ready on the shore
near the sea-waves, newly placed on the headland, made fast by having
its entrances skillfully hidden. The keeper of the rings carried in the part
of his riches worthy of hoarding, plated gold; he spoke few words:

"Hold now, you earth, now that men may not, the possession of earls.
What, from you good men got it first! War-death has taken each man of
my people, evil dreadful and deadly, each of those who has given up this
life, the hall-joys of men. I have none who wears sword or cleans the
plated cup, rich drinking vessel. The company of retainers has gone
elsewhere. The hard helmet must be stripped of its fair-wrought gold, of
its plating. The polishers are asleep who should make the war-mask
shine. And even so the coat of mail, which withstood the bite of swords
after the crashing of the shields, decays like its warrior. Nor may the ring-
mail travel wide on the war-chief beside his warriors. There is no harp-
delight, no mirth of the singing wood, no good hawk flies through the
hall, no swift horse stamps in the castle court. Baleful death has sent
away many races of men."

So, sad of mind, he spoke his sorrow, alone of them all, moved joyless
through day and night until death's flood reached his heart. The ancient
night-ravager found the hoard-joy standing open, he who burning seeks
barrows, the smooth hateful dragon who flies at night wrapped in flame.

9. This part of the manuscript is badly damaged, and the text within brackets is highly conjectural.
1. The dragon.
2. The dragon.
3. Several lines of the text have been lost.

Earth-dwellers much dread him. He it is who must seek a hoard in the earth where he will guard heathen gold, wise for his winters: he is none the better for it.

So for three hundred winters the harmer of folk held in the earth one of its treasure-houses, huge and mighty, until one man angered his heart. He bore to his master a plated cup, asked his lord for a compact of peace: thus was the hoard searched, the store of treasures diminished. His requests were granted the wretched man: the lord for the first time looked on the ancient work of men. Then the worm woke; cause of strife was renewed: for then he moved over the stones, hard-hearted beheld his foe's footprints—with secret stealth he had stepped forth too near the dragon's head. (So may an undoomed man who holds favor from the Ruler easily come through his woes and misery.) The hoard-guard sought him eagerly over the ground, would find the man who had done him injury while he slept. Hot and fierce-hearted, often he moved all about the outside of the barrow. No man at all was in the emptiness. Yet he took joy in the thought of war, in the work of fighting. At times he turned back into the barrow, sought his rich cup. Straightway he found that some man had tampered with his gold, his splendid treasure. The hoard-guard waited restless until evening came; then the barrow-keeper was in rage: he would requite that precious drinking cup with vengeful fire. Then the day was gone—to the joy of the worm. He would not wait long on the sea-wall, but set out with fire, ready with flame. The beginning was terrible to the folk on the land, as the ending was soon to be sore to their giver of treasure.

(XXXIII.) Then the evil spirit began to vomit flames, burn bright dwellings; blaze of fire rose, to the horror of men; there the deadly flying thing would leave nothing alive. The worm's warfare was wide-seen, his cruel malice, near and far—how the destroyer hated and hurt the people of the Geats. He winged back to the hoard, his hidden hall, before the time of day. He had circled the land-dwellers with flame, with fire and burning. He had trust in his barrow, in his war and his wall: his expectation deceived him.

Then the terror was made known to Beowulf, quickly in its truth, that his own home, best of buildings, had melted in surging flames, the throne-seat of the Geats. That was anguish of spirit to the good man, the greatest of heart-sorrows. The wise one supposed that he had bitterly offended the Ruler, the Eternal Lord, against old law. His breast within boiled with dark thoughts—as was not for him customary. The fiery dragon with his flames had destroyed the people's stronghold, the land along the sea, the heart of the country. Because of that the war-king, the lord of the Weather-Geats, devised punishment for him. The protector of fighting men, lord of earls, commanded that a wonderful battle-shield be made all of iron. Well he knew that the wood of the forest might not help him—linden against flame. The prince good from old times was to come to the end of the days that had been lent him, life in the world, and the worm with him, though he had long held the hoarded wealth. Then the ring-prince scorned to seek the far-flier with a troop, a large army. He had no fear for himself of the combat, nor did he think the worm's war-power anything great, his strength and his courage, because he himself had come through many battles before, dared perilous straits, clashes of war, after he had purged Hrothgar's hall, victorious warrior, and in combat crushed to death Grendel's kin, loathsome race.

Nor was that the least of his hand-combats where Hygelac was slain, when the king of the Geats, the noble lord of the people, the son of Hrethel, died of sword-strokes in the war-storm among the Frisians, laid low by the blade. From there Beowulf came away by means of his own strength, performed a feat of swimming; he had on his arm the armor of thirty earls when he turned back to the sea. There was no need for the Hetware[4] to exult in the foot-battle when they bore their shields against him: few came again from that warrior to seek their homes. Then the son of Ecgtheow swam over the water's expanse, forlorn and alone, back to his people. There Hygd offered him hoard and king-dom, rings and a prince's throne. She had no trust in her son, that he could hold his native throne against foreigners now that Hygelac was dead. By no means the sooner might the lordless ones get consent from the noble that he would become lord of Heardred or that he would accept royal power.[5] Yet he held him up among the people by friend-ly counsel, kindly with honor, until he became older,[6] ruled the Weather-Geats.

Outcasts from over the sea sought him, sons of Ohthere.[7] They had rebelled against the protector of the Scylfings, the best of the sea-kings of those who gave treasure in Sweden, a famous lord. For Heardred that became his life's limit: because of his hospitality there the son of Hygelac got his life's wound from the strokes of a sword. And the son of Ongentheow went back to seek his home after Heardred lay dead, let Beowulf hold the royal throne, rule the Geats: that was a good king.

(XXXIV.) In later days he was mindful of repaying the prince's fall, became the friends of the destitute Eadgils;[8] with folk he supported the son of Ohthere over the wide sea, with warriors and weapons. Afterwards he got vengeance by forays that brought with them cold care: he took the king's life.

---

4. I.e., a tribe with whom the Frisians were allied.
5. I.e., Beowulf refused to take the throne from the rightful heir Heardred.
6. I.e., Beowulf supported the young Heardred.
7. Ohthere succeeded his father, Ongentheow, as king of the Scylfings (Swedes), but after his death his brother, Onela, seized the throne, driving out Ohthere's sons, Eanmund and Eadgils. They were given refuge at the Geatish court by Heardred, whom Onela attacked for this act of hospitality. In the fight Eanmund and Heardred were killed, and Onela left the kingdom in Beowulf's charge.
8. The surviving son of Ohthere was befriended by Beowulf, who supported him in his successful attempt to gain the Swedish throne and who killed the usurper Onela.

Thus he had survived every combat, every dangerous battle, every deed of courage, the son of Ecgtheow, until that one day when he should fight with the worm. Then, one of twelve, the lord of the Geats, swollen with anger, went to look on the dragon. He had learned then from what the feud arose, the fierce malice to men: the glorious cup had come to his possession from the hand of the finder: he was the thirteenth of that company, the man who had brought on the beginning of the war, the sad-hearted slave—wretched, he must direct them to the place. Against his will he went to where he knew of an earth-hall, a barrow beneath the ground close to the sea-surge, to the struggling waves: within, it was full of ornaments and gold chains. The terrible guardian, ready for combat, held the gold treasure, old under the earth. It was no easy bargain for any man to obtain. Then the king, hardy in fight, sat down on the headland; there he saluted his hearth-companions, gold-friend of the Geats. His mind was mournful, restless and ripe for death: very close was the fate which should come to the old man, seek his soul's hoard, divide life from his body; not for long then was the life of the noble one wound in his flesh.

Beowulf spoke, the son of Ecgtheow: "In youth I lived through many battle-storms, times of war. I remember all that. I was seven winters old when the lord of treasure, the beloved king of the folk, received me from my father: King Hrethel had me and kept me, gave me treasure and feast, mindful of kinship. During his life I was no more hated by him as a man in his castle than any of his own sons, Herebeald and Haethcyn, or my own Hygelac. For the eldest a murder-bed was wrongfully spread through the deed of a kinsman, when Haethcyn struck him down with an arrow from his horned bow—his friend and his lord—missed the mark and shot his kinsman dead, one brother the other, with the bloody arrowhead. That was a fatal fight, without hope of recompense, a deed wrongly done, baffling to the heart; yet it had happened that a prince had to lose life unavenged.

"So it is sad for an old man to endure that his son should ride young on the gallows. Then he may speak a story, a sorrowful song, when his son hangs for the joy of the raven,[9] and, old in years and knowing, he can find no help for him. Always with every morning he is reminded of his son's journey elsewhere. He cares not to wait for another heir in his hall, when the first through death's force has come to the end of his deeds. Sorrowful he sees in his son's dwelling the empty wine-hall, the windy resting place without joy—the riders sleep, the warriors in the grave. There is no sound of the harp, no joy in the dwelling, as there was of old. (XXXV.) Then he goes to his couch, sings a song of sorrow, one alone for one gone. To him all too wide has seemed the land and the dwelling.

---

9. In Old English poetry, the raven was one of the traditional beasts of battle that devoured the corpses of the slain. Other such beasts included the wolf and the eagle.

"So the protector of the Weather-Geats bore in his heart swelling sor-
row for Herebeald. In no way could he settle his feud with the life-
slayer; not the sooner could he wound the warrior with deeds of hatred,
though he was not dear to him. Then for the sorrow that had too bitter-
ly befallen him he gave up the joys of men, chose God's light. To his
sons he left—as a happy man does—his land and his town when he went
from life.

*can't
take
vengeance
on own
family*

"Then there was battle and strife of Swedes and Geats, over the wide
water a quarrel shared, hatred between hardy ones, after Hrethel died.
And the sons of Ongentheow[1] were bold and active in war, wanted to
have no peace over the seas, but about Hreosnabeorh often devised
awful slaughter. That my friends and kinsmen avenged, both the feud
and the crime, as is well-known, though one of them bought it with his
life, a hard bargain: the war was mortal to Haethcyn, lord of the Geats.[2]
Then in the morning, I have heard, one kinsman avenged the other on
his slayer with the sword's edge, when Ongentheow attacked Eofor: the
war-helm split, the old Scylfing fell mortally wounded: his hand remem-
bered feuds enough, did not withstand the life-blow.

"I repaid in war the treasures that he[3] gave me—with my bright sword,
as was granted me by fate: he had given me land, a pleasant dwelling.
There was not any need for him, any reason, that he should have to seek
among the Gifthas[4] or the Spear-Danes or in Sweden in order to buy
with treasure a worse warrior. I would always go before him in the troop,
alone in the front. And so all my life I shall wage battle while this sword
endures that has served me early and late ever since I became
Daeghrefn's slayer in the press—the warrior of the Hugas.[5] He could not
bring armor to the king of the Frisians, breast ornament, but fell in the
fight, keeper of the standard, a noble man. Nor was my sword's edge his
slayer, but my warlike grip broke open his heart-streams, his bone-house.
Now shall the sword's edge, the hand and hard blade, fight for the
hoard."

[Beowulf attacks the Dragon]

Beowulf spoke, for the last time spoke words in boast: "In my youth I
engaged in many wars. Old guardian of the people, I shall still seek bat-
tle, perform a deed of fame, if the evil-doer will come to me out of the
earth-hall."

---

1. I.e., the Swedes Onela and Ohthere: the reference is, of course, to a time earlier than that
   referred to in section XXXIII, note 7.
2. Haethcyn had succeeded his father, Hrethel, as king of the Geats after his accidental killing of
   his brother Herebeald. When Haethcyn was killed while attacking the Swedes, he was suc-
   ceeded by Hygelac, who, as the next sentence relates, avenged Haethcyn's death on
   Ongentheow. The death of Ongentheow is described below, sections XL and XLI.
3. Hygelac.
4. An East Germanic tribe known as a common source of mercenaries.
5. I.e., the Franks.

Then he saluted each of the warriors, the bold helmet-bearers, for the last time—his own dear companions. "I would not bear sword, weapon, to the worm, if I knew how else according to my boast I might grapple with the monster, as I did of old with Grendel. But I expect here hot battle-fire, steam and poison. Therefore I have on me shield and mail-shirt. I will not flee a footstep from the barrow-ward, but it shall be with us at the wall as fate allots, the ruler of every man. I am confident in heart, so I forgo help against the war-flier. Wait on the barrow, safe in your mail-shirts, men in armor—which of us two may better bear wounds after our bloody meeting. This is not your venture, nor is it right for any man except me alone that he should spend his strength against the monster, do this man's deed. By my courage I shall get gold, or war will take your king, dire life-evil."

Then the brave warrior arose by his shield; hardy under helmet he went in his mail-shirt beneath the stone-cliffs, had trust in his strength—that of one man: such is not the way of the cowardly. Then he saw by the wall—he who had come through many wars, good in his great-heartedness, many clashes in battle when troops meet together—a stone arch standing, through it a stream bursting out of the barrow: there war welling of a current hot with killing fires, and he might not endure any while unburnt by the dragon's flame the hollow near the hoard. Then the man of the Weather-Geats, enraged as he was, let a word break from his breast. Stout-hearted he shouted; his voice went roaring, clear in battle, in under the gray stone. Hate was stirred up, the hoard's guard knew the voice of a man. No more time was there to ask for peace. First the monster's breath came out of the stone, the hot war-steam. The earth resounded. The man below the barrow, the lord of the Geats, swung his shield against the dreadful visitor. Then the heart of the coiled thing was aroused to seek combat. The good war-king had drawn his sword, the old heirloom, not blunt of edge. To each of them as they threatened destruction there was terror of the other. Firm-hearted he stood with his shield high, the lord of friends, while quickly the worm coiled itself; he waited in his armor. Then, coiling in flames, he came gliding on, hastening to his fate. The good shield protected the life and body of the famous prince, but for a shorter while than his wish was. There for the first time, the first day in his life, he might not prevail, since fate did not assign him such glory in battle. The lord of the Geats raised his hand, struck the shining horror so with his forged blade that the edge failed, bright on the bone, bit less surely than its folk-king had need, hard-pressed in perils. Then because of the battle-stroke the barrow-ward's heart was savage, he exhaled death-fire—the war-flames sprang wide. The gold-friend of the Geats boasted of no great victories: the war blade had failed, naked at need, as it ought not to have done, iron good from old times. That was no pleasant journey, not one on which the famous son of

Ecgtheow would wish to leave his land; against his will he must take up a dwelling-place elsewhere—as every man must give up the days that are lent him.

It was not long until they came together again, dreadful foes. The hoard-guard took heart, once more his breast swelled with his breathing. Encircled with flames, he who before had ruled a folk felt harsh pain. Nor did his companions, sons of nobles, take up their stand in a troop about him with the courage of fighting men, but they crept to the wood, protected their lives. In only one of them the heart surged with sorrows: nothing can ever set aside kinship in him who means well.

(XXXVI.) He was called Wiglaf, son of Weohstan, a rare shield-warrior, a man of the Scylfings, kinsman of Aelfhere.[6] He saw his liege lord under his war-mask suffer the heat. Then he was mindful of the honors he had given him before, the rich dwelling-place of the Waegmundings, every folk-right such as his father possessed. He might not then hold back, his hand seized his shield, the yellow linden-wood; he drew his ancient sword. Among men it was the heirloom of Eanmund, the son of Ohthere:[7] Weohstan had become his slayer in battle with sword's edge—an exile without friends; and he bore off to his kin the bright-shining helmet, the ringed mail-armor, the old sword made by giants that Onela had given him,[8] his kinsman's war-armor, ready battle-gear: he did not speak of the feud, though he had killed his brother's son.[9] He[1] held the armor many half-years, the blade and the battle-dress, until his son might do manly deeds like his old father. Then he gave him among the Geats war-armor of every kind, numberless, when, old, he went forth on the way from life. For the young warrior this was the first time that he should enter the war-storm with his dear lord. His heart's courage did not slacken, nor did the heirloom of his kinsman fail in the battle. That the worm found when they had come together.

Wiglaf spoke, said many fit words to his companions—his mind was mournful: "I remember that time we drank mead, when we promised our lord in the beer-hall—him who gave us these rings—that we would repay him for the war-arms if a need like this befell him—the helmets

---

6. Though in the next sentence Wiglaf is said to belong to the family of the Waegmundings, the Geatish family to which Beowulf belonged, he is here called a Scylfing (Swede), and immediately below his father, Weohstan, is represented as having fought for the Swede Onela in his attack on the Geats. But for a man to change his nation was not unusual, and Weohstan, who may have had both Swedish and Geatish blood, had evidently become a Geat long enough before to have brought up his son, Wiglaf, as one. The identity of Aelfhere is not known.
7. See above, section XXXIII, note 7. Not only did Weohstan support Onela's attack on the Geat king Heardred, but actually killed Eanmund whom Heardred was supporting, and it is Eanmund's sword that Wiglaf is now wielding.
8. The spoils of war belonged to the victorious king, who apportioned them among his fighters: thus Onela gave Weohstan the armor of Eanmund, whom Weohstan had killed.
9. This ironic remark points out that Onela did not claim wergild or seek vengeance from Weohstan, as in other circumstances he ought to have done inasmuch as Weohstan had killed Onela's close kinsman, his nephew Eanmund: but Onela was himself trying to kill Eanmund.
1. Weohstan.

and the hard swords. Of his own will he chose us among the host for this venture, thought us worthy of fame—and gave me these treasures—because he counted us good war-makers, brave helm-bearers, though our lord intended to do this work of courage alone, as keeper of the folk, because among men he had performed the greatest deeds of glory, daring actions. Now the day has come that our liege lord has need of the strength of good fighters. Let us go to him, help our war-chief while the grim terrible fire persists. God knows of me that I should rather that the flame enfold my body with my gold-giver. It does not seem right to me for us to bear our shields home again unless we can first fell the foe, defend the life of the prince of the Weather-Geats. I know well that it would be no recompense for past deeds that he alone of the company of the Geats should suffer pain, fall in the fight. For us both shall there be a part in the work of sword and helmet, of battle-shirt and war-clothing."

Then he waded through the deadly smoke, bore his war-helmet to the aid of his king, spoke in few words: "Beloved Beowulf, do all well, for, long since in your youth, you said that you would not let your glory fail while you lived. Now, great-spirited noble, brave of deeds, you must protect your life with all your might. I shall help you."

After these words, the worm came on, angry, the terrible malice-filled foe, shining with surging flames, to seek for the second time his enemies, hated men. Fire advanced in waves; shield burned to the boss; mail-shirt might give no help to the young spear-warrior; but the young man went quickly under his kinsman's shield when his own was consumed with flames. Then the war-king was again mindful of fame, struck with his war-sword with great strength so that it stuck in the head-bone, driven with force: Naegling broke, the sword of Beowulf failed in the fight, old and steel-gray. It was not ordained for him that iron edges might help in the combat. Too strong was the hand that I have heard strained every sword with its stroke, when he bore wound-hardened weapon to battle: he was none the better for it.

Then for the third time the folk-harmer, the fearful fire-dragon, was mindful of feuds, set upon the brave one when the chance came, hot and battle-grim seized all his neck with his sharp fangs: he was smeared with life-blood, gore welled out in waves.

(XXXVII.) Then, I have heard, at the need of the folk-king the earl at his side made his courage known, his might and his keenness—as was natural to him. He took no heed for that head,[2] but the hand of the brave man was burned as he helped his kinsman, as the man in armor struck the hateful foe a little lower down, so that the sword sank in, shining and engraved; and then the fire began to subside. The king himself then still controlled his senses, drew the battle-knife, biting and war-sharp, that he wore on his mail-shirt: the protector of the Weather-Geats cut the worm

---

2. I.e., the dragon's flame-breathing head.

through the middle. They felled the foe, courage drove his life out, and they had destroyed him together, the two noble kinsmen. So ought a man be, a thane at need. To the prince that was the last moment of victory for his own deeds, of work in the world.

Then the wound that the earth-dragon had caused began to burn and to swell; at once he felt dire evil boil in his breast, poison within him. Then the prince, wise of thought, went to where he might sit on a seat near the wall. He looked on the work of giants, how the timeless earth-hall held within it stone-arches fast on pillars. Then with his hands the thane, good without limit, washed him with water, blood-besmeared, the famous prince, his beloved lord, sated with battle; and he unfastened his helmet.

Beowulf spoke—despite his wounds spoke, his mortal hurts. He knew well he had lived out his days' time, joy on earth; all passed was the number of his days, death very near. "Now I would wish to give my son my war-clothing, if any heir after me, part of my flesh, were granted. I held this people fifty winters. There was no folk-king of those dwelling about who dared approach me with swords, threaten me with fears. In my land I awaited what fate brought me, held my own well, sought no treacherous quarrels, nor did I swear many oaths unrightfully. Sick with life-wounds, I may have joy of all this, for the Ruler of Men need not blame me for the slaughter of kinsmen when life goes from my body. Now quickly go to look at the hoard under the gray stone, beloved Wiglaf, now that the worm lies sleeping from sore wounds, bereft of his treasure. Be quick now, so that I may see the ancient wealth, the golden things, may clearly look on the bright curious gems, so that for that, because of the treasure's richness, I may the more easily leave life and nation I have long held."

(XXXVIII.) Then I have heard that the son of Weohstan straightway obeyed his lord, sick with battle-wounds, according to the words he had spoken, went wearing his ring-armor, woven battle-shirt, under the barrow's roof. Then he saw, as he went by the seat, the brave young retainer, triumphant in heart, many precious jewels, glittering gold lying on the ground, wonders on the wall, and the worm's lair, the old night-flier's—cups standing there, vessels of men of old, with none to polish them, stripped of their ornaments. There was many a helmet old and rusty, many an arm-ring skillfully twisted. (Easily may treasure, gold in the ground, betray each one of the race of men, hide it who will.) Also he saw a standard all gold hang high over the hoard, the greatest of hand-wonders, linked with fingers' skill. From it came a light so that he might see the ground, look on the works of craft. There was no trace of the worm, for the blade had taken him. Then I have heard that one man in the mound pillaged the hoard, the old work of giants, loaded in his bosom cups and plates at his own desire. He took also the standard, brightest of banners. The sword of the old lord—its edge was iron—had already wounded the one who for a long time had been guardian of the treasure, waged his fire-terror, hot for the hoard, rising up fiercely at midnight, till he died in the slaughter.

The messenger was in haste, eager to return, urged on by the treasures. Curiosity tormented him, whether eagerly seeking he should find the lord of the Weather-Geats, strength gone, alive in the place where he had left him before. Then with the treasures he found the great prince, his lord, bleeding, at the end of his life. Again he began to sprinkle him with water until this word's point broke through his breast-hoard—he spoke, the king, old man in sorrow, looked on the gold: "I speak with my words thanks to the Lord of All for these treasures, to the King of Glory, Eternal Prince, for what I gaze on here, that I might get such for my people before my death-day. Now that I have bought the hoard of treasures with my old life, you attend to the people's needs hereafter: I can be here no longer. Bid the battle-renowned make a mound, bright after the funeral fire, on the sea's cape. It shall stand high on Hronesness as a reminder to my people, so that sea-travelers later will call it Beowulf's barrow, when they drive their ships far over the darkness of the seas."

He took off his neck the golden necklace, bold-hearted prince, gave it to the thane, to the young spear-warrior—gold-gleaming helmet, ring, and mail-shirt, bade him use them well. "You are the last left of our race, of the Waegmundings. Fate has swept away all my kinsmen, earls in their strength, to destined death. I have to go after." That was the last word of the old man, of the thoughts of his heart, before he should taste the funeral pyre, hot hostile flames. The soul went from his breast to seek the doom of those fast in truth.

[Beowulf's Funeral]

(XXXIX.) Then sorrow came to the young man that he saw him whom he most loved on the earth, at the end of his life, suffering piteously. His slayer likewise lay dead, the awful earth-dragon bereft of life, overtaken by evil. No longer should the coiled worm rule the ring-hoard, for iron edges had taken him, hard and battle-sharp work of the hammers, so that the wide-flier, stilled by wounds, had fallen on the earth near the treasure-house. He did not go flying through the air at midnight, proud of his property, showing his aspect, but he fell to earth through the work of the chief's hands. Yet I have heard of no man of might on land, though he was bold of every deed, whom it should prosper to rush against the breath of the venomous foe or disturb with hands the ring-hall, if he found the guard awake who lived in the barrow. The share of the rich treasures became Beowulf's, paid for by death: each of the two had journeyed to the end of life's loan.

Then it was not long before the battle-slack ones left the woods, ten weak troth-breakers together, who had not dared fight with their spears in their liege lord's great need. But they bore their shields, ashamed, their war-clothes, to where the old man lay, looked on Wiglaf. He sat wearied, the foot-soldier near the shoulders of his lord, would waken him with water: it gained him nothing. He might not, though he much wished it, hold life in his chieftain on earth nor change anything of the Ruler's: the judgment of God would control the deeds of every man, just as it still does now. Then it was easy to get from the young man a grim answer to him who before had lost courage. Wiglaf spoke, the son of Weohstan, a man sad at heart, looked on the unloved ones:

"Yes, he who will speak truth may say that the liege lord who gave you treasure, the war-gear that you stand in there, when he used often to hand out to hall-sitters on the ale-benches, a prince to his thanes, helmets and war-shirts such as he could find mightiest anywhere, both far and near—that he quite threw away the war-gear, to his distress when war came upon him. The folk-king had no need to boast of his war-comrades. Yet God, Ruler of Victories, granted him that he might avenge himself, alone with his sword, when there was need for his courage. I was able to give him little life-protection in the fight, and yet beyond my power I did begin to help my kinsman. The deadly foe was ever the weaker after I struck him with my sword, fire poured less strongly from his head. Too few defenders thronged about the prince when the hard time came upon him. Now there shall cease for your race the receiving of treasure and the giving of swords, all enjoyment of pleasant homes, comfort. Each man of your kindred must go deprived of his land-right when nobles from afar learn of your flight, your inglorious deed. Death is better for any earl than a life of blame."

(XL.) Then he bade that the battle-deed be announced in the city, up over the cliff-edge, where the band of warriors sat the whole morning of the day, sad-hearted, shield-bearers in doubt whether it was the beloved man's last day or whether he would come again. Little did he fail to speak of new tidings, he who rode up the hill, but spoke to them all truthfully: "Now the joy-giver of the people of the Weathers, the lord of the Geats, is fast on his deathbed, lies on his slaughter-couch through deeds of the worm. Beside him lies his life-enemy, struck down with dagger-wounds—with his sword he might not work wounds of any kind on the monster. Wiglaf son of Weohstan sits over Beowulf, one earl by the lifeless other, in weariness of heart holds death-watch over the loved and the hated.

"Now may the people expect a time of war, when the king's fall becomes wide-known to the Franks and the Frisians. A harsh quarrel was begun with the Hugas when Hygelac came traveling with his sea-army to the land of the Frisians, where the Hetware assailed him in battle, quickly, with stronger forces, made the mailed warrior bow; he fell in the ranks: that chief gave no treasure to his retainers. Ever since then the good will of the Merewioing king has been denied us.

"Nor do I expect any peace or trust from the Swedish people, for it is wide-known that Ongentheow took the life of Haethcyn, Hrethel's son, near Ravenswood when in their over-pride the people of the Geats first went against the War-Scylfings. Straightway the wary father of Ohthere,[3] old and terrible, gave a blow in return, cut down the sea-king,[4] rescued his wife, old woman of times past, bereft of her gold, mother of Onela and Ohthere, and then he followed his life-foes until they escaped, lord-less, painfully, to Ravenswood. Then with a great army he besieged those whom the sword had left, weary with wounds, often vowed woes to the wretched band the livelong night, said that in the morning he would cut them apart with sword-blades, [hang] some on gallows-trees as sport for birds. Relief came in turn to the sorry-hearted together with dawn when they heard Hygelac's horn and trumpet, his sound as the good man came on their track with a body of retainers. (XLI.) Wide-seen was the bloody track of Swedes and Geats, the slaughter-strife of men, how the peoples stirred up the feud between them. Then the good man went with his kinsmen, old and much-mourning, to seek his stronghold: the earl Ongentheow moved further away. He had heard of the warring of Hygelac, of the war-power of the proud one. He did not trust in resis-tance, that he might fight off the sea-men, defend his hoard against the war-sailors, his children and wife. Instead he drew back, the old man behind his earth-wall.

"Then pursuit was offered to the people of the Swedes, the standards of Hygelac overran the stronghold as Hrethel's people pressed forward to the citadel. There Ongentheow the gray-haired was brought to bay by sword-blades, and the people's king had to submit to the judgment of Eofor alone. Wulf[5] son of Wonred had struck him angrily with his weapon so that for the blow the blood sprang forth in streams beneath his hair. Yet not for that was he afraid, the old Scylfing, but he quickly repaid the assault with worse exchange, the folk-king, when he turned toward him. The strong son of Wonred could not give the old man a return blow, for Ongentheow had first cut through the helmet of his head so that he had to sink down, smeared with blood—fell on the earth: he was not yet doomed, for he recovered, though the wound hurt him. The hardy thane of Hygelac,[6] when his brother lay low, let his broad sword, old blade made by giants, break the great helmet across the shield-wall; then the king bowed, the keeper of the folk was hit to the quick.

---

3. I.e., Ongentheow.
4. I.e., Haethcyn, king of the Geats. Haethcyn's brother Hygelac, who succeeded him, was not present at this battle, but arrived after the death of Haethcyn with reinforcements to relieve the survivors and to pursue Ongentheow in his retreat to his city.
5. The two sons of Wonred, Wulf and Eofor, attacked Ongentheow in turn. Wulf was struck down but not killed by the old Swedish king, who was then slain by Eofor.
6. I.e., Eofor.

"Then there were many who bound up the brother, quickly raised him up after it was granted them to control the battlefield. Then one warrior stripped the other, took from Ongentheow his iron-mail, hard-hilted sword, and his helmet, too; he bore the arms of the hoary one to Hygelac. He accepted that treasure and fairly promised him rewards among the people, and he stood by it thus: the lord of the Geats, the son of Hrethel, when he came home, repaid Wulf and Eofor for their battle-assault with much treasure, gave each of them a hundred thousand [units] of land and linked rings: there was no need for any man on middle-earth to blame him for the rewards, since they had performed great deeds. And then he gave Eofor his only daughter as a pledge of friendship—a fair thing for his home.

"That is the feud and the enmity, the death-hatred of men, for which I expect that the people of the Swedes, bold shield-warriors after the fall of princes, will set upon us after they learn that our prince has gone from life, he who before held hoard and kingdom against our enemies, did good to the people, and further still, did what a man should. Now haste is best, that we look on the people's king there and bring him who gave us rings on his way to the funeral pyre. Nor shall only a small share melt with the great-hearted one, but there is a hoard of treasure, gold uncounted, grimly purchased, and rings bought at the last now with his own life. These shall the fire devour, flames enfold—no earl to wear ornament in remembrance, nor any bright maiden add to her beauty with neck-ring; but mournful-hearted, stripped of gold, they shall walk, often, not once, in strange countries—now that the army-leader has laid aside laughter, his game and his mirth. Therefore many a spear, cold in the morning, shall be grasped with fingers, raised by hands; no sound of harp shall waken the warriors, but the dark raven, low over the doomed, shall tell many tales, say to the eagle how he fared at the feast when with the wolf he spoiled the slain bodies."

Thus the bold man was a speaker of hateful news, nor did he much lie in his words or his prophecies. The company all arose. Without joy they went below Earnaness[7] to look on the wonder with welling tears. Then they found on the sand, soulless, keeping his bed of rest, him who in former times had given them rings. Then the last day of the good man had come, when the war-king, prince of the Weather-Geats, died a wonderful death. First they saw the stranger creature, the worm lying loathsome, opposite him in the place. The fire-dragon was grimly terrible with his many colors, burned by the flames; he was fifty feet long in the place where he lay. Once he had joy of the air at night, came back down to seek his den. Then he was made fast by death, had made use of the last of his earth-caves. Beside him stood cups and pitchers, plates and rich swords lay eaten through by rust, just as they had been there in the

7. The headland near where Beowulf had fought the dragon.

bosom of the earth for a thousand winters. Then that huge heritage, gold
of men of old, was wound in a spell, so that no one of men must touch
the ring-hall unless God himself, the True King of Victories—He is
men's protection—should grant to whom He wished to open the
hoard—whatever man seemed fit to Him.

(XLII.) Then it was seen that the act did not profit him who wrongly
kept hidden the handiworks under the wall. The keeper had first slain a
man like few others, then the feud had been fiercely avenged. It is a
wonder where an earl famed for courage may reach the end of his allot-
ted life—then may dwell no longer in the mead-hall, man with his kin.
So it was with Beowulf when he sought quarrels, the barrow's ward: he
himself did not then know in what way his parting with the world should
come. The great princes who had put it[8] there had laid on it so deep a
curse until doomsday that the man who should plunder the place
should be guilty of sins, imprisoned in idol-shrines, fixed with hell-
bonds, punished with evils—unless the Possessor's favor were first shown
the more clearly to him who desired the gold.

Wiglaf spoke, the son of Weohstan: "Often many a man must suffer
distress for the will of one man, as has happened to us. We might by no
counsel persuade our dear prince, keeper of the kingdom, not to
approach the gold-guardian, let him lie where he long was, live in his
dwelling to the world's end. He held to his high destiny. The hoard has
been made visible, grimly got. What drove the folk-king thither was too
powerfully fated. I have been therein and looked at it all, the rare things
of the chamber, when it was granted me—not at all friendly was the
journey that I was permitted beneath the earth-wall. In haste I seized
with my hands a huge burden of hoard-treasures, of great size, bore it out
here to my king. He was then still alive, sound-minded and aware. He
spoke many things, old man in sorrow, and bade greet you, command-
ed that for your lord's deeds you make a high barrow in the place of his
pyre, large and conspicuous, since he was of men the worthiest warrior
through the wide earth, while he might enjoy wealth in his castle.

"Let us now hasten to see and visit for the second time the heap of pre-
cious jewels, the wonder under the walls. I shall direct you so that you
may look on enough of them from near at hand—rings and broad gold.
Let the bier be made ready, speedily prepared, when we come out, and
then let us carry our prince, beloved man, where he shall long dwell in
the Ruler's protection."

Then the son of Weohstan, man brave in battle, bade command many
warriors, men who owned houses, leaders of the people, that they carry
wood from afar for the pyre for the good man. "Now shall flame eat the
chief of warriors—the fire shall grow dark—who often survived the iron-
shower when the storm of arrows driven from bow-strings passed over the

---

8. The treasure.

shield-wall—the shaft did its task, made eager by feather-gear served the arrowhead."

And then the wise son of Weohstan summoned from the host thanes of the king, seven together, the best; one of eight warriors, he went beneath the evil roof. One who walked before bore a torch in his hands. Then there was no lot to decide who should plunder that hoard, since the men could see that every part of it rested in the hall without guardian, lay wasting. Little did any man mourn that hastily they should bear out the rare treasure. Also they pushed the dragon, the worm, over the cliff-wall, let the wave take him, the flood enfold the keeper of the treasure. Then twisted gold was loaded on a wagon, an uncounted number of things, and the prince, hoary warrior, borne to Hronesness.

(XLIII.) Then the people of the Geats made ready for him a funeral pyre on the earth, no small one, hung with helmets, battle-shields, bright mail-shirts, just as he had asked. Then in the midst they laid the great prince, lamenting their hero, their beloved lord. Then warriors began to awaken on the barrow the greatest of funeral fires; the wood-smoke climbed, black over the fire; the roaring flame mixed with weeping—the wind-surge died down—until it had broken the bone-house, hot at its heart. Sad in spirit they lamented their heart-care, the death of their liege lord. And the Geatish woman, wavy-haired, sang a sorrowful song about Beowulf, said[9] again and again that she sorely feared for herself invasions of armies, many slaughters, terror of troops, humiliation, and captivity. Heaven swallowed the smoke.

Then the people of the Weather-Geats built a mound on the promontory, one that was high and broad, wide-seen by seafarers, and in ten days completed a monument for the bold in battle, surrounded the remains of the fire with a wall, the most splendid that men most skilled might devise. In the barrow they placed rings and jewels, all such ornaments as troubled men had earlier taken from the hoard. They let the earth hold the wealth of earls, gold in the ground, where now it still dwells, as useless to men as it was before. Then the brave in battle rode round the mound, children of nobles, twelve in all, would bewail their sorrow and mourn their king, recite dirges and speak of the man. They praised his great deeds and his acts of courage, judged well of his prowess. So it is fitting that man honor his liege lord with words, love him in heart when he must be led forth from the body. Thus the people of the Geats, his hearth-companions, lamented the death of their lord. They said that he was of world-kings the mildest of men and the gentlest, kindest to his people, and most eager for fame.

---

9. The manuscript is badly damaged and the interpretation conjectural.

BACKGROUNDS AND
CONTEXTS

The *Beowulf* Manuscript

First Folio of the Cotton *Beowulf* (Reproduced by permission of the Board of the British Library)

Nothing is known of the history of the only existing manuscript of *Beo-wulf* before it came into the possession of Sir Robert Cotton (1571–1631). In 1731 the MS was damaged by a fire and was moved, together with the rest of the Cotton Collection, from Ashburnham House to the British Museum, where it now resides. Note the charred edges on this repro-duction of a facsimile of the first page.

Here is a transliteration:

H WÆT WE GARDE
na ingear dagum þeod cyninga
þrym ge frunon huða æþelingas elle[n]
fre medon. Oft scyld scefing sceathe[na]
þreatum monegum mægþum meodo setla
of teah egsode eorl syððan ærest wear[ð]
fea sceaft funden he þaes frofre geba[d]
weox under wolcnum weorð myndum þah
oð þæt him æghwylc þara ymb sittendra
ofer hron rade hyran scolde gomban
gyldan þæt wæs god cyning. ðæm eafera wæs
æfter cenned geong in geardum þone god
sende folce tofrofre fyren ðearfe on
geat þæt hie ær drugon aldor [le]ase. lange
hwile him þæs lif frea wuldres wealdend
worold are forgeaf. beowulf wæs breme
blæd wide sprang scyldes eafera sc̈ede
landum in. Swa sceal [geong g]uma gode
ge wyrcean fromum feoh giftum. on fæder

In modern editions of Old English verse in the original, such as those of *Beowulf* by Klaeber, Dobbie, Wrenn, and others, the lines are com-monly laid out in a manner which clearly shows the poetic half-lines and the alliterative patterns:

Hwæt we Gar-Dena   in geardagum
þeodcyninga   þrym gefrunon,
hu ða æþelingas   ellen fremedon!
Oft Scyld Scefing   sceaþena þreatum,
monegum mægþum   meodosetla ofteah,
egsode eorl[as],   syððan ærest wearð
feasceaft funden;   he þæs frofre gebad,
weox under wolcnum,   weorðmyndum þah,
oðþæt him æghwylc   þara ymbsittendra
ofer hronrade   hyran scolde,
gomban gyldan;   þæt wæs god cyning!
Ðæm eafera wæs   æfter cenned
geong in geardum,   þone God sende

folce to frofre;   fyrenðearfe ongeat,
þæt hie ær drugon   aldor[le]ase
lange hwile;   him þæs Liffrea,
wuldres Wealdend,   woroldare forgeaf;
Beowulf wæs breme   —blæd wide sprang—
Scyldes eafera   Scedelandum in.
Swa sceal [geong g]uma   gode gewyrcean,
fromum feohgiftum   on fæder

Tribes and Genealogies[†]

I. The Danes (Bright-, Half-, Ring-, Spear-, North-, East-, South-, West-Danes; Scyldings, Honor-, Victor-, War-Scyldings; Ing's friends).
IV. Miscellaneous.

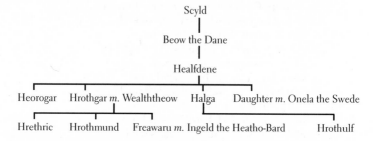

II. The Geats (Sea-, War-, Weather-Geats)

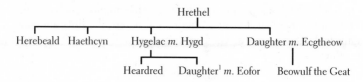

III. The Swedes.

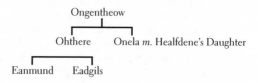

---

† From *Beowulf*, a new prose translation by E. Talbot Donaldson, pp. 57–58. Copyright © 1966 by W. W. Norton & Co., Inc. Reprinted by permission of the publisher.
1. The daughter of Hygelac who was given to Eofor may have been born to him by a former wife, older than Hygd.

A. The Half-Danes (also called Scyldings) involved in the fight at Finnsburg may represent a different tribe from the Danes of paragraph I, above. Their king Hoc had a son, Hnaef, who succeeded him, and a daughter Hildeburh, who married Finn, king of the Jutes.

B. The Jutes or Frisians are represented as enemies of the Danes in the fight at Finnsburg and as allies of the Franks or Hugas at the time Hygelac the Geat made the attack in which he lost his life and from which Beowulf swam home. Also allied with the Franks at this time were the Hetware.

C. The Heatho-Bards (i.e., "Battle-Bards") are represented as inveterate enemies of the Danes. Their king Froda had been killed in an attack on the Danes, and Hrothgar's attempt to make peace with them by marrying his daughter, Freawaru, to Froda's son, Ingeld, failed when the latter attacked Heorot. The attack was repulsed, though Heorot was burned.

A. Karl

Miles
0   50   100

Vendel
Uppsala

Heatho-
Ræmas

SWEDES   UPPLAND

Vänern

Vättern

Gotland

Göteborg

Vendsyssel

GEATS

Öland

JUTLAND

EOTAN
(JUTES)

Skåney

DANES   (København)

North Sea

Heorot

ANGLES   ZEALAND

Baltic Sea

Schleswig

Eider

Gifths

Heathobards

Wendle(?)
(Vandals)

Vistula

Wylfings (?)

N

Frisians

Ems

Oder

Hetware

Elbe

FRANCAN

Meuse   Rhine

(After Fr. Klaeber, *Beowulf*)

Map from *Medieval English Literature*, edited by J. B. Trapp, vol. I of *The Oxford Anthology of English Literature*. Copyright © 1973 by Oxford University Press, Inc. Original version of map first appeared in Fr. Klaeber, *Beowulf*, 3rd ed. Reprinted by permission of Oxford University Press, Inc., and D. C. Heath & Co.

ROBERT C. HUGHES

The Origins of Old English to 800 A.D. [†]

Pre-history of England and the Celtic Settlements

By the best available estimates, the land we now call England had been inhabited for 50 to 250 thousand years before the recorded history of the English-speaking peoples. Paleolithic man roamed the area when the North Sea was only a minor river and when no channel separated England from the Continent. Neolithic man from the Mediterranean with his polished and ground stone implements, his agrarian interests, his domesticated animals, and his rituals of burial lived in these lands from ca. 5000 B.C. The Stone Age lasted in this region until ca. 2000 B.C., and the Bronze Age settlements continued probably to ca. 500 B.C. The early Celts made their way to this land in the last centuries of the Bronze Age and remained the chief population through the early centuries of the Iron Age in England.

By the time of Christ, Celtic peoples lived not only in England, but also had migrated throughout many other parts of western Europe. Although, as far as we know, the Celts had no single name for England, early Latin writers referred to these western lands as "Britannia" ("island of the Bretons"). The Celts lived in small groups or tribes of kinsmen without the larger political unity necessary for a nation or empire. The language of the Celts in England, near kinsmen of the Celts in Gaul, was probably first Gaelic and then later Britannic, from which Welsh, Breton, and Cornish derived.

Roman Occupation of England

In 55 B.C. and again in 54 B.C., Julius Caesar invaded the Celtic lands in England, not necessarily to conquer the islands, but perhaps to retaliate for the British fellowship with the Gallic Celts who had fought him on the Continent. Neither invasion was successful even though Caesar established his forces for a time in the southeast and demanded tribute which the Britannic Celts never paid. Not until 43 A.D. did the Romans

† Copyright © 1975 by Robert C. Hughes and printed with his permission. This essay first appeared in the original Norton Critical Edition of *Beowulf* (1975).

   This brief review of the Old English language and peoples is extensively indebted to Albert C. Baugh, *A History of the English Language,* 2nd ed. (New York: Appleton, 1957). For additional material on the internal and external history of Old English, see Henry Alexander, *The Story of Our Language* (1940; rpt. New York: Anchor, 1969); Otto Jespersen, *Growth and Structure of the English Language,* 9th ed. (New York: Anchor, 1955); Samuel Moore and Thomas A. Knott, *The Elements of Old English,* 10th ed. (Ann Arbor: Wahr, 1965); John Nist, *A Structural History of English,* (New York: St. Martin's 1966); Thomas Pyles, *The Origins and Development of the English Language,* 2nd ed. (New York: Harcourt, 1971); and Stuart Robertson and Frederic G. Cassidy, *The Development of Modern English,* 2nd ed. (Englewood Cliffs, N. J.: Prentice-Hall, 1954).

under Emperor Claudius seriously attempt to occupy Britannia. Between 78 and 85 A.D., the Roman governor of Britain, Agricola, completed the conquest of the southern and midland Celtic populace; however, the Roman forces never entirely overcame the Celts in the northern mountains and in the far western land of Wales, where many Celts had retreated in the face of Roman advances. The Roman occupation was challenged from time to time from the North and from the West; for instance, in the second century the Celts from the North revolted and pushed the Romans south of the Humber River. In reaction, after the northern Celts were driven back, the Emperor Hadrian came to England and constructed "Hadrian's Wall" (73 miles long) from Wallsend on the Tyne River to the head of the Solway Firth, ca. 121–27 A.D., a line of fortifications which helped the Romans defend themselves later against the Picts.

By the end of the fourth century, the Roman rulers had begun to recall their military forces from the frontiers of the Empire to help defend the homeland from the increasing hostility of the Germanic tribes on the move, kinsmen of the Teutons who would settle in England from the second half of the fifth century. The Angles, Saxons, and Jutes (L. *Iuti*) shared a common Germanic history and culture with other migratory peoples who challenged Roman sovereignty in western Europe, with tribes such as the Goths, Vandals, Franks, and Danes.[1]

By ca. 410, the last of the Roman legions were recalled from Britannia and left the British Celts without protection from their own kinsmen in the North and West. With the end of the Roman sovereignty in England and with the British Celts weakened militarily after over three centuries of Roman occupation, the Gaelic Scots (Irishmen) from the West and the Britannic Picts from the North began to encroach upon the Celtic dominance south of the Humber. For a narrative account of what then happened in Britain, we have Venerable Bede (673?–735) to thank for his history of these times in his *Ecclesiastical History of the English People*.

Germanic Invasions

In his Latin work written in 731, Bede relates that the Celtic chieftain Vortigern offered the Germanic Jutes the island of Thanet in exchange for military support against the Picts and the Scots. The Jutes, led by the brothers Hengest[2] and Horsa, came in force and fulfilled their obligation to the Celts, but they decided to stay and settled in Kent and on the Isle of Wight. This first Germanic tribe to occupy part of England seems to have come from the Frankish Rhineland and

---

1. Note how stories and figures from all these related Germanic cultures are interwoven in *Beowulf* [*Editor*].
2. He may be the same Hengest referred to in the Finn Episode in *Beowulf* (see pp. 19–22) and in the *Fight at Finnsburg* [*Editor*].

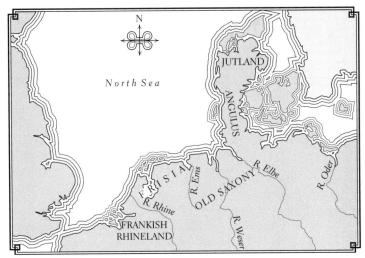

The continental homelands of the Germanic invaders
(From Ralph Arnold, *A Social History of England*)

was closely related to the Frisians, many of whom had joined with the
Jutes in their military adventures.

Within a generation, the Saxons came to England in great numbers
and settled in Sussex by 477 and in Wessex by 495. The mythic King
Arthur from Wales supposedly helped fight off the Saxon advance to the
West; in the fifth century, many Celts were driven into Wales and Corn-
wall and over to Brittany by the Saxons. These Saxons, sea-raiders of the
English coasts from the fourth century, migrated from the area between
the Rhine and Elbe Rivers.

Within another generation after the Saxon invasions, the Angles
from South Denmark had invaded East Anglia and the midland
between the Humber and the Thames. By 547 the Angles had set up
yet another area of dominance in Northumbria. The tribal divisions of
England and the European homes of the Germanic tribes are matters
of scholarly opinion and should be understood as probable rather than
historical locations. For instance, by the end of the fifth century both
Saxons and Angles inhabited the midland regions in England. By the
seventh century, the Anglo-Saxon heptarchy constituted the main polit-
ical divisions of the land later named after the Angles: Northumbria,
Mercia, and East Anglia populated by the Angles; Kent settled by the
Jutes; and Essex, Wessex, and Sussex controlled by the Saxons. In the
seventh century, Northumbria dominated politically; in the eighth cen-
tury, Mercia; and in the ninth century, Wessex, first under Egbert
(802–39), and then under King Alfred, who ruled the West Saxons and
hence the heptarchy from 871 to 899.

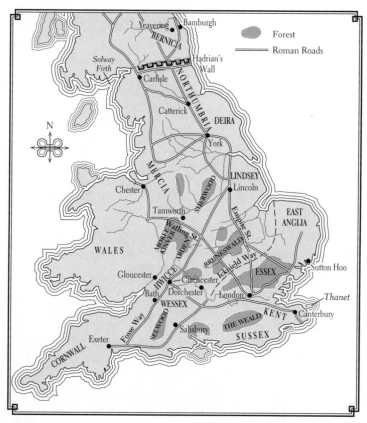

The English kingdoms at the beginning of the seventh century A.D. (From Ralph Arnold, *A Social History of England*)

The name "Anglo-Saxon" originally referred to Saxons in England as distinct from those on the Continent, but by the sixteenth century the term was used in reference to both the peoples and the language of England after the Germanic migration. In 601, Pope Gregory I referred to Ethelbert, the Jutish king, as "Rex Anglorum" ("King of the Angles"), and a century later Bede entitled his work *Historia Ecclesiastica Gentis Anglorum*. By the year 1000, the English people were often called "Angul-cynn" ("race of the Angles"). The word "Englisc" actually predates the term "Englalond" which came into use about 1000.[3]

3. Baugh, p. 57.

Christianity in England

The Celts had their first contact with Christianity through the Roman occupation of the third century, before the Germanic invasions. Some of the Celts in the North and West remained Christian even after the Teutons settled in England in the fifth century. Irish missionaries from Iona in the Hebrides, a mission established in the sixth century by St. Columba to convert the Scots, helped to introduce the Northumbrians to Christianity through the work of St. Aidan and his missionaries from 635 to 655.

In 597, Pope Gregory I appointed St. Augustine, a Roman Benedictine monk, to convert the central and southern regions of England to Christianity. With some forty monks, Augustine first arrived in Kent at the reluctant invitation of King Ethelbert, who had married Bertha, a Christian Frankish princess. At the end of the sixth century, King Ethelbert was the strongest overlord in the lands south of the Humber. After Ethelbert granted Augustine some lands in Canterbury, Augustine began his work for which he was later called the "Apostle of the English"; within three months, the king himself became one of Augustine's first English converts to Christianity. By the end of the seventh century, almost all of the English had been converted by missionaries through the efforts of Aidan in the North and of Augustine's monks in the South. For centuries thereafter, the Germanic myths and pagan rituals survived barely beneath the surface of Christian philosophy and theology, with Wyrd ("fate, doom") and Providence often scarcely distinguishable.

The "Englisc" Language

The language that the Germanic tribes spoke at the time of their invasions of England sprang from a common language used by the early Teutonic peoples in prehistoric times. By the fifth century, the Angles, Saxons, and Jutes spoke dialects of the same language understandable in large measure by each of the tribes. Old English (OE), as the shared language is called, belongs to the low West Teutonic (Germanic) branch of the Indo-European family of languages. OE is related to the North Teutonic languages (Icelandic and the Scandinavian tongues, Danish, Norwegian, and Swedish), to the East Teutonic (Gothic, now extinct), and to other West Teutonic languages such as Frisian and Franconian. OE, like Latin and Greek, was a highly inflected, synthetic language in which person, number, and tense in verbs, and case, number, and gender in nouns, adjectives, and pronouns were established by adding special endings to words or by making internal changes in words. As is the case with modern German, the major method of word formation in OE was the compounding of base forms with one another or with affixes.

With the exception of place names, the British Celts contributed only a small number of words to OE, the language of their conquerors. The Latin influence upon the Germanic dialects when these tribes were on the Continent amounted to several hundred words. Although Latin contributed over six hundred words to the British Celts, very few of these words found their way from Celtic to OE. The greatest influence of Latin upon OE before the Norman invasion came about coincident with English conversion to Christianity, and with the subsequent introduction of philosophical, theological, liturgical, and administrative vocabulary used by the Roman Church in England. To the tenth century, OE dialects (Northumbrian, Mercian, and West Saxon) only reluctantly and sparingly borrowed from other languages, and even then usually only in vocabulary, with a few important exceptions from the Scandinavian languages.

Literature and Learning

Since the West Saxon dialect became the literary standard of OE in the eighth and ninth centuries, it is the dialect in which the vernacular literature is preserved. When they invaded England, the Germanic tribes apparently did not keep written records, but relied on a strong oral tradition for the transmission of their depository of literary and historical matters to later generations. Not until the conversion of the Anglo-Saxons to Christianity with its use of the Roman alphabet and with its commitment to the preservation of written historical records do we have extant examples of OE vernacular. The earliest OE work extant is a code of laws promulgated by King Ethelbert, the first Christian King of the Jutes, ca. 600. Since nearly all OE works are preserved in copies compiled years after their composition, it is very difficult to ascertain a definite chronology for them and to testify to their authorship with certainty. The earliest and most important Germanic epic, *Beowulf*, was probably composed in the oral tradition at a time roughly contemporaneous with Bede's *Ecclesiastical History* in the first half of the eighth century.

From the end of the seventh century to the close of the eighth, York and Canterbury were the main centers of learning in England. Both Alcuin (735?–804), who established a school in the court of Charlemagne ca. 781, and Venerable Bede, who did his work in Northumbria, were from the school at York. The scholars at Canterbury spent much of their efforts in teaching Latin and Greek. Cædmon, who is our first known English poet, flourished ca. 670 at the Abbey of Whitby. Bede quotes a Latin version of Cædmon's "Hymn" in his *Ecclesiastical History*. *Widsith* also belongs to this early period of OE literature, ca. 650–700; in this poem of less than 150 lines, the scop, who is the "far traveller," describes his visits to famous

Germanic kings and praises their generosity in the gifts they gave him in return for his works. The chieftains looked to the poets in the oral tradition for the recording of their heroic deeds, thereby to attain immortality through succeeding generations who would marvel over the exploits of their ancestors.

From these works emerges a portrait of the Germanic tribes not very different from Tacitus' description of the continental Teutons in his *Germania*, written in 98 A.D. The Germanic traditions in the legal payments for offenses (such as the *wergild*, or "man-price," paid by a murderer to the bereaved family), in the composition of the society as a *comitatus*, or brotherhood of men who owed allegiance to a chieftain and expected his benevolence in return, and in the heroic ideal of excellence in kingly behavior form some of the basic tenets of the Old English society from the fifth to the eighth century. Even with this heroic ethic established, however, the atmosphere remains dark and ominous as heroic man struggles against the natural and supernatural forces that are perhaps malevolent or, what is worse, indifferent to his survival, honor, and nobility. Heroic literature, typified by *Beowulf*, at least held out the possibility of the dignity that comes alone from demonstrated skill and courage in struggles engaged in for the manly values of the community.

E. TALBOT DONALDSON

[Old English Prosody and Cædmon's *Hymn*]†

All the poetry of Old English is in the same verse form. The verse unit is the single line, since rhyme was not used to link one line to another, except very occasionally in late Old English. The organizing device of the line is alliteration, the beginning of several words with the same sound ("Foemen fled"). The Old English alliterative line contains four principal stresses, and is divided into two half-lines of two stresses each by a strong medial caesura, or pause. These two half-lines are linked to each other by the alliteration: at least one of the two stressed words in the first half-line, and usually both of them, begin with the same sound as the first stressed word of the second half-line (the second stressed word is generally non-alliterative). The fourth line of *Beowulf* is an example:

† Adapted from *The Norton Anthology of English Literature*, M. H. Abrams and others, eds., 3rd ed. (New York: W. W. Norton & Co., Inc., 1974), I, 18, 21–22. Copyright © 1974, 1968, 1962 by W. W. Norton & Co., Inc. Reprinted by permission of the publisher. For a more detailed discussion of Old English prosody see J. R. R. Tolkien's classic Prefatory Remarks to *Beowulf and the Finnesburg Fragment*, John R. Clark Hall, trans., ed. with notes and an introduction by C. L. Wrenn (London: Allen & Unwin, 1950).

Oft Scyld Scefing   sceaþena þreatum.

[As can be seen in lines 4, 5, and 8 of Cædmon's *Hymn*, any vowel allit-
erates with any other vowel (*Editor*).] In addition to the alliteration, the
length of the unstressed syllables and their number and pattern are gov-
erned by a highly complex set of rules. When sung or intoned—as it
was—to the rhythmic strumming of a harp, Old English poetry must have
been wonderfully impressive in the dignified, highly formalized way
which aptly fits both its subject matter and tone.

Cædmon's *Hymn* is one of the oldest of preserved English poems,
having been written between 658 and 680. Bede, the great cleric of
Old English times, tells the story of its composition in his *Ecclesiastical
History of the English People* (completed in 731). Cædmon, a
Northumbrian layman, had all his life felt himself incompetent in the
art of verse, and when, according to the custom that was used at feasts,
the harp was passed around the table so that each guest might enter-
tain the others with a song, Cædmon always found a pretext to take
himself from the table before the harp reached him. One night when
he had thus avoided singing, he fell asleep in the stable where he had
gone to tend the animals. He dreamed that someone came to him and
said: "Cædmon, sing me something," and when Cædmon excused
himself, the other insisted that he sing, directing him to celebrate the
beginning of created things. Cædmon at once sang the *Hymn*. On wak-
ing, he remembered his verses; and thereafter, Bede tells us, he was
able to express any given sacred topic in excellent poetry after only a
few hours of work. He became a monk and devoted his life to the com-
position of Christian verse, but none of the religious poetry in Old
English that has been preserved may surely be ascribed to him except
his first short work.

[Cædmon's *Hymn* is an early example of the revolutionary transforma-
tion that took place as Germanic verse form and vocabulary were turned
to Christian usage after the conversion of the Anglo-Saxons. Cædmon
seems to have been the first to use this form for Christian subjects, and to
use words like *Weard* ("Guardian"), *Driht* ("Lord"), *and Frea* ("Ruler") in
a Christian rather than earthly connotation. These and words like them
also appear frequently in the Christian sense in *Beowulf*, most likely as a
result of the influence of Cædmon and his poetic followers. Perhaps the
Beowulf-poet had Cædmon's *Hymn* in mind when he made the scop at
Hrothgar's court sing of the creation of the world (lines 90–98) (*Editor*).]

The poem is given here in a West Saxon form with a literal inter-
linear translation. In Old English spelling, *æ* (as in Cædmon's name
and line 3) is a vowel symbol that has not survived; it represented both
a short *a* sound and a long open *e* sound. *þ* (line 2) and *ð* both rep-
resented the sound *th*. The large space in the middle of the line indi-
cates the caesura.

Cædmon's Hymn

Nu sculon herigean
Now we must praise

heofonrices Weard,
heaven-kingdom's Guardian,

Meotodes meahte
the Creator's might

and his modgeþanc,
and his mind-plans,

weorc Wuldor-Fæder,
the work of the Glory-Father,

swa he wundra gehwæs,
when he of wonders of everyone,

ece Drihten,
eternal Lord,

or onstealde.
the beginning established.[1]

He ærest sceop
He first created

ielda[2] bearnum
for men's sons

heofon to hrofe,
heaven as a roof,

halig Scyppend;
holy Creator;

ða middangeard,
then middle-earth,

moncynnes Weard,
mankind's Guardian,

ece Drihten,
eternal Lord,

æfter teode
afterwards made—

firum foldan
for men earth,

Frea ælmihtig.
Master almighty.

1. I.e., "established the beginning of every one of wonders."
2. The later manuscript copies read *eorpan* "earth," for *ælda* (West Saxon *ielda*), "men's."

CRITICISM

FRED C. ROBINSON

Appositive Style and the Theme of *Beowulf*[†]

A recent edition of John C. Hodges's *Harbrace College Handbook* defines "appositive" as "a noun or noun substitute set beside another noun or noun substitute and identifying or explaining it."[1] Thus in the sentence "the hero of the poem is Beowulf, king of the Geatas," "Beowulf" and "king of the Geatas" are in apposition, since they stand next to one another, have no word connecting them, and have the same referent, one element explaining or identifying the other. Etymologically *The Harbrace College Handbook* is correct in saying that an appositive is "set beside" another noun, for the Latin *appositus* means "placed (next) to." But in practice appositives can sometimes be separated from the word to which they refer, as in "Beowulf was there, the king of the Geatas." Also, some grammarians extend the meaning of "appositive" to include parts of speech other than the noun and to include even phrases and clauses.[2] What is essential, apparently, is that the two elements in an appositive construction be the same part of speech, have the same referent, and not be connected except by syntactical parallelism within the sentence in which they occur. "Appositive" in this broad sense describes fairly accurately what Anglo-Saxon scholars term "variation" in Old English poetry. "Variation" has been defined as "syntactically parallel words or word-groups which share a common referent and which occur within a single clause.[3] A ubiquitous feature in Old Germanic poetry, variation is, according to Frederick Klaeber, "the very soul of the Old English poetical style."[4]

The distinguishing feature of apposition (or variation) is its parataxis — its lack of an expressed logical connection between the apposed elements. "Beowulf, king of the Geatas" is apposition; "Beowulf was king of the Geatas" is not. The relationship between the elements of an appositive construction and the relevance of these elements to the sentence at large must be inferred from their proximate and parallel status. In Old English poetry, where apposition is used so heavily, the construction

---

[†] From *Beowulf and the Appositive Style* (Knoxville: U of Tennessee P, 1985) 3–28; 84–89. Translations appearing in brackets are the editor's. Footnotes are the author's except where followed by [*Editor*].

1. John C. Hodges and Mary E. Whitten, *Harbrace College Handbook*, 8th ed. (New York, 1977), 425.

2. E.g., H. Poutsma, *A Grammar of Late Modern English*, 2d ed. (Groningen, Netherlands, 1928), 278.

3. Fred C. Robinson, "Two Aspects of Variation in Old English Poetry," in *Old English Poetry: Essays on Style*, ed. Daniel G. Calder (Berkeley, 1979), 129.

4. Frederick Klaeber, "Studies in the Textual Interpretation of *Beowulf*," *MP* 3 (1905), 237. Cf. Frederick Klaeber, ed., *Beowulf and the Fight at Finnsburg*, 3d ed. with 1st and 2nd supps. (Boston, 1950), lxv. All quotations from *Beowulf* are drawn from this edition and are cited by simple line number(s). I have not reproduced Klaeber's macrons and other diacritics, and I occasionally disregard his use of capital letters.

often seems especially rich in implicit meaning, as the following examples from *Beowulf* may suggest.

> Nealles him on heape   handgesteallan,
> æðelinga bearn   ymbe gestodon   [2596–97]

"The comrades, the sons of noblemen, did not stand by him together at all." Only so much is overtly stated about the cowardly retainers who abandoned Beowulf in his time of need. But implicit are the logical relationships among the apposed elements: "Although sons of noblemen and thus especially obligated to stand firm at the hand of the leader, they did not stand by him together at all." This rendition of the poet's logically reticent paratactic sentence into an elaborately explicit hypotactic version is not entirely arbitrary; it is, I believe, implied in the selection of the two terms in apposition and especially by the implied relationship between the components of the compound *handgesteallan*.[5] Similarly implicit relationships may be suspected in Wiglaf's appositions in his rueful comment about the Geatas' efforts to dissuade Beowulf from facing the dragon:

> Ne meahton we gelæran   leofne þeoden,
> rices hyrde   ræd ænigne,
> þæt he ne grette   goldweard þone

"We could not persuade the dear prince, the guardian of the kingdom, that he should leave the dragon unchallenged." The appositives "leofne þeoden" and "rices hyrde" seem to supply the respective motivations of the persuading subjects and the unpersuaded king: "Because the prince was beloved to us, we begged him not to fight the dragon, but since he was a conscientious guardian of his kingdom, he insisted on doing so." The poet says only that Beowulf was a prince beloved by his subjects and a guardian of his kingdom; he leaves to inference the relevance these juxtaposed descriptive phrases have in their context.

Occasionally, when a character in the poem wishes to suggest logical relationships without overtly stating them, this suggestive power of apposition becomes a part of the dramatic action. In his farewell speech to Hrothgar, Beowulf wishes to assure the Danish king that the Geatas stand ready to help him in the event of either attack from without or treachery from within. If foreign armies resume hostilities, declares Beowulf, he will bring to Hrothgar's defense "a forest of spears, the support of an army."[6] Turning to the other source of danger, the incipient power struggle at which Wealhtheow has persistently hinted,[7] Beowulf dares not

---

5. BTD, s.v. *handgestealla*, brings out well the elemental meaning of the compound with its definition "one whose parts is close at one's hand."

6. For this interpretation of "garholt . . . mægenes fultum" (1834–35), see Robinson, "Two Aspects of Variation," 134–35.

7. Some reasons for dissenting from Kenneth Sisam's popular argument that there is no treachery afoot in Heorot (in *The Structure of "Beowulf"* [Oxford, 1965]) are set forth in my essay "Teaching the Backgrounds: History, Religion, and Culture," in *Approaches to Teaching "Beowulf"*, ed. Jess B. Bessinger, Jr., and Robert F. Yeager (New York, 1984), 109, 111–12.

speak so openly. In order to convey his meaning without declaring it in the full hearing of Hrothulf and the other Danes, he resorts to an implicitly significant apposition:

> Gif him þonne Hreþric   to hofum Geata
> geþingeð þeodnes bearn,   he mæg þær fela
> freonda findan   [1836–38]

This has usually been taken as merely a polite invitation: if Hrethric should come to Geatland, he will find friends there. But the appositive "þeodnes bearn" subtly calls attention to Hrethric's standing in the line of succession to the Danish throne: he is the eldest son of Hrothgar. Wealhtheow's anxious allusions to her sons' succession and her appeals to Beowulf to support them (1178–87, 1219–20, 1226–27) give special significance to this seemingly casual appositive. Moreover, Beowulf describes Hrethric's visit with the curious expression "him . . . geþingeð [MS geþinged]," implying arrangements or negotiations rather than a casual visit,[8] while the cryptic maxim with which Beowulf concludes the speech ("feorcyþðe beoð / selran gesohte þæm þe him selfa deah") seems to hint at more serious purposes than a pleasure trip. The unique compound *feorcyþðu* could mean "close friends who are afar" (i.e., distant allies) as well as the usually assumed "far countries" and would then refer to the same people as *freonda* in the first half of the verse. Beowulf's carefully phrased advice and veiled assurances prompt Hrothgar to sudden and enthusiastic praise of his wisdom and his skill at speech. (He praises Beowulf's *wordcwydas* twice in five lines: 1841–45.) If my reading is correct, then this passage depicts a character in the poem using an appositive phrase with subtle significance and another character reacting to that use. If the poet has his characters use apposition with calculated effect, then it should not seem oversubtle to see such effects in his own use of the construction when he is speaking in his own voice.

As we shall soon see, the logically open, implicit quality of apposition is shared by other stylistic devices in the poem, and in concert these create a reticent, appositive style which is intimately cooperative with the tone and theme of the poem. Before we turn to these other appositive devices, however, we should perhaps address the question of the theme of *Beowulf*, since after doing so we shall find it easier to relate the stylistic devices to that theme.

What is the theme of *Beowulf*? There will never be universal agreement on this question, and yet there is considerable common ground among critics of the poem, especially those who, like me, start from a gen-

---

8. Assuming that a finite form of *geþingian* lies behind the MS *geþinged*, I translate "him . . . to hofum Geata / geþinged" as "makes arrangements (or negotiates) for himself at the courts of the Geatas" (*to* being used as in 1990). Although indirectly phrased so as not to alarm Hrothulf, Beowulf's statement makes clear that if the king's son opens negotiations with the Geatas, he will find that he has allies there.

eral acceptance of the landmark essay by J.R.R. Tolkien, "*Beowulf:* The Monsters and the Critics."[9] Central to this Tolkienian view of the poem is the contrast between the time and milieu of the poet and the time and milieu of the characters in his poem. Like most heroic poems of Western culture—the *Iliad and Odyssey, the Aeneid,* the *Song of Roland,* the *Nibelungenlied*[1] —*Beowulf* is about a bygone era. The action of the poem is set in the fifth and sixth centuries, and the people it describes are remote pagan ancestors of the Anglo-Saxons, living on the continent of Europe in and near the lands whence the English migrated to the British Isles and, after many generations, became Christians. The events recounted conform in outline and in some detail with what we know of the history of pagan Germania, and yet the time and the setting are sufficiently distant that monsters and dragons can assume a place in the narrative without disturbing the verisimilitude of the more historical elements, partly, no doubt, because everything in the poem is felt to have taken place in a far lost, primordial past.

Exactly how much time elapsed between the action of *Beowulf* and the time of the poet and his audience depends upon the exact date of the poem's composition. Until recently there was a broad scholarly consensus that *Beowulf* reached more or less its present form sometime in the eighth century. In the wake of Ashley Crandell Amos's crucially important reassessment of linguistic methods of dating Old English texts, however, a series of radical reappraisals of the bases for dating the poem have now reopened the question of date in an almost dismaying fashion.[2] Some authorities stubbornly cling to the conviction that the poem was composed in the eighth century, while others (most prominently Kevin Kiernan) argue that the poem could not have been written before A.D. 1016. And there are arguments for various dates between these extremes. I am inclined to favor an earlier rather than a later date. The alliteration of palatal and velar *g*, which Amos confirms is still a valid criterion of early poetry,[3] implies a date probably before the early to mid tenth century, when the allophones of *g* began to be perceived by poets as two distinct sounds. Moreover, while it is true that scholars have demolished the old argument that *Beowulf* could not have been composed after the period of Scandinavian invasions and settlement,[4] I do not believe the case is strong for a post-invasion *Beowulf* poet's having taken his story from contemporary Scandinavian sources. The forms of the proper names in

---

9. J. R. R. Tolkien, "*Beowulf:* The Monsters and the Critics," *Proceedings of the British Academy* 22 (1936), 245–95.
1. Only *El Cid,* the great Spanish epic, is close in time to the events it describes, and its heroic quality is accordingly diminished. The most charming and realistic of medieval epics, *El Cid* is the least heroic in outlook and temper.
2. See Amos's *Linguistic Means of Determining the Dates of Old English Texts* (Cambridge, Mass., 1980); Colin Chase, ed., *The Dating of "Beowulf"* (Toronto, 1981); Kevin S. Kiernan, "*Beowulf*" *and the "Beowulf" Manuscript* (New Brunswick, 1981).
3. Amos, pp. 100–2.
4. See especially the essays by R. I. Page and Roberta Frank in *The Dating of "Beowulf,"* 113–39.

the Old English poem bear no traces of transmission through ninth- or tenth-century Norse, and the stories in *Beowulf* and the manner of their telling do not closely resemble surviving Norse poetry. But these arguments are not probative, and when such learned and formidable challenges to an early date have been posed, minds must remain open. Whatever the poem's date, everyone will agree that there is a chasm of time—two to four centuries—separating the poet from the dramatic action of his poem, and during that time there was a transforming migration, both geographical and theological. Few readers would deny that *Beowulf* is a profoundly retrospective narrative.

Why does the poet reach back so far in time for his subject matter? Why does a person living in a settled realm, with church and coinage and law codes to help order his existence and written documents to protect his interests and enrich his mind—why should such a person compose a poem about barely literate tribes striving for fame and hegemony in the ancient Germanic lands of the north? The poet's life was far different from that of his characters, not least because he and his contemporaries were Christian, with a rich Christian literature to comfort them and a clear Christian formula to explain the hopeless plight of their heathen ancestors, while the characters in the poem are these very heathen ancestors, living in a benighted and violent world. They were deprived of the revelation which offered the poet and his audience escape from the damnation which awaits all heathens, including, apparently, the heroes of *Beowulf.*

In the poet's Christian world there was no uncertainty as to the nature of heathenism as contrasted with that of Christianity. Christianity is the Truth. Paganism is a network of deceptions and lies fabricated by the Devil to ensnare the ignorant. Through Christianity a person can find salvation. Without Christianity, according to the voices that spoke for the Church, a person is lost eternally. The three damnatory clauses distributed throughout the Athanasian Creed reiterate ominously the sure perdition which awaits those who have not heard and accepted the articles of the faith.[5] Mark 16:16 gives powerful scriptural support to this view,[6] as do Church Fathers such as St. Cyprian, who insisted quite simply that "there is no salvation outside the Church." In his letter describing the pagan Saxons as being "of one blood and one bone" with the Christian English, St. Boniface makes it clear that without conversion these Germanic brethren were forever lost to the Devil.[7]

---

5. The threefold anathema—"quicumque vult salvus esse: ante omnia opus est, ut teneat catholicam fidem. . . . Quam nisi quisque integram inviolatamque servaverit: absque dubio in æternum peribit. . . . Hæc est fides catholica: quam nisi quisque fideliter firmiterque crediderit, salvus esse non poterit"—was widely known through, inter alia, the liturgy.
6. "He that believeth and is baptised shall be saved; but he that believeth not shall be damned."
7. *Sancti Bonifatii et Lullii epistolae,* ed. M. Tangl, Monumenta historica Germaniae, Epistolae selectae, I (1916), no. 46.

English kings who traced their lineage back to Woden, and English aristocrats who took pride in the works and wisdom of their continental forebears, had, then, to acknowledge upon becoming Christians that their ancestors were consigned to eternal damnation. More than that, the Christian mentors of the Anglo-Saxons demanded that the ancestors be consigned to oblivion as well. Alcuin's frequently cited letter to the monks of Lindisfarne remains the locus classicus for this view: "Let the words of God be read at the meal of the clergy. There it is proper to listen to the lector, not a harp-player; the sermons of the Fathers, not songs of the people. For what has Ingeld to do with Christ? Narrow is the house; it cannot hold both. The King of Heaven wants nothing to do with so-called kings who are pagan and damned. For the eternal King reigns in heaven; the damned pagan laments in hell."[8] Some critics have felt that too much has been made of this passage, arguing that Alcuin speaks only for himself when he exhorts the monks at Lindisfarne. But in fact Alcuin's statement about the importance of divorcing oneself utterly from the traditions of non-Christians is merely an adaptation of a widely expressed medieval Christian doctrine. In Corinthians II, 6:14–15, St. Paul provides the biblical paradigm for this tenet: "Be ye not unequally yoked together with unbelievers: for what fellowship hath righteousness with unrighteousness? and what communion hath light with darkness? and what concord hath Christ with Belial, or what part hath he that believeth with an infidel?" Among the Church Fathers who repeated this injunction is Tertullian, who seems almost obsessed with it. In De spectaculis, chapters 26–27, he condemns those who listen to a tragedian at heathen assemblies with the challenge "What fellowship has light with darkness, life with death?" Elsewhere he reiterates the antithesis in various forms: "What has Athens to do with Jerusalem?" "What communion has Christ with Belial?" "What part has a believer with an infidel?" "What commerce have the condemners with those who are condemned? The same, I assume, as Christ with Belial."[9] St. Jerome adopts Tertullian's antithesis, adding the query, "What has Horace to do with the Psalter?"[1] Pope Zacharias in a letter to St. Boniface had also used the antithesis, and the eighth-century biographer of St. Eligius asks what use there could be for the nonsense of Homer and Virgil or the writings of heathens like Sallust and Herodotus[2] The phrasing of the question in the Gemma animae seems to owe something to Alcuin: "Of what benefit to the soul are the battles of Hector or the disputations of Plato or the poems of Virgil or the songs of Ovid, all of whom are wailing with their ilk in the prison of the

8. Monumenta Germaniae historica: Epistolae Karolini Aevi, II (1895), ed. E. Dümmler, 183.
9. For a compilation of Tertullian's uses of this antithesis, see Jean-Claude Fredouille, Tertullien et la conversion de la culture antique (Paris, 1972), 320–22.
1. Epistola 22, 29, PL, XX, col. 416: "Quae enim communicatio luci ad tenebras? Qui consensus Christo cum Belial? Quid facit cum Psalterio Horatius?"
2. Sancti Bonifatii, no. 87, and Luc d'Achery, Spicilegium; sive, Collectio veterum aliquot scriptorum qui in Galliæ bibliothecis delituerant (Paris, 1723), II, 77.

infernal Babylon under the grim rule of Pluto?" (*PL* CLXXII, cols. 543–44). The exhortation to Christians to reject the pre-Christian past— whether Hector or Horace or Athens or Ingeld—is in no sense, then, an aberration of Alcuin's. It is a serious Christian belief grafted deeply into Anglo-Saxon thought, but with reference to Germanic rather than to Classical paganism. The proscription continues into the later Anglo-Saxon period, with Ælfric instructing his fellow priests, "Forbeode ge þa hæðenan sangas þæra læwedra manna" ["I forbid you the heathen songs of laymen"], and Wulfstan proclaiming, "And we læraŏ þæt man geswice freolsdagum hæþenra leoŏa and deofles gamena" "[And we teach one should desist from the feast days of heathen peoples and the pleasures of the devil"].[3]

And yet it is precisely the condemned, pre-Christian past to which the *Beowulf* poet devotes his poem. Though a Christian addressing Christians, he does not treat the Christian heroes celebrated by so many of his fellow poets but turns his gaze instead back to the dark and hopeless epoch and recreates for his own age the times and people whom the churchmen wanted forgotten. He cannot pretend these people were Christian, nor can he just quietly ignore their desperate spiritual state, as some modern critics have wanted to believe. From the very beginning, when the poem is set temporally "in geardagum" ["in past days"] and geographically "Scedelandum in" ["in the land of the Danes"], the audience would assume that the subject of the narrative is pre-Christian Germanic folk, and when they hear the names of Scyld Scefing, Beowulf, Healfdene, Hrothgar, Heorogar, and Halga in swift succession, names familiar to them from other poems and from genealogies, their assumption would have been confirmed. The impressive funeral of Scyld would have seemed the appropriate rite for this pagan people, and their bewilderment at the attacks by Grendel would have been expected, since they (unlike the audience) had no knowledge of his descent from Cain. Noting these clear signs of a pagan setting, the audience would have felt less surprise, I believe, than most modern readers seem to feel at the poet's account in 175–88 of the Scylding's worship at pagan shrines, vow to make sacrifices to their demon gods, and ignorant commission of their souls to hell by their tragically misguided piety. The reason modern readers have been surprised by the "pagan excursus" and have even wanted to excise this passage as a later interpolation is, I believe, that they have not been sufficiently aware of just how persistently the poet has included

3. See *Die Hirtenbriefe Ælfrics in altenglischer und lateinischer Fassung*, ed. Bernhard Fehr, reprinted with a supplement to the introduction by Peter Clemoes, Bibliothek der angelsächsischen Prosa 9 (Darmstadt, 1966), 25, and *Wulfstan's Canons of Edgar*, ed. Roger Fowler, EETS, o.s. 266 (London, 1972), 6. For further demonstration that Alcuin's letter accurately represents Christian teaching in Anglo-Saxon England, see now Patrick Wormald, "Bede, *Beowulf*, and the Conversion of the Anglo-Saxon Aristocracy," in *Bede and Anglo-Saxon England: Papers in Honour of the 1300th Anniversary of the Birth of Bede, Given at Cornell University in 1973 and 1974*, ed. Robert T. Farrell, British Archaeological Reports 46 (Oxford, 1978), 43–48.

details of heathen life in *Beowulf,* both before the pagan excursus and
throughout the ensuing poem. It may be well to review some of these de-
tails and then to suggest why they have seemed inconspicuous to most
readers.

The cremations which are described or are alluded to in 1107–24,
2126, 2802–8, 2818, 3097, and 3110–80 would themselves assure that the
audience could not lose sight of the paganism of the poem's characters.[4]
The references to burying treasure or other grave goods with the dead
would also have identified the Danes and Geatas as non-Christian,[5] and
indeed the buried treasure of the dragon's hoard is specifically called
"hæðen gold" ["heathen gold"] and "hæðen hord" ["heathen hoard"] in
2216 and 2276. Reading omens of various kinds to divine the future or to
determine the best times for traveling is regularly condemned in laws, ser-
mons, and other writings of the period,[6] and so when the Geatas are in-
troduced to us in the act of reading the omens before Beowulf's
embarking for Denmark, their theological status is made clear. When the
scene of the poem shifts to Geatland, the poet again specifies the Geatas'
paganism, if we agree with Håkan Ringbom that the original manuscript
reading *hæðnum,* "heathens" (with ð erased), should displace the editors'
emendations in 1983.[7] Such an emphatic reaffirmation of their hea-
thenism here would be interesting but not necessary, since their pre-
Christian status is made clear generally, if more subtly, elsewhere in the
poem. The allusion to totemic animals (boar, hart, and "snake swords")[8]
in the context of other pagan practices would likely have assumed hea-

---

4. Gale R. Owen's chapter "Pagan Inhumation and Cremation Rites" in her *Rites and Religions of the Anglo-Saxons* (London, 1981), 67–95, provides a summary of pertinent facts. Even genera-
   tions after the Anglo-Saxon abandoned cremation, they could not have forgotten that it was the
   way of the heathen, for they continued to encounter it in their contacts with pagan Germanic
   tribes on the continent: see Boniface's letter to Æthelbald, king of Mercia (*Sancti Bonifatii,* no.
   73.) Wormald, p. 40, rightly observes that cremation never had been "remotely tolerable in
   Christian circles." See his documentation on p. 75, n. 36.
5. See Owen, pp. 74–75, and Francis Peabody Magoun, Jr., "On Some Survivals of Pagan Beliefs
   in Anglo-Saxon England," *Harvard Theological Review* 40 (1947), 46, who demonstrates further
   that the ritually mourning woman and the perambulation of Beowulf's barrow would also have
   been recognized as distinctively pagan features of the practices in *Beowulf.*
6. Following the passage on Ingeld in his letter to the monks of Lindisfarne, Alcuin vigorously de-
   nounces the pagan practice of reading auguries and omens. See also *Sancti Bonifatii,* nos. 50,
   51, 56, and 78, and Felix Liebermann, ed., *Die Gesetze der Angelsachsen* (Halle, 1903–13), II,
   pt. 2, p. 574. Ælfric condemns pagan divination in "De auguriis" in *Ælfric's Lives of Saints,* ed.
   Walter W. Skeat, 2 vols, EETS, o.s. 76, 82, 94, 114 (London, 1881–1900), I, 364–83 (see p. 370
   for explicit prohibition against calculating the best days for travel), and in *Homilies of Ælfric: A
   Supplementary Collection,* ed. John C. Pope, II, EETS, o.s. 260 (London, 1968), 790–96. The
   Old English *Distichs of Cato,* no. 30, warn against divining future events by casting lots: see
   R. S. Cox, "The Old English Dicts of Cato," *Anglia* 90 (1972), 9. Prohibitions against casting of
   lots were so pervasive that metaphorical uses of terms like *hleotan* [receive], *hlytm* [lot], and
   unhlitme [without lot(?), involuntarily(?)] in *Beowulf* may have carried an undertone of pagan
   associations. See René Derolez, "La divination chez les Germains," in *La divination,* ed. André
   Caquot and Marcel Leiborici (Paris, 1968), I, 293.
7. Håkan Ringbom, *Studies in the Narrative Technique of "Beowulf" and Lawman's "Brut,"* Acta
   Academia Aboensis, ser. A Humaniora, XXXVI, no. 2 (Åbo, Finland, 1968), 18, n. 10. For the
   form *hæðnum,* cf. *Beowulf* 2216.
8. See A. T. Hatto, "Snake-swords and Boar-helms in *Beowulf,*" *English Studies* 38 (1957), 145–60,
   257–59.

then associations, and Beowulf's speeches about the preferability of blood vengeance to mourning and about the importance of fame after death would certainly have carried such connotations.

Given the frequency and repetition of such pagan details throughout the poem, we might well ask why readers have so often overlooked them and have tried to imagine a Christian setting for the poem or a setting devoid of any religious coloration at all. One reason is that the poet has by design selected the more inconspicuous, inoffensive tokens of heathenism for iteration throughout *Beowulf* because he does not wish his audience to lose sympathy with the poem's characters. He wants them to accept the heathenism of the men of old and to join him in regretting it, but then he wishes to take his audience beyond this recognition of their spiritual status to a sympathetic evaluation of them for what they were. He does not show his heroes exposing children, performing human sacrifice,[9] or practicing witchcraft, and except for the one description of the Danes' idol worship (175–78), we are not made to see them at their pagan rites. He avoids calling the pagan gods by name,[1] and he even uses terms like *hæðen* somewhat sparingly,[2] in order that his portrayal of his characters will not repel the very audience whose sympathetic hearing he wants to engage. Another reason why readers have tended to pass over the mild yet pervasive signs of paganism in Beowulfian society is that the pagan characters use pious expressions and Christian-sounding allusions which have given some people the impression that Beowulf, Hrothgar, and other characters in the poem are in fact Christians, despite the anachronistic absurdity of such an assumption. This problem is the subject of my second chapter, where I shall try to show that the pseudo-Christian language used by characters in the poem is, like the inconspicuous pagan details, a calculated effect of the poet's and, indeed, perhaps his greatest achievement in adapting his pagan heroes for a devoutly Christian audience in such a way that the audience can admire those heroes while remaining fully aware of their hopeless paganism.

It will be argued throughout this study that a combined admiration and regret is the dominant tone in *Beowulf* and that one of the poet's signal

9. We do see the Swedish King Ongentheow threatening to sacrifice warriors to Odin (2939–41), perhaps. See Hilda Ellis Davidson, *Gods and Myths of Northern Europe* (Harmondsworth, England, 1964), 51, and Hans Kuhn, "Gaut," in *Festschrift für Jost Trier zu seinem 60. Geburtstag*, ed. Benno von Weise and Karl Heinz Borck (Meisenheim, West Germany, 1954), 417–33. It seems likely that Ongentheow was alluding more to pagan sacrifices than to some kind of punishment for war crimes.

1. It may have been regarded as impious as well as shocking to name the pagan gods. See Exodus 23:13, Joshua 23:7, Psalms 16:4, Hosea 2:17, and Zachariah 13:2. Tertullian alludes to this scriptural injunction when he says, "The Law prohibits the gods of the nations from being named" (*De idololatria*, ch. 20), and Cynewulf, in his *Juliana*, deletes from his poem the names of pagan gods which are present in his source.

2. *Hæðen* occurs but five times in the entire poem (six if we restore the erased MS reading at 1983). That the word had special force may be suggested by the capital *H* used with the word at *Beowulf* 852 (according to Thorkelin A), which Kemp Malone finds "particularly striking." See *The Nowell Codex*, Early English Manuscripts in Facsimile, XII, ed. Kemp Malone (Copenhagen, 1963), 20.

triumphs was to adopt the precisely appropriate style for striking that tone. Admiration for pagans, however, has often been judged a highly improbable attitude for medieval Christians to assume. Many readers have held that moral revulsion is the only possible reaction that a converted Anglo-Saxon could have when confronted with pagans. But Larry D. Benson has skillfully demonstrated that this is not the case.[3] Citing, among other sources, the letters of St. Boniface, Benson shows that Anglo-Saxons often reacted to the paganism of their continental cousins compassionately and with "intense sympathy for their plight" (p. 201). The description of the Danes' heathenism in *Beowulf*, Benson notes, emphasizes the blameless ignorance of the idol worshipers, who are "ensnared in devilish errors through no fault of their own." This view seems to be supported by a text which was published after "The Pagan Coloring of *Beowulf*" was in print. In his sermon *De falsis diis*, Ælfric describes how the Devil first induced people to euhemerize famous men and build idols to them and then entered those idols and spoke through them deceptively to the worshipers, whose souls were thus betrayed into hell's punishment. Ælfric's attitudes call to mind the passage in *Beowulf*: "Þa gesawon þa deoflu, þe hi beswicon on ær, / þa fægran anlicnyssa, and flugon þarto, / and þurh þa anlicnyssa spræcon to þam earmum mannum, / and hi swa forlæddon mid heora leasungum, / and to hellicum suslum heora sawla gebrohtan."[4] Here as in *Beowulf* the Devil is blamed and the heathens are pitied: the demons "spoke through the idols to those poor people and misled them with their deceptions and brought their souls to the torments of hell." If even so stern a Christian as Ælfric could join in this compassionate attitude toward benighted, idol-worshiping pagans, there seems little reason to doubt that *Beowulf*, Boniface, and other sources cited by Benson could, at an earlier time, have reflected a similar attitude. The virtues of the Beowulfian heroes are extolled and are even held up as models for behavior in the poet's own day ("Swa sceal mæg don," "Swa sceal geong guma," "Swa sceal man don" ["So ought a kinsman do," "So ought a young man," "So ought a man do"]), while at the same time the poet never loses sight of the hard fact that these are pagans, and pagans, say the churchmen, are damned.

Not every medieval Christian, it is true, was content to consign all virtuous pagans to hell. Dante's sadness about Virgil's status in the afterlife, and his apparent view that the righteous pagan Ripheus gained entry into Heaven (*Paradiso* XX, 122–24), bear witness to his agonized concern for the fate of the good heathen.[5] In at least one version of Jacobus de Voragine's *Legenda aurea*, Trajan seems to have gained salvation through the prayers of Gregory, although there is considerable disagreement about

3. Larry D. Benson, "The Pagan Coloring of *Beowulf*," in *Old English Poetry: Fifteen Essays*, ed. Robert P. Creed (Providence, R. I., 1967), 193–213.
4. *Homilies of Ælfric*, ed. Pope, II, 687–88.
5. Cf. the similar concern for Cato's soul in *Purgatorio I*, 73–75.

the conditions and even the possibility of Trajan's salvation.[6] Later, the problem of the virtuous heathen is raised in *Piers Plowman*.[7] It is hardly surprising, then, that, as early as the Anglo-Saxon period, some thinkers may have been looking for ways to save the virtuous heathen. Charles Donahue's articles on Irish speculations as to how good heathens might gain entry to Heaven show that the stern Augustinian attitude toward heathens was not the only one possible among Christians,[8] and the persistence of the Pelagian heresy[9] in the British Isles would suggest some discomfort with the notion that every unbaptized soul was damned. But as Benson has well demonstrated, the central tradition was in accord with the views of St. Augustine, Bede, Boniface, and other churchmen who agreed that salvation without conversion was impossible.[1] If the *Beowulf* poet knew about a softer theological position on the heathen, he did not appeal to it in his poem. It is true, as Morton Bloomfield has noted, that there is an implicit parallel between the pre-Mosaic patriarchs of the Old Testament and the Beowulfian characters, since both lived without knowledge of either the Old Law or the New.[2] But while this parallel may give the Christian English room for a certain pride of ancestry, it does not grant salvation. For all the *Beowulf* poet says, we are left with heroes who are pathetic in their heathenism while being at the same time noble in their thoughts and actions; they are exemplary but cannot save themselves. Statius says to Virgil (*Purgatorio* XXII, 67–73), "You were like one who goes by night and carries the light behind him and profits not himself, but makes those wise who follow him,"[3] and a Christian Anglo-Saxon might say the same to Beowulf.

From this complex attitude toward his subject, the poet of *Beowulf* attempts to build a place in his people's collective memory for their lost ancestors. This lofty and challenging theme requires for its expression an appositive style, a style more suggestive than assertive, more oblique than direct. A poet who, in a deeply Christian age, wants to acknowledge his

---

6. E. G. Stanley, "Hæthenra Hyht in *Beowulf*," in *Studies in Old English Literature in Honor of Arthur G. Brodeur*, ed. S. B. Greenfield (Eugene, Ore., 1963), 147, points out that the Anglo-Saxon monk of Whitby who wrote the life of Pope Gregory alludes to the Trajan story. See also Charles S. Singleton, trans., *The Divine Comedy: Purgatorio, II: Commentary* (Princeton, 1973), 210–13.

7. See G. H. Russell, "The Salvation of the Heathen: The Exploration of a Theme in *Piers Plowman*," *Journal of the Warburg and Courtauld Institute* 29 (1966), 101–16, and R. W. Chambers, "Long Will, Dante, and the Righteous Heathen," *Essays and Studies by Members of the English Association* 9 (1924), 50–69.

8. See Charles Donahue, "Beowulf, Ireland, and the Natural Good," *Traditio* 7 (1949–51), 263–77, and "Beowulf and Christian Tradition: A Reconsideration from a Celtic Stance," *Traditio* 21 (1965), 55–116.

9. The belief, taught by Pelagius in the fifth century, that all human beings are born without sin and thus there in no need for infant baptism to ensure salvation [*Editor*].

1. Benson, "The Pagan Coloring," 202–4.

2. Morton Bloomfield, "Patristics and Old English Literature: Notes on Some Poems," in *Studies in Old English Literature in Honor of Arthur G. Brodeur*, ed. Stanley B. Greenfield (Eugene, Ore., 1963), 39–41.

3. The translation is that of Charles S. Singleton, *Purgatorio, I: Italian Text and Translation*, 239.

heroes' damnation while insisting on their dignity must find and exercise in his listeners' minds the powers of inference and the ability to entertain two simultaneous points of view that are necessary for the resolution of poignant cultural tensions. As we turn now to a systematic examination of the elements of appositive style, we shall see that common to them all is this quality of implicitness or logical openness. Not every ambiguity or deliberate indeterminacy is directly related to the paradoxical portrayal of the poem's characters as people to be both admired and regretted, but each such effect makes its contribution toward the creation of a general atmosphere in the poem where such a complex attitude toward a people can be made both understandable and comforting to an Anglo-Saxon audience.

We have already given attention to some of the inferential demands made by grammatical apposition. Another basic element of the *Beowulf* poet's style which is juxtapositional in character and requires more inferences than is often noted is the compound, a cardinal feature of traditional Old English poetic diction.[4] That compounds are in a real sense appositional has been noted before.[5] Nominal compounds in particular seem to achieve their effect by a simple juxtaposing of independent elements, with the reader or audience being left to infer the relationship of the two and their composite meaning. Deducing the logical relationship between compound elements is not always as simple as we might expect. Thomas J. Gardner's study *Semantic Patterns in Old English Substantival Compounds* and Charles T. Carr's analysis of the semantic types of Germanic nominal compounds[6] show that the elements of a compound can stand in any one of various possible relationships with each other, and context must guide the reader or audience in electing the most appropriate one. Consider, for example, words like *deaðcwalu* [death, killing], *deaðcwealm* [death, killing], *freadrihten* [lord], *gryreboga* [horror], *gumman* [man], *modsefa* [mind, spirit], *wældeað* [murderous, death], and *winedrihten* [lord and friend] in *Beowulf*. In these compounds the two elements seem to refer more or less equally to the same referent. (This does not mean, of course, that the words are merely tautological; a *wældeað* is not the same as a death from natural causes, and a *winedrihten*, or lord and friend, is more than just a lord.) In other, seemingly similar compounds

4. Klaeber, *Beowulf and the Fight at Finnsburg*, observes, "Obviously, composition is one of the most striking and inherently significant elements of the diction. . . . Fully one third of the entire vocabulary, or some 1070 words, are compounds, so that in point of numbers, the *Beowulf* stands practically in the front rank of Old English poems" (p. lxiv).
5. See Charles T. Carr, *Nominal Compounds in Germanic*, St. Andrews University Publications 41 (London, 1939), 320–21, 324–43. In Hermann Paul's *Principles of the History of Language*, trans H. A. Strong (London, 1888), various types of compounds are described as "the appositional connexion of two substantives" and "the appositional . . . connexion of two adjectives," etc. (p. 369). A relevant contemporary definition is that of Baxter Hathaway, A *Transformational Syntax* (New York, 1967): "Compound—A construction . . . in which words are juxtaposed without inflectional, derivational, or analytic signals of relationship" (p. 288).
6. Thomas J. Gardner, *Semantic Patterns in Old English Substantival Compounds* (Hamburg, 1968); Carr, *Nominal Compounds in Germanic*, 319–43.

the first element appears to have a different, genitival relationship with the second: *gumdrihten* and *mondrihten* probably mean not "man and lord" (as we might assume from the pattern of *gumman*, "man-person") but rather "lord of men" (following the pattern of *folccyning* and *þeod-cyning*). *Beorncyning*, on the other hand, is ambiguous in syntactical structure. Some scholars take it to mean "hero-king," while others interpret it as "king of heroes." Ever since the first performance of *Beowulf*, readers or listeners have had to exercise their individual judgment as to how to construe this and many similar compounds.

The individual judgments forced upon the audience by the compounds in *Beowulf* constantly remind us of how syntactically open, how "appositional" the style of the poem is, especially if we free our minds of the false certainties with which modern glossaries beguile us. Klaeber's edition, for example, instructs us that *eorðcyning* means "king of the land," while *wyruldcyning* means "(earthly) king." But compounding being the open structure that it is, do not both words in fact mean both things, readers being forced to choose the more appropriate sense in any given context? Sometimes the poet uses the same compound in two separate contexts, one of which induces the reader to assign one kind of syntactic analysis and the other of which requires a different kind. When Heremod is exiled and punished by his nation, he is said to suffer *leodbealu*, "woe from his people" (*leod-* standing in a subjective-genitival relationship with *-bealu*); but when Modþryð (or Þryð)[7] curbs her behavior as a tyrannical and murderous queen, we are told that she inflicted less *leodbealu*—that is, less woe against her people (*leod-* standing here in an objective-genitival relationship with *-bealu*). Similarly, the nicor [water-monster] killed by the Geatas is said to have been separated from his swimming or his thrashing on the water (*yðgewinn*, 1434), but when we are told at 2412 that the dragon's hoard lay near the *yðgewinn* (which stands in apposition with *holmwylm*), we know that the elements of the compound must be related differently ("tumult of the waves," that is, "restless sea"), since no swimming takes place at this point. Depending on how we choose to analyze the compound *heofodweard* syntactically and semantically, the word can mean "bodyguard," "chapter," "chief protector," or "watch over the head." Klaeber's glossary definition "head-watch . . . (i.e., 'death-watch')" obscures from us the play of mind that the word required from an Anglo-Saxon audience, which had to exclude three common meanings before arriving at a fourth that satisfied the context. We may compare the effect that the word had on contemporary listeners or readers with the effect that "overrul'd" would have on readers of Marlowe's *Hero and Leander* (167–68) in his own time or ours:

7. Or possibly Hygd: see Norman E. Eliason, "The 'Thryth-Offa Digression' in *Beowulf*," in *Franciplegius: Medieval and Linguistic Studies in Honor of Francis Peabody Magoun, Jr.*, ed. Jess B. Bessinger, Jr., and Robert P. Creed (New York, 1965), 124–38.

"It lies not in our power to love or hate, / For will in us is *overrul'd* by fate." Context here forces the reader to exclude the common meaning "pronounce invalid" and adopt the more primitive sense "rule over, control." But the common meaning is faintly present, so that our experience of the sentence is slightly more complex than it would have been had Marlowe used a univocal word like "controlled" or "governed" rather than "overrul'd."

The variety of syntactic relationships that can exist between compound elements is further illustrated by the three compounds with the base word *-lufu* in *Beowulf*: *wiflufu*, *modlufu*, and *eardlufu*. Each of these entails a different syntactical relationship between its component elements: "love for a woman," "heart's love," and "beloved thing that is home, beloved home." The series *goldgyfa* [gold-giver, lord], *goldmaððum* [gold treasure], and *goldwine* [gold-friend, generous lord] exhibits a similarly varied range of internal syntactical relationships. At times the syntactical structure of compounds remains unresolved in most readers' minds. Is a *wundorsmið* a smith who works by wondrous power or a smith who makes wondrous things? Is a *geosceaftgast* a creature serving fate's cruel purposes or a fated, doomed creature? Klaeber glosses *deaðscua* simply as "death-shadow," but what does that mean exactly—a deadly shadow, or the shadow of death, or a deadly thing that moves in darkness? In compounds like *meodustig and meoduwong*, the implicit relationship between the compound elements requires that the audience supply a good deal that is unexpressed: "path (to) the mead(-hall)," "plain (near) the mead(-hall)." These two words, like others discussed in this paragraph, are unique to *Beowulf*, as far as surviving records allow us to judge, and so the audience would probably have encountered them in few if any other contexts. It is likely, then, that the audience of *Beowulf* frequently had to infer the composite meaning of collocations which the listeners had rarely or never encountered before.

In emphasizing the syntactical openness of the poem's diction, I am not suggesting that the poet has no clearly defined meaning for the words he uses or that he is inviting us to impart to his poem whatever meaning we wish. Wherever the meanings of compounds are important (which is most of the time), context forces us to select one interpretation of the compound over other possible ones. *Mondrihten* in *Beowulf* almost certainly means "a lord who rules men" rather than "a lord who is a man"; *wiflufu* means "(a man's) love for a woman" rather than "a woman's love (for a man)," although in isolation from context all these meanings are possible. The difference between compounds and some other syntactical strategy for expressing relationships is not that the compound *in context* is less specifically meaningful but that part of the meaning is implicit rather than explicit, thus requiring of the reader more inferences and logical deductions than another linguistic form would demand.

One way of bringing into prominence the implicit quality of com-
pounding is to imitate the method of some twentieth-century linguists for
displaying the underlying structure and meaning of nominal com-
pounds.[8] This method is based upon the assumption that compounds can
best be regarded as reduced sentences or as transforms of complete sen-
tences. Thus *wiflufu*, in its context in *Beowulf* 2065, implies a sentence
"he lufað þæt wif" ["he loves the woman"]; underlying the two contrast-
ing uses of *yðgewinn* [swimming, turbulent water] in *Beowulf* 1434 and
2412 are the sentences "he winneð in þam yðum" ["he strives in the
waves" = "he swims"] and "þa yða winnað" ["the waves struggle" = "tur-
bulent water"]. The two possible interpretations of *beorncyning* remarked
above can be expressed as "se cyning is beorn" and "se cyning wealdeð
beornum."[9] Viewing the Beowulfian compounds in this way not only
brings to light the variety of contrasting syntactical relationships latent in
the juxtapositions which make up many compounds; it also reminds us
of the wealth of verbal action which is implicit in the seemingly static
nominalizations of Old English poetic diction. Indeed, in both nominal
and adjectival compounds there are various kinds of verbal relationships
implied (cf. *beadurun* [hostile utterance], *hordwyrðe* [worthy of being
hoarded], *lifbysig* [struggling for life], *nathhwylc* [some one], *sadolbeorht*
[with bright saddles], *sarigmod* [sad-hearted]), and if we add to the com-
pounds the parallel system of forming nominal phrases—the noun-plus-
genitival-noun collocations such as "yða gewinn" cf. *yðgewinn*, "gumena
cynn" cf. *gumcynn*, "mægenes cræft cf. *mægencræft*—we become aware
that the often-remarked static quality of *Beowulf* is partly an illusion cre-
ated by the chosen style. At the level of surface structure it is true that Old
English verse is poetry of the noun and not of the verb, a grammatical
propensity fostered in part by the accentual verse form. But beneath the
surface, implicit in all these compounds and nominal phrases, the dic-
tion is alive with verbal activity. Both perspectives on the diction are im-
portant. At the level of meaning, the poet communicates all the verbal
action and relationships his subject requires, but at the level of style he
seems to avoid predications. This feature together with other elements of
his paratactic style creates the impression of restraint and reticence in the
poet's voice, a voice which seems often to supply facts without an ac-
companying interpretation of them. The syntactical ambiguities of com-
pounds, which are so often overlooked by modern readers, make a
modest and yet pervasive contribution to this restrained tone of the nar-
rative.

8. See Hans Marchand, *The Categories and Types of Present-Day English Word-Formation*, 2d rev.
   ed. (Munich, 1969), 31–95; cf. Robert B. Lees, *The Grammar of English Nominalizations*
   (Bloomington, Ind., 1960), and Laurie Bauer, *The Grammar of Nominal Compounding*, Odense
   University Studies in Linguistics 4 (Odense, Denmark, 1978).
9. For important cautionary strictures on transformational analysis of Old English compounds, see
   Gardner, *Semantic Patterns*, 31–33.

As we have seen, one reason why modern readers tend to lose sight of the fundamentally ambiguous relation between the elements of nominal compounds is that glossaries and dictionaries systematically disambiguate these structures. At another level of expression, the modern punctuation which editors introduce into Old English texts serves a similar disambiguating function and further blinds readers to an underlying multiplicity of grammatical relationships which informs Old English poetic language. An important essay by Bruce Mitchell has recently called attention to ambiguous clause juncture in the syntax of the poetic language in general and of *Beowulf* in particular.[1] In a passage like *Beowulf* 1233–38 (here unpunctuated)

> Wyrd ne cuþon
> geosceaft grim*me*   swa hit agangen wearð
> eorla manegum   syþðan æfen cwom
> ond him Hroþgar gewat   to hofe sinum
> rice to reste   reced weardode
> unrim eorla   swa hie oft ær dydon

[They did not know the fate, the grim decree made long before, as it came to pass to many of the earls after evening had come and Hrothgar had gone to his chambers, the noble one to his rest. A great number of men remained in the hall, just as they had often done before.]

some editors punctuate so as to make the clause "syþðan . . . reste" dependent upon the preceding main clause and some upon the following. Mitchell argues that the *syþðan* clause more likely stands *apo koinou*[2] and serves as a pivot between the two main clauses. At other times there is a syntactic openness in the very status of clauses, nothing in the original language indicating whether a clause is dependent or independent. But modern punctuation cannot tolerate such openness. Therefore, in passages like

> se æt Heorote fand
> wæccendne wer   wiges bidan
> þær him aglæca   ætgræpe wearð   [1267–69]

[who at Heorot found a waking man waiting his warfare. There the monster had laid hold upon him]

and

> hwilum heaþorofe   hleapan leton
> on geflit faran   fealwe mearas
> ðær him foldwegas   fægere þuhton
> cystum cuðe   [864–67]

1. Bruce Mitchell, "The Dangers of Disguise: Old English Texts in Modern Punctuation," *RES*, n.s. 31 (1980), 385–413.
2. A syntactical construction in which a word or group of words simultaneously serves two grammatical functions [*Editor*].

[At times battle-famed men let their brown horses gallop, let them
race where the paths seemed fair, known for their excellence.]

editors have variously interpreted the *þær* clauses as independent ("there
the monster laid hold on him") or dependent ("where the paths seemed
pleasant to them"), with no apparent basis for their decisions. In fact, it is
only the rules of modern punctuation that force a decision in the first
place. The Old English sentences were probably more fluid and struc-
turally ambiguous, and the scribal practices of the time preserved that flu-
idity. The numerous examples of such openness which Mitchell sets out
in his study (pp. 395–412) show that the language was permeated by si-
multaneous reference of this kind. The Anglo-Saxon audience, Mitchell
implies, expected and appreciated such amphibolies, while modern edi-
tors' punctuation is constantly "eliminating options and blurring alter-
native connections and associations which were present in the poem
created by the poet" (p. 411). It is important to notice that Mitchell says
not that the syntax is uncontrolled but rather that it is capable of multi-
ple reference and requires of the contemporary Anglo-Saxon audience
that same attention to syntactic relationships which we have already seen
to be requisite in the nominal compounds. "As in the structure of com-
pounds, so also in the structure of sentences much is left to the sympa-
thetic imagination of the hearer," observed Otto Jespersen long ago,[3] and
Mitchell's study shows that this is truer of Old English than anyone had
suspected as long as the punctuation of modern editions blinded us to the
actual genius of the language.

Another syntactic device which enlists the "sympathetic imagination
of the hearer" of *Beowulf* is clausal apposition, the type of construction
which Walther Paetzel called *Satzvariationen* and *Gruppenvariationen*
(pp. 17–24).[4] In clausal appositions phrases and even entire independent
clauses stand in the same relation to each other as do individual words in
simple appositions. Thus parallel restatement of a verb and its object may
occur (I italicize the apposed elements):

> ðy he *þone feond ofercwom,*
> *gehnægde helle gast*   [1273–74]

[by that he overcome the foe, subdued the hell-spirit.]

> ðonne *forstes bend*   Fæder *onlæteð,*
> *onwindeð wælrapas*   [1609–10]

[when the father loosens the frost's fetters, undoes the water-bonds]

The verb-object construction may include parallel instrumental nouns:

---

3. Otto Jespersen, *Philosophy of Grammar* (London, 1924), 310.
4. "Satzvariationen" are clausal variations, as in *Beowulf*, lines 340–41; "Gruppenvariationen" are
word-group variations, as in *Beowulf*, lines 467–68. These terms derive from Walther Paetzel,
Die Variationen in der altgermanischen Alliterationspoesie (Berlin: Mayer und Muller, 1913)
[*Editor*].

> his freawine   flane geswencte,
> miste mercelses   ond his mæg ofscet,
> . . .   blodigan gare   [2438–40]

[struck him down with an arrow . . . —his friend and his lord—
missed the mark and shot his kinsman dead . . . with the bloody
arrowhead]

The parallel construction can consist of subject and predicate adjective:

> ða wæs Heregar dead,
> min yldra mæg   unlifigende   [467–68]

[Heorogar had died then, gone from life, my older brother]

or of object and predicate adjective:

> syðþan he aldorðegn   unlyfigendne,
> þone deorestan   deadne wisse   [1308–9]

[when he learned that his chief thane was lifeless, his dearest man
dead]

or of entire independent clauses:

> Metod hie ne cuþon,
> dæda Demend,   ne wiston hie Drihten God   [180–81]

[they knew not the Ruler, the Judge of Deeds, they recognized not
the Lord God]

> Him þa ellenrof   andswarode,
> wlanc Wedera leod   word æfter spræc   [340–41][5]

[The man known for his courage replied to him; the proud man of
the Geats . . . spoke words in return]

> ofer þæm hongiað   hrinde bearwas,
> wudu wyrtum fæst   wæter oferhelmað   [1363–64]

[over it hang frost-covered woods, trees fast of root close over the
water]

Besides illustrating the variety of types of clausal apposition in *Beowulf*,
these examples show how these collocations, like the simple collocations
discussed earlier in this chapter, are not merely tautological but rather
supply various kinds of information if we reflect on the implications of
the parallel structures. In the first example the initial predication "þone
feond ofercwom" describes the victory from the hero's point of view,
while the restatement "gehnægde helle gast" emphasizes the Christian
narrator's ampler perspective on the vanquished monster. The poet in his
own voice often specifies the hellish nature of the monsters, something

---

5. I omit Klaeber's comma after *leod*, which obscures the parallel sentence construction.

of which the characters in the poem are unaware. In the second example the verbs give successive stages of the action, and the restated noun phrases develop the metaphor for frost. In the third, *freawine* and *mæg* bring out different aspects of the relationship between the two men — "lord and friend" and "kinsman" — while the words used to describe the arrow suggest progressive stages in the projectile's course. *Flan* is alliteratively linked with words for "flight" so frequently in Old English that it probably suggested "arrow in flight."[6] "Blodigan gare" presents the arrow after it has completed its flight and has found its victim. The restatement "dead, unlifigende" seems emotive, suggesting that the bereaved survivor was trying to come to terms with a painful loss. (Cf. the apposition in Wordsworth's "No motion has she now, no force.") "Aldorþegn unlyfigendne" also involves a mournful quibble on *aldor-*, which means "life" as well as "lord."

The poet's penchant for parallel statements which carry contrasting versions of the same action makes itself felt at times in simple successions of sentences:

> Beornas gearwe
>   on stefn stigon . . .
>   secgas bæron
>   on bearm nacan   beorhte frætwe,
>   guðsearo geatolic   [211–15]

[The warriors eagerly climbed on the prow . . . men bore bright weapons into the ship's bosom, splendid armor.]

> Let ða of breostum,   ða he gebolgen wæs,
> Weder-Geata leod   word ut faran,
> stearcheort styrmde   [2550–52]

[Then the man of the Weather-Geats, enraged as he was, let a word break from his breast. Stout-hearted he shouted]

> Swa se secg hwata   secggende wæs
> laðra spella;   he ne leag fela
> wyrda ne worda   [3028–30]

[Thus the bold man was a speaker of hateful news, nor did he much lie in his words or his prophecies.]

These are not clausal appositions in any strict sense, but the rhetoric of such parallel clauses may have been influenced by the poet's appositional propensity. Two statements relating to the same event are juxtaposed without a connecting element. The reader is left to infer whatever sig-

---

6. See "fleogan flana scuras" in *Judith* 221, "fleogende flane" in *Charms* 4:11, "flanes flyht" in *Maldon* 71, "flacor flangeweorc" in *Christ* 676, and "flacor flanþracu" in *Guthlac* 1144. All quotations from poems other than *Beowulf* refer to *The Anglo-Saxon Poetic Records*, ed. George Philip Krapp and Elliott Van Kirk Dobbie (New York, 1931–53), 6 vols.

nificance the juxtaposition may have. The third example, with its char-
acteristic collocation of a negative statement following a positive one, is
an instance of apposed sentences conveying an especially important im-
plicit meaning: The messenger said grievous things. The messenger said
things that were not lies. In these two sentences the poet validates the
messenger's dire predictions, informing us that the grim future foretold
for the Geatas is indeed imminent.

Not only are independent sentences juxtaposed with significant effect;
the poet at times extends this device to large segments of narrative. A fa-
vorite means of characterization in *Beowulf*[7] is the drawing of parallel
portraits so that the juxtaposed descriptions imply through similarity or
contrast the essential qualities of a character. Upon first meeting Hygd,
the queen of the Geatas, for example, the poet tells us she was not like
Thryth and then proceeds to explain who Thryth is and why she is unlike
Hygd. The essential contrast between them may be underlined by their
quasi-allegorical names. Old English *hygd* means "forethought, reflec-
tion," one of the ideal qualities of a Germanic woman, while *þryð* means
"force, vehemence," a less queenly quality which proved fatal to the re-
tainers who displeased Queen Thryth.[8]

This appositive method is used repeatedly to characterize Beowulf.
After the hero's victory over Grendel, a scop celebrates his prowess by
singing not about Beowulf but about two earlier figures from Germanic
legend: Sigemund, the prototype of Germanic heroes, and then Here-
mod, the violent ruler who turned on his own subjects, by whom he was
ultimately banished. The point of this curiously indirect way of charac-
terizing Beowulf is never spelled out, but the implication is clear: Be-
owulf is like Sigemund, unlike Heremod. And here again the names of
the two apposed figures signal a contrast. *Sigemund* means "victorious
protector" (a precise description of the man who has just saved the Danes
from Grendel's depredations), while *Heremod* means "hostile temper"
(the defect of character which Beowulf, near the end of his life, prides
himself on having avoided [2741–43]).[9] Scholars have seen a similar con-

7. Alistair Campbell, "The Use in *Beowulf* of Earlier Heroic Verse," in *England before the Con-
quest: Studies in Primary Sources presented to Dorothy Whitelock*, ed. Peter Clemoes and Kath-
leen Hughes (Cambridge, 1971), observes that "the *Beowulf* poet stands practically alone in
using the Homeric-Virgilian device of an inserted narrative in its original structural function" of
illuminating "the character and background of their heroes" (pp. 283–84). Campbell's examples
are different from mine.
8. *Þruðr*, the Old Icelandic equivalent of *þryð*, is the name of a pagan deity. If there were a corre-
sponding figure in the pre-Christian English pantheon, this could have added to the ominous
connotations of the name. A further connection with German *Drude*, "witch, evil demon," has
been proposed but is etymologically problematic. As Eliason has shown (see n. 7, [above, p. 85],
the status of *Þryð* is questionable. If the name is taken as Modþryð, its significance is no less neg-
ative: see BTD, s.v. *modþryðu* and *higeþryð*. On Hygd's name, see R. E. Kaske, " 'Hygelac' and
'Hygd,' "in *Studies in Honor of Arthur G. Brodeur*, ed. S. B. Greenfield, reprinted with new "Au-
thor's Note" (New York, 1973), 200–6.
9. For the literary uses of names in *Beowulf* and in Old English in general, see Fred C. Robinson,
"The Significance of Names in Old English Literature," *Anglia* 86 (1968), 14–58, and "Some Uses
of Name-Meanings in Old English Poetry," *Neuphilologische Mitteilungen* 69 (1968), 161–71.

trastive intent in the Hama-Hygelac passage in *Beowulf* 1197–1214,[1] and the character Unferth has been seen as existing primarily to serve as a foil to Beowulf.[2]

Characterization is not the only purpose served by significant juxtapositions in *Beowulf*. In 2444–69 the account of an unnamed father grieving for a hanged son is interposed as a parable of Hrethel's grief over Herebeald. A seemingly uncalled-for reflection on how each man must leave the banquet of life and sleep the sleep of death (1002–8) is given relevance by the immediately following description of the actual banquet in Heorot, where all rejoice in blissful ignorance of the death which will soon invade the hall while they are sleeping. In presenting Beowulf's report to Hygelac after the Geatas' triumphant return from Denmark, the poet contrives to have two remarkably similar scenes of royal reception and hospitality stand in proximity, so that as Beowulf recounts the courtly rituals in Heorot (2011–13, 2020–24), those same rituals are being enacted around him in the Geatish meadhall (1976–83). The phrasal echoes between the two passages assure that the audience will sense how the men of old lived in a world of ineluctable recurrence and may even lead some members of the audience to think of fateful parallels between the places and characters juxtaposed: just as Beowulf's valor was needed to save the Danish king's realm, so will it be needed to save Hygelac's realm; just as young Freawaru will lose her husband to old enmities (2065–66), so will young Hygd lose her husband to the strife in Frisia. In another artful juxtaposition the poet places Beowulf's refusal of the Geatish throne (in deference to the young scion of the royal family) alongside the description of the Geatas' war with Onela years later (2373 ff.). The resulting contrast displays dramatically the social norm against which Beowulf demonstrates his magnanimity: Onela had banished his nephews and seized the Swedish throne for himself, while Beowulf declines the Geatish throne and acts as protector to his young cousin Heardred, who takes the crown.[3]

I have discussed elsewhere[4] how Beowulf's great speech in 1384–89 acquires much of its power from the poet's simple device of positioning it after the famous description of Grendel's mere. Here it need only be remarked that this narrative collocation is typical of the poet's use of appositive style to express theme. The convictions underlying Beowulf's speech are wholly un-Christian—importance of blood vengeance, personal fame the highest good—but the juxtaposition of the hero's enunci-

---

1. Robert E. Kaske, "The Sigemund-Heremod and Hama-Hygelac Passages in *Beowulf*," *PMLA* 74 (1959), 489–94.
2. J.D.A. Ogilvy, "Unferth: Foil to Beowulf?" *PMLA* 79 (1964), 370–75.
3. Contrasts and comparisons between characters in the poem have been skillfully analyzed by Adrien Bonjour, *The Digressions in "Beowulf"*, Medium Ævum Monographs 5 (Oxford, 1950).
4. Fred C. Robinson, "An Introduction to *Beowulf*," in *"Beowulf": A Verse Translation with Treasures of the Ancient North* by Marijane Osborn (Berkeley, 1983), xiv–xv.

ation of his heathen courage with the depiction of the evil forces against which he must prove that courage exacts respect even from an audience which sadly regrets his heathen ignorance of true Christian values. As is the case elsewhere in the poem, the narrator avoids direct comment on the hero's pagan virtue; rather he apposes without comment episodes which force us to admire the men of old no matter how deeply we regret their theological predicament. Here appositive style enables the poet to present pre-Christian heroism honestly yet sympathetically to his Christian world.

Besides narrative segments which stand juxtaposed in *Beowulf*, there are other passages and subjects which seem to stand in a significant but unexpressed relationship even though they are widely separated. The impressive funeral described near the beginning of the poem finds a kind of appositional restatement in the funeral which ends the poem. The symmetry of the two has long impressed scholars as intentional and meaningful, and Klaeber (p. 228) notes that verbal echoes of Scyld's funeral preparations and those for Beowulf further emphasize the implied connection between them. A similar strategy of repeated epithets brings certain characters in the poem into implicit contrast or comparison with each other. Beowulf echoes Unferth's phrasing when he puts forth his version of a story which he wants compared with Unferth's. The aged King Hrothgar and his young champion Beowulf in the first part of the poem seem mirrored by the aged King Beowulf and his young stalwart Wiglaf in the second part, as the formulas which had earlier described the Danish king ("æðeling ærgod" [prince good from olden times], "eald eþelweard" [old guardian of the native land], "eorla drihten" [lord of noblemen], "folces hyrde" [guardian of the people], "gumcystum god" [good one in manly virtue], "har hilderinc" [old warrior], "frod cyning" [wise king], "mære þeoden" [famous lord], "rices hyrde" [guardian of the kingdom], "þeoden mærne" [famous lord]) are transferred to old Beowulf, and terms which had been applied to the youthful Beowulf (e.g., "hæle hildedeor" [battle-brave warrior], "secg on searwum" [man in armor], and "feþe-cempa" [foot warrior]) are inherited by Wiglaf.[5] The poet makes no explicit comment about these significant role shifts, but the symmetry of both character and phrase suggests clearly the inexorable generational cycles in heroic life and the pathos of ageing.

The most forceful expression of the youth-and-age theme in the poem is yet another apposition of narrative segments, the apposition that controls the structure of the entire narrative. *Beowulf* consists of two starkly juxtaposed episodes in the hero's life divided chronologically by a chasm of fifty years and hinged together across that chasm by a single transitional sentence (2200–9). Tolkien describes the structure precisely: "It is essen-

---

5. William Whallon, *Formula, Character, and Context: Studies in Homeric, Old English, and Old Testament Poetry* (Cambridge, Mass., 1969), 98–101, lists nominal formulas for warriors and kings in *Beowulf* and indicates the characters to whom they are applied.

tially a balance, an opposition of ends and beginnings. In its simplest terms it is a contrasted description of two moments in a great life, rising and setting; an elaboration of the ancient and intensely moving contrast between youth and age, first achievement and final death. It is divided in consequence into two opposed portions" (p. 271). From the smallest element of microstructure—the compounds, the grammatical appositions, the metrical line with its apposed hemistichs—to the comprehensive arc of macrostructure, the poem seems built on apposed segments. And the collocation of the segments usually implies a tacit meaning.

If we look beyond the macrostructure of *Beowulf*, we may see one further juxtaposition which is implicit in any reading or rendition of the poem. The highly traditional nature of the subject matter of *Beowulf*, the poet's allusive and sometimes cryptic manner of telling the story, and his frequent abandonment of sequential narration (especially in the last thousand lines) have all persuaded readers from the earliest day of *Beowulf* scholarship that the poem as we have it is a retelling of material familiar to the audience.[6] And an audience perceives a retelling differently from a first telling. On first hearing, people listen for the story; on later hearings they listen for differences between the present and previous versions. Keeping two versions in mind at one time, people notice what the present teller does with the story. Literature as a retelling is of course familiar to students of the Middle Ages, a new treatment of the old story being what most medieval narrative poets purport to be giving to their audiences. But in the case of *Beowulf*, this dimension of the narrative has special significance, since the old stories are ultimately pagan stories and the poet is telling them to a Christian audience which been warned against too much interest in pagan times. A Christian poet who takes up a narrative such as *Beowulf* would need special tact and sensitivity as a teller, and his audience would probably be alert to his way of handling the old heroes and the old themes.

That the poet was emphasizing that his poem is a retelling is suggested by the fact that he includes so much retelling within *Beowulf*. Repeatedly we are asked to listen to one account of an event and to compare it with another. First Unferth tells the story of Beowulf's swim with Breca, and then Beowulf immediately retells it, asking us to notice the differences, to correct in our minds the inaccuracies of Unferth's telling. Near the end of the first long segment of the narrative dealing with Beowulf's adventures in Denmark, the poet has the hero retell in his own words the events which the poet has just finished narrating himself (1999–2151). Scholars have offered various aesthetic justifications for this curious narrative strategy, but whatever else may have been its purpose, one effect of the retelling is to exercise us once again in comparing narrative versions, in

6. Alistair Campbell, "The Use . . . of Earlier Heroic Verse," 283–92, attempts to identify those portions of *Beowulf* which are drawn from preexisting heroic poems.

attending to how the poet's own telling differs from the story as it is re-
fracted through the consciousness of Beowulf. The things Beowulf does
not include in his version (e.g., the Unferth episode, the sword that failed
him, and the defection of the Danes at the mere) give us insights into the
hero's magnanimity which are as revealing as the details he adds to the
poet's telling (e.g., his identification of the one Geatish casualty as a man
named Hondscioh who was dear to him, his sympathetic account of
Hrothgar's lamenting his old age at the harp playing, and his concern for
the ill-fated marriage between Freawaru and Ingeld). Again the poet
forces us to assess a retelling of a known tale when he gives his curiously
slanted summary of the scop's story of Finnsburg. We know from the cryp-
tic and omissive way he tells the story that he assumes his audience knows
it from another source, and we know from the surviving fragment of *The
Fight at Finnsburg* that other tellings of the story were in circulation in
Anglo-Saxon England. From a reading of fragment and episode we re-
ceive the impression that the original story primarily concerned treach-
ery and revenge for treachery, with the heroic code surviving intact after
a severe test. But from the way in which the *Beowulf* poet tells the story,
it seems to have more to do with woman's grief in a world of dark-age vi-
olence. The theme of vengeance taken and honor preserved is overlaid
in the poet's summary with the tragedy of Hildeburh. Since the Finn
episode is carefully juxtaposd with Wealhtheow's major scene in the
poem—her appeal to Beowulf to support her sons—we can assume that
the poet's telling of the story has been shaped for the purpose of stressing
a poignant parallel with Wealhtheow's tragic fate, which remains untold
in the poem but which was apparently known to the audience. On the
level of the factual content of the Finnsburg story as it is represented in
the fragment, there is an obvious parallel between the heroic ethos and
exploits of the Half-Danes on the one hand and those of the people in
Heorot on the other; on the level of the poet's slanted summary, there is
an equally obvious parallel between the tragic fates of Hildeburh and
Wealhtheow. The Finn lay is appropriate on one level to the public oc-
casion being celebrated in Heorot and on another to the tragic irony
which poet and audience see in the future of the Danes. The audience
was to entertain simultaneously the emphases of both tellings and to
apply each as was appropriate to the situation in Hrothgar's Denmark.[7]

Such exercises in the nuances and emphases of retellings inevitably
call our attention to the poet's own strategies of retelling in his manage-
ment of the narration of *Beowulf*. By planting within his poem significant
retellings, he reminds us that, like the scop in Heorot (867 ff.), he is
putting old sagas (*ealdgesegena*) into new words, and he encourages us to
explore the distance between the story he has taken up and his own

---

7. Bonjour, *The Digressions*, 57–61, summarizes the parallels and emphases to which I allude here.
   For more recent comment, see Donald K. Fry, ed., *Finnsburg: Fragment and Episode* (London,
   1974).

telling of it. In particular, we have been disciplined by the retold tales within *Beowulf* to heed the poet's perspective on his story as that perspective is conveyed through his own personal use of the poetic language at his disposal. * * *

In the present chapter I have tried to suggest that in *Beowulf* the poet is concerned with confronting his Christian nation with the heroic age of their heathen ancestors; that to achieve this confrontation (and ultimately reconciliation) he exploits in a unique way the paratactic, juxtapositional character of Old English poetic style; and that his attention to retellings within his poem repeatedly alerts his audience to the fact that *Beowulf* is itself a retelling and hence his audience must remain sensitive to his own perspective on the characters and events he is presenting. It is noteworthy that these three topics—the appositional style, the theme of present time confronting past time, and the status of *Beowulf* as a retelling of known tales—are all to be found in the majestic opening sentence of the poem:

> Hwæt, we Gar-Dena   in geardagum,
> Þeodcyninga   þrym gefrunon,
> hu ða æþelingas   ellen fremedon!

[Yes, we have heard of the glory of the Spear-Danes' kings in the old days—how the princes of that people did brave deeds.]

In form this sentence exemplifies the artfully congested syntax, the heavily nominal surface structure, and the martialing of juxtapositions so characteristic of Old English poetic style. The strong juxtapositional effect of the verse form is highlighted ornamentally, as if the poet were calling his audience's attention to the way verses stand independently in Old English, each hemistich defining itself within its own prosodic boundaries and emphasizing the syntactical appositions which the verses demarcate. The highlighting is achieved through the rhetorical device which Latin rhetoricians term *similiter desinens* [similarity of endings or suffixes], the feature which led ultimately to the development of end rhyme. The chiming suffixes of *þeodcyningas* and *æðelingas* and the repetition of preterite plural endings in *gefrunon and fremedon* emphasize the grammetrical pauses and parallelisms of the verse, as if attuning the audience's ear to the binary contrasts and juxtapositions of metrical lines, appositions, and compounds in Old English poetry.

Simultaneously the poet initiates the theme of present time confronting past time. The pronoun *we* unites the audience with the poet in his own time, while the preterite *fremedon*, intensified by the temporal phrase "in geardagum," places the subject of the poem firmly in the past in "days of yore." This emphasis on the contrasting time periods is maintained by various devices throughout the remainder of the poem. The repeated phrase "on þæm dæge þysses lifes" [in the day/time of this life]

(197, 790, 806) and the phrase "þy dogore" [this day/time] underscore the temporal gulf between Christian present and Germanic past by the abnormal stress on the deictic pronouns.[8] Terms like *fyrndagum*, "in days of old," *fyrnmenn*, "men of old," *ærgeweorc* and *fyrngeweorc*, "works of old," also keep reminding us of the bygone age in which the poem is set, as do, perhaps, the repeated formulas "hyrde ic" [I heard] and "ic gefrægn" [I learned by asking; I heard of] and their variants, which emphasize that we are hearing reports of a distant past.

Finally, the whole point of the opening sentence of *Beowulf* is that the poem is a retelling of exploits already known to the audience. "We have heard[9] of the greatness of the spear-Danes, of kings of nations in days of yore, of how the noblemen wrought deeds of valor." In this characteristically resumptive, appositional sentence reminding us of the great gap of time between the tale and the teller, the poet invites us to read his poem as a pensive reconsideration of things known.   *   *   *

ROBERTA FRANK

The *Beowulf* Poet's Sense of History[†]

> I don't know how humanity stands it
> with a painted paradise at the end of it
> without a painted paradise at the end of it
>
> Ezra Pound, *Canto* LXXIV

Awareness of historical change, of the pastness of a past that itself has depth, is not instinctive to man; there is nothing natural about a sense of

8. Late in the preparation of these lectures for the press, I came upon Roberta Frank's splendid essay "The *Beowulf* Poet's Sense of History," in *The Wisdom of Poetry: Essays in Early English Literature in Honor of Morton W. Bloomfield*, ed. Larry Benson and Siegfried Wenzel (Kalamazoo, 1982), 53–65, which treats these phrases as well as other aspects of the *Beowulf* poet's perspective on the heathen past. I have eliminated the discussion of a number of points developed in my original lecture because Frank has dealt with them more skillfully than I did. For a list of the poet's allusions to the fact that this plot takes place in an earlier age, see Klaeber, *Beowulf and the Fight at Finnsburg*, cxxiii, n. 4.

9. "Heard" is the usual rendering, but it is actually imprecise. *Gefrunon* means "asked and received answers," or "learned by asking," the prefix *ge-* imparting perfective sense to the verb *frignan*, "ask." Implicit in *gefrunon*, then, is a confessed eagerness to hear the deeds from olden days, an active interest in the story, and thus *gefrunon* is a bolder word than, say *gehyrdon* [heard] when considered in the context of ecclesiastical condemnation of those who listen to songs about the pagan heroes of *geardagum* [days past]. This hint at persistent curiosity about the old heroes is carried on in the recurring "ic gefrægn" formula, which contrasts with "ic gehyrde" [I heard], a verb denoting passive hearing. In other contexts, too, *gefrignan* [learn by asking, hear of] should be accorded its full semantic force. It is noteworthy, e.g., Beowulf *gefrægn* [learned by asking, heard of] rather than *hyrde* [heard] the challenge posed by Grendel (194).

† From *The Wisdom of Poetry: Essays in Early English Literature in Honor of Morton W. Bloomfield*, ed. Larry D. Benson and Siegfried Wenzel (Kalamazoo, MI: Medieval Institute Publications, 1982) 53–65, 271–77. Translations appearing in brackets are the editor's. Footnotes are the author's except where followed by [*Editor*].

history. Anthropologists report that the lack of historical perspective is a feature of primitive thought, and historians that its absence characterizes medieval thinking: Herod in the Wakefield Cycle swears "by Mahoun in heaven," the medieval Alexander is a knight, and heathen Orléans boasts a university.[1] Morton Bloomfield has shown that a sense of history, even a tentative, underdeveloped one, was a rare thing in fourteenth-century England, and that Chaucer's attention to chronology and his preoccupation with cultural diversity have affinities with aspects of the early Italian Renaissance.[2] But what in the Anglo-Saxon period stimulated a monastic author to stress the differences between ancient days and his own, to paint the past as if it were something other than the present?[3] The *Beowulf* poet's reconstruction of a northern heroic age is chronologically sophisticated, rich in local color and fitting speeches. The poet avoids obvious anachronisms and presents such an internally consistent picture of Scandinavian society around A.D. 500 that his illusion of historical truth has been taken for the reality.[4]

The poet's heroic age is full of men both "emphatically pagan and exceptionally good," men who believe in a God whom they thank at every imaginable opportunity.[5] Yet they perform all the pagan rites known to Tacitus, and are not Christian. The temporal distance between past and present, acknowledged in the opening words of the poem—"in geardagum" ("in days of yore")—is heard again when Beowulf, as yet unnamed, makes his entrance. He is the strongest of men "on þæm dæge þysses lifes" ("on that day of this life" 197, 790).[6] The alliterating demonstratives stress the remoteness of the past, here and later when a hall-servant in Heorot looks after all the visitors' bedtime needs "swylce þy dogore heaþoliðende habban scoldon" ("such as in those days seafarers were wont to have" 1797–98). The descriptive clause distances but also glosses over, shadowing with vagueness an unknown corner of the past. The poet is so attracted by the aristocratic rituals of life in the hall, so in-

1. Peter Burke, *The Renaissance Sense of the Past* (London, 1969), pp. 1–6; Michael Hunter, "Germanic and Roman Antiquity and the Sense of the Past in Anglo-Saxon England," *ASE* 3 (1974), 45–48.
2. "Chaucer's Sense of History," *JEGP* 51 (1952), 301–13; rpt. in Morton Bloomfield, *Essays and Explorations: Studies in Ideas, Language, and Literature* (Cambridge, Mass., 1970), pp. 13–26.
3. In assuming that literate composition indicates authorship by a cleric, I am following, among others, C. P. Wormald, "The Uses of Literacy in Anglo-Saxon England and its Neighbours," *TRHS*, 5th ser., 27 (1977), 95–114.
4. On the use of *Beowulf* as a historical document, see J. R. R. Tolkien, "*Beowulf*: The Monsters and the Critics," *PBA* 22 (1936), 245–51; sep. rpt. (London, 1937, 1958, 1960), pp. 1–6; Robert T. Farrell, "*Beowulf*, Swedes and Geats," *SBVS* 18 (1972), 225–86. Kemp Malone found the most remarkable feature of *Beowulf* to be its "high standard of historical accuracy": the anachronisms "that one would expect in a poem of the eighth century" are missing ("Beowulf," *ES* 29 [1948], 161–72, esp. 164). But the *Beowulf* poet occasionally nodded; see Walter Goffart, "Hetware and Hugas: Datable Anachronisms in *Beowulf*" in *The Dating of Beowulf*, ed. Colin Chase, Toronto Old English Series, 6 (1981), pp. 83–100.
5. Larry D. Benson, "The Pagan Coloring of *Beowulf*" in *Old English Poetry: Fifteen Essays*, ed. Robert P. Creed (Providence, 1967), p. 194.
6. The same line is used to place Grendel's downfall in the distant past (806). Citations of *Beowulf* refer to Frederick Klaeber, ed., *Beowulf and The Fight at Finnsburg*, 3rd ed. (Boston, 1950).

tent on historical verisimilitude, that he imagines everything, even basic human needs, to have changed over time. His proposition that golden tapestries hanging in the hall were a wondrous sight for the partying sixth-century retainers is quickly modified in the direction of reality: "þara þe on swylc stara" ("for those who look upon such things" 996); even in Heorot not all beefy breakers-of-rings in their cups would have had an eye for interior design. The vividness of the past underlines, paradoxically, its distance.

The *Beowulf* poet has a strong sense of cultural diversity, as strong perhaps as Chaucer's. Three times in the "Knight's Tale" Chaucer explains the behavior of characters with the clause "as was tho the gyse" [as was then the custom]; in "The Legend of Cleopatra" he has Anthony sent out to win kingdoms and honor "as was usance" [as was the custom]; and in "The Legend of Lucrece" he notes approvingly that Roman wives prized a good name "at thilke tyme" [at that time].[7] The Old English poet maintains a similar perspective. He praises the Geats for their ancient custom of keeping armor and weapons at their sides at all times: "They were always prepared for war, whether at home or in the field, as their lord required" (1246–50). He has Hrothgar admire their steadfastness, the dependability of men who live blameless "ealde wisan" ("in the old fashion" 1865). When the dragon's ravages begin, the poet makes the aged Beowulf fear that he has transgressed "ofer ealde riht" ("against ancient law" 2330): pagans have their own moral code, separating them from the author and us. The poet emphasizes cultural differences not only between present and past but also between coeval peoples. He depicts the Swedes and Geats as more authentically primitive, more pagan in outlook and idiom, than the Danes. When a roughhewn Beowulf arrives at the Danish court he puts himself in the hands of a skilled local who "knew the custom of the retainers" (359). Ongentheow, the grizzled king of the Swedes, threatens to pierce ("getan" 2940) captives on the gallows for the pleasure of carrion birds.[8] The Geats consult auspices (204); Beowulf, like the Scandinavian heroes of old, trusts in his own might (418, 670, 1270, 1533); the messenger imagines a raven boasting to an eagle of carnage-feasts (3024–27); and Hæðcyn's slaying of Herebeald (2435–43) imitates a fratricide in the Norse pantheon: euhemerism becomes, in the poet's hands, an aid to historical research.[9]

---

7. Morton W. Bloomfield observes that Chaucer employs "as was tho the gyse" to qualify pagan funeral customs (line 993), sacrificial rites (line 2279), and cremations (line 2911) (*Essays and Explorations*, p. 21). Citations from *The Legend of Good Women* are to lines 586 and 1813 in the second edition of F. N. Robinson (Boston, 1957).

8. Hans Kuhn relates Ongentheow's threat (*getan* = *gautian*) to a boast by the pagan tenth-century skald Helgi trausti Ólafsson: "I paid to the gallows-prince [Odin] Gautr's [Odin's] sacrifice" ("Gaut," *Festschrift für Jost Trier zu seinem 60. Geburtstag*, ed. Benno von Wiese and Karl Heinz Borck [Meisenheim, 1954], pp. 417–33).

9. Ursula Dronke points out that *Beowulf* contains human analogues for two additional mythological incidents recorded in Norse poetry ("*Beowulf* and Ragnarok," *SBVS* 17 [1969], 322–25). On Scandinavian heroes' faith in their own *megin* (OE *mægen*), see Peter Foote and David M. Wil-

The poet's sense of anachronism is revealed in his characters' speeches, utterances that avoid all distinctively Christian names and terms. The actors themselves have a sense of the past and of the future. They are able to look back two generations, tracing the origins of the feud between the Geats and the Swedes (2379–96, 2472–89, 2611–19, 2379–96). They can also forecast the feuds of the next generation. There is a fine display of chronological wit when Beowulf, on the basis of a piece of information picked up at the Danish court, turns the Ingeld legend into a political prophecy, a sequence of events likely to occur in the near future (2024–69). The poet's sense of historic succession is so strong and the internal chronology of the poem so carefully worked out that his audience knows why Hrothulf and Heoroweard have to be kept in the wings a little while longer. After Beowulf's death, it is clear even to the messenger that Eadgils is not likely to sit for long on the Swedish throne without avenging his brother's murder on the new king of the Geats, son of the slayer. The poet does not make earlier Danish and Germanic heroes like Scyld, Heremod, Finn, Offa, Sigemund, Eormenric and Hama contemporaneous with the sixth-century events narrated, but sets them in a distant mirror, conveying the illusion of a many-storied long-ago. Such chronological tidiness is all the more remarkable for its appearance in a poetic vernacular that has no distinctive future tense, and whose chief adverbs of recollection and continuation — "þa" and "siððan" ("thereupon": looking forward; "at that time," "from the time that": looking back) — are almost always ambiguous.[1]

Philosophically, in order to have a sense of history at all, the *Beowulf* poet had to hold certain premises about man and his role on earth. Despite his professional concern with the timeless, he had to be engaged to some extent with the things of this world; he needed a positive attitude toward secular wisdom and some notion of natural law. Above all, he had to believe that pagan Germanic legend had intellectual value and interest for Christians. These concepts were available to twelfth-century humanists. Christian Platonists like William of Conches, Bernard Silvestris, and Alan of Lille shared an unpolemical attitude toward the pagan past and stressed the importance of earthly understanding as the base of all human knowledge.[2] But in the central theological traditions of the early medieval West and, more specifically, in the teachings of Aldhelm, Bede, and Alcuin, there is no trace of this liberal mentality.[3] No contemporary

son, *The Viking Achievement* (London, 1970), p. 404. A raven, "oath-brother of the eagle," converses again in a section of the tenth-century pagan Norse *Hrafnsmál* (or *Haraldskvæði*) attributed to the skald þórbjǫrn Hornklofi.

1. Noted by E. G. Stanley, "The Narrative Art of *Beowulf*," in *Medieval Narrative: A Symposium,* ed. Hans Bekker-Nielsen et al. (Odense, 1979), pp. 59–60.
2. See Ursula and Peter Dronke, "The Prologue of the Prose *Edda:* Explorations of a Latin Background" in *Sjötíu ritgerðir helgaðar Jakobi Benediktssyni* (Reykjavik, 1977), pp. 169–70.
3. See H. M. and N. K. Chadwick, *The Growth of Literature* (Cambridge, Eng., 1932–40), 1:556–57; Patrick Wormald, "Bede, *Beowulf,* and the Conversion of the Anglo-Saxon Aristocracy" in *Bede and Anglo-Saxon England,* ed. Robert T. Farrell, British Archaeological Reports,

of these three concerned himself with man on earth, looking upon hea-
then virtues and customs with an indulgent eye, and had his vision sur-
vive. The patristic tradition that pagan story is diabolically inspired, that
unbaptized pagans lie lamenting in hell, was too strong.

Purely from the perspective of the history of ideas, the *Beowulf* poet's
chronological acrobatics and fascination with cultural diversity, his posi-
tive view of those who lived "while men loved the lawe of kinde," needs
explanation.[4] We cannot, wielding editorial knives, remove these ideas
from the text the way other late-seeming growths have been excised solely
on the grounds that the poem is early.[5] "It is a dangerous principle
to adopt in literary investigation that nothing we do not readily under-
stand can be rationally explained. We must as a working principle assume
that everything in a work of art is capable of explanation even at the cost
of oversubtlety and even error. . . . We must not assume, unless we are
finally forced to it, that the writer or composer did not know what he was
doing."[6] Professor Bloomfield offered this guidance in a review of Ken-
neth Sisam's *The Structure of Beowulf*. Sisam contends that "great diffi-
culties stand in the way of all explanations that make the poet a deep
thinker, attempting themes and ways of conveying them that might be
tried on a select body of readers in a more advanced age."[7] The fact re-
mains, however, that the poem, for an early composition, is full of oddly
advanced notions. Twenty years ago Morton Bloomfield observed that
"ealde riht" ("old law" 2330) in *Beowulf* referred not to the Mosaic Code,
the Old Law, but to natural law, and noted that the moral laws of the Old
Testament were often equated with this natural law, "although in general
this equation is later than the early Middle Ages."[8] More recently, he has
seen behind Beowulf's single combat with Grendel the concept of the *iu-
dicium Dei*, a calling upon God to decide the justice of an action: "Let
wise God, the holy Lord, adjudge the glory to whichever side he thinks

---

46 (1978), pp. 42–49. [Aldhelm (c. 639–709), Bede (c. 673–735), and Alcuin (c. 735–804) were
three of the greatest Anglo-Saxon scholars (*Editor*).]
4. Chaucer, *The Book of the Duchess*, line 56 (*The Works of Geoffrey Chaucer*, ed. F. N. Robinson,
2nd ed. [Boston, 1957]).
5. Kenneth Sisam long ago interpreted the Scyld Scefing preamble to *Beowulf* as a contemporary
allusion to the West Saxon dynasty; but since he took *Beowulf* as a whole to be seventh or eighth
century, the opening episode had to be a late, post-Alfredian addition: better a composite poem
than a Viking one. See Sisam, "Anglo-Saxon Royal Genealogies," *PBA* 39 (1953), 287–346, esp.
339. The Offa digression of *Beowulf*—a probable allusion to the great ancestor of the Mercian
house—would have flattered not only Offa of Mercia but also the descendants of Alfred who had
succeeded to the rule of Mercia and who were themselves descendants of the Mercian royal line.
But commentators, reluctant to look outside the age of Bede, either reject the Mercian associa-
tions of this digression or declare it, too, a later interpolation. See the important article by Nico-
las Jacobs, "Anglo-Danish Relations, Poetic Archaism and the Date of *Beowulf*: A
Reconsideration of the Evidence," *Poetica* (Tokyo) 8 (1977) [1978], 23–43. Jacobs demonstrates
that no linguistic or historical fact compels us to anchor *Beowulf* before the tenth century.
6. *Speculum* 41 (1966), 368–71.
7. *The Structure of Beowulf* (New York and Oxford, 1965), p. 77.
8. "Patristics and Old English Literature: Notes on Some Poems," *CL* 14 (Winter 1962), 36–43;
rpt. twice in its entirety, and partially in *An Anthology of Beowulf Criticism*, ed. Lewis E. Nichol-
son (Notre Dame, 1963), p. 370.

fit," says Beowulf (685–87); the champion will rely in the coming strug-
gle on the judgment of God (440–41).[9] Something like the judicial duel
appears to have been a feature of medieval Scandinavian society. Yet all
the early evidence for trial by combat from Tacitus to Pope Nicholas I is
Continental; there is no documentation for multilateral ordeal in Eng-
land before the Norman Conquest. The *Beowulf* poet's use of the form
and spirit of the judicial duel, whether he derived the concept from Tac-
itus, from the Franks, or from the Danelaw, emphasizes—like his au-
guries, sacrifices, and exotic cremations—the temporal and cultural
distance between the pagan Scandinavian past and the England of his
own day. His backward glance is both admiring and antiquarian.

Anglo-Saxon scholarship has done its best to read *Beowulf* as the sev-
enth and eighth centuries would have. Because Aldhelm and Bede in-
sisted that the only suitable subject for poetry was a religious one, and
because secular epics and long historical poems only started to appear
in the later ninth century, Margaret Goldsmith had little choice but to
interpret *Beowulf* allegorically.[1] Alcuin's only known comment on heroic
literature in ecclesiastical contexts is an orthodox denunciation of it as a
heathen distraction.[2] W.F. Bolton's new book on *Alcuin and Beowulf* dis-
covers, predictably, that the great schoolmaster would have found Beo-
wulf guilty, flawed, vengeful, incapable even of protecting his people.[3]
Charles Donahue attempts to account for the existence of an eighth-
century Old English poem about noble pagans by invoking Irish views of
pre-Christian goodness, legends that tell of virtuous pagans and their nat-
ural knowledge of God.[4] Yet the stories of Cormac and Morand that he
cites are not easy to date (that of Cormac is surely no earlier than the last
quarter of the tenth century), and Donahue concedes that they are "later
than *Beowulf* and can be viewed only as parallel developments of that
early insular Christian humanism. . . ."[5] Patrick Wormald has recently
located a social and cultural context for the composition of heroic litera-
ture in the aristocratic climate of early English Christianity, in the inte-
gration of monastic and royal houses.[6] Yet the aristocratic nature of the
early English church is, if anything, more pronounced with the passage
of time, reaching a kind of culmination under the successors of Alfred.[7]

---

9. "Beowulf, Byrhtnoth, and the Judgment of God: Trial by Combat in Anglo-Saxon England,"
   Speculum 44 (1969), 545–59.
1. *The Mode and Meaning of 'Beowulf'* (London, 1970).
2. *Alcuini Epistolae*, 124, ed. Ernest Dümmler, MGH, *Epistolae* IV.2 (Berlin, 1895), p. 183.
3. *Alcuin and Beowulf: An Eighth-Century View* (New Brunswick, N. J., 1978), esp. pp. 152–54,
   165–70.
4. "*Beowulf*, Ireland, and the Natural Good," *Traditio* 7 (1949–51), 263–77; "*Beowulf* and Christ-
   ian Tradition: A Reconsideration from a Celtic Stance," *Traditio* 21 (1965), 55–116.
5. "*Beowulf*, Ireland, and the Natural Good," p. 277.
6. "Bede, *Beowulf*, and the Conversion of the Anglo-Saxon Aristocracy," esp. pp. 49–58.
7. According to Wormald, "the aristocratic climate of early English Christianity is, if anything,
   more apparent in the age of Offa [second half of the eighth century (*Editor*)] than in the age of
   Bede [early eighth century (*Editor*)]" ("Bede, *Beowulf*, and the Conversion of the Anglo-Saxon
   Aristocracy," p. 94). Royal and monastic interests seem even more closely integrated in the age

The "vast zone of silence" Wormald observes existing between Bede and the *Beowulf* poet[8] may be due not only to Bede's fundamentalism but also to the centuries separating the two authors.

When in the Anglo-Saxon period did pagans become palatable? A positive attitude toward the pagans of classical antiquity is visible in translations of the Alfredian period. While the real Orosius, writing in the first decades of the fifth century, was as reluctant as Bede to say anything good about those who lived before the Christian Era, the Old English paraphrase of *Orosius* from around 900 contemplates with pleasure the bravery, honorable behavior, and renown of several early Romans, adds references to Julius Caesar's clemency, generosity, and courage, and even suggests that in some of their customs the Romans of the Christian Era were worse than their pagan ancestors.[9] Unlike his source, the Old English translator does not think in an exclusively religious way: what matters is how rulers of the past served God's purpose, not whether they were Christians or pagans.[1]

Boethius' *Consolation of Philosophy*, translated by King Alfred himself, resorted to pre-Christian human history and to pagan mythology for some fifty illustrations, finding archetypal patterns in the behavior of a Nero or a Hercules just as the *Beowulf* poet locates exemplary models in Heremod and Beowulf. In the late ninth and early tenth centuries, the *Consolation* enjoyed a considerable vogue among Carolingian commentators, at least one of whom, Remigius of Auxerre, Alfred may have used.[2] Alfred thrusts aside much of Remigius' Neoplatonic speculation along with his scientif-

---

of Athelstan [first half of the tenth century (*Editor*)]. Accompanying that king on his military expedition to Scotland in 934 were the two archbishops, fourteen bishops, seven ealdormen, six jarls with Norse names, three Welsh kings, and twenty-four others including eleven royal thegns. One of Athelstan's laws commanded that every Friday at every monastery all monks were to sing fifty psalms "for the king and those who want what he wants. . . ." See P. H. Sawyer, *From Roman Britain to Norman England* (New York, 1978), pp. 126, 192, 243. For a glimpse of aristocratic climates in tenth-century Saxony, see K. J. Leyser, *Rule and Conflict in an Early Medieval Society: Ottonian Saxony* (London, 1979).

8. "Bede, *Beowulf*, and the Conversion of the Anglo-Saxon Aristocracy," p. 36.
9. See Dorothy Whitelock, "The Prose of Alfred's Reign" in *Continuations and Beginnings: Studies in Old English Literature*, ed. E. G. Stanley (London, 1966), p. 91. For the Old English text, see *The Old English Orosius*, ed. Janet Bately, EETS, s. s. 6 (Oxford, 1980), p. xcix; for the Latin, *Pauli Orosii Presbyteri Hispani adversum Paganos Historiarum Libri Septem*, ed. Karl Zangemeister, CSEL, 5 (Vienna, 1882). [Orosius was the author of the Latin *History against the Pagans*, a work written at the behest of St. Augustine of Hippo (*Editor*).]
1. See J. M. Wallace-Hadrill, *Early Germanic Kingship in England and on the Continent* (Oxford, 1971), pp. 145–46.
2. Kurt Otten surveys attempts from Schepss (1881) to Courcelle (1937) to locate the Remigian commentaries available to Alfred (*König Alfreds Boethius*, Studien zur englischen Philologie, N. F. 3 [Tübingen, 1964], pp. 4–9). See also Brian Donaghey, "The Sources of King Alfred's Translation of Boethius' *De Consolatione Philosophiae*," *Anglia* 82 (1964), 23–57. Pierre Courcelle favors a ninth-century commentary by an anonymous monk of St. Gall (*La Consolation de Philosophie dans la tradition littéraire: antécédents et postérité de Boèce* [Paris, 1967]). But even if Alfred (d. 899) did not have access to Remigius' work in its final Parisian form (c. 902–908), he could have followed a version modelled on Remigius' earlier teaching at Auxerre and Rheims. See Diane Bolton, "Remigian Commentaries on the *Consolation of Philosophy* and their Sources," *Traditio* 33 (1977), 381–94, and "The Study of the *Consolation of Philosophy* in Anglo-Saxon England," *Archives d'histoire doctrinale et littéraire du Moyen Age* 44 (1977), [1978], 33–78.

ic and theological information, but is quick to insert commentary material having to do with classical myths. He occasionally gives a pagan analogy for a Christian concept, something Alcuin never managed to do.[3] Alfred's story of Orpheus teaches that a man who wishes to see the true light of God must not turn back to his old errors.[4] Boethius' tale of Jupiter overthrowing the giants who warred on heaven is shown by Alfred to reflect—*secundum fidem gentilium* [in the terms of pagan belief]—Nimrod's building of the Tower of Babel and God's subsequent division of tongues.[5] Alfred stresses the underlying truthfulness of Boethius' pagan fables. The details of Hercules' taming the Centaurs, burning the Hydra's poisonous heads, and slaying Cacus are skipped, but the myth itself is universalized into a philosophic reflection on life and on the meaning of victory and defeat: good men fight for honor in this world, to win glory and fame; for their deeds, they dwell beyond the stars in eternal bliss.[6] Circe in Alfred's paraphrase is no longer the wicked enchantress of Boethius, but a vulnerable goddess who falls violently in love with Odysseus at first sight; she turns his men into animals only after they, out of homesickness, plot to abandon their lord.[7] Alfred, like the *Beowulf* poet, looks for the moral and psychological laws of things, tries to understand and learn rather than condemn. Only once in his paraphrase does he abandon the world of classical paganism for a Germanic allusion; it is a small step, but full of significance for the future of Old English poetry. He translates Boethius' "Where now are the bones of faithful Fabricius?" as "Where now are the bones of the famous and wise goldsmith Weland?"[8]

When in the Anglo-Saxon period could a Christian author exploit pagan Germanic legend for its intellectual and moral values? Seventh- and eighth-century sources furnish evidence that English monks were overfond of harpists, secular tales, eating and drinking; but such worldly tastes provoked the scorn and hostility of their superiors: "What has Ingeld to do with Christ? The House is narrow, it cannot hold both. The King of Heaven wishes to have no fellowship with so-called kings, who are pagan and lost."[9] But by the late ninth century, even an archbishop—Fulk of Rheims, who recruited Remigius of Auxerre, corresponded with

3. Bolton, *Alcuin and Beowulf*, pp. 139, 177.
4. *Anicii Manlii Severini Boethii Philosphiae Consolatio*, ed. L. Bieler, CC, 94 (Turnhout, 1957), III, m. 12, lines 52–58; *King Alfred's Old English Version of Boethius' De Consolatione Philosophiae*, ed. W. J. Sedgefield (Oxford, 1900), p. 103, lines 14–16. Otten, *König Alfreds Boethius*, p. 133.
5. *De Consolatione Philosophiae*, III, pr. 12, lines 64–65; *King Alfred's Old English Version*, p. 99, lines 4–20. Otten, *König Alfreds Boethius*, pp. 129–32.
6. *De Consolatione Philosophiae*, IV, m. 7; *King Alfred's Old English Version*, p. 139, lines 5–18. Otten, *König Alfreds Boethius*, p. 38.
7. *King Alfred's Old English Version*, p. 116, lines 2–34.
8. *De Consolatione Philosophiae*, II, m. 7; *King Alfred's Old English Version*, p. 46, lines 16–17.
9. See n. 2 [above, p. 103]. The Council of Clovesho (746/7) specified that priests were not to chatter in church like secular poets (*Councils and Ecclesiastical Documents Relating to Great Britain and Ireland*, ed. A. W. Haddan and W. Stubbs [Oxford, 1869–78], 3:366); for additional examples, including one from the early eleventh century, see Wormald, "Bede, *Beowulf*, and the Conversion of the Anglo-Saxon Aristocracy," pp. 51–52.

King Alfred and sent Grimbald to him—could in one and the same sentence refer to a letter of Gregory the Great on kingship and to "Teutonic books regarding a certain King Hermenric."[1] A century and a half later, puritanical youth can be seen shaking its fist at reckless middle age in a letter that one cleric of Bamberg Cathedral wrote to another complaining of their bishop, Gunther, who spent all his time reading of Attila and Theodoric when not composing epics himself.[2]

The Beowulf poet insists on the virtue and paganism of his characters, and is unusually explicit about their heathen rites, describing them lovingly and at length.[3] A slender tradition of extolling the good customs of Germanic pagans can be traced in Roman authors, but this tradition does not enjoy a continuous run through the medieval period. The first known use of Tacitus' Germania after Cassiodorus occurs in the mid-ninth-century Translatio Sancti Alexandri by the monk Rudolf of Fulda.[4] This work, commissioned by the aristocratic abbot of the monastery of Wildeshausen in Saxony, opens with a description of the moral practices and brave deeds of the early pagan ancestors of the Saxons. Bede, monk of Wearmouth-Jarrow and historian of the English church and people (c. 731), is reticent about the doings of the Anglo-Saxons before their conversion and shows no inclination to celebrate heathens or their habits.[5] Widukind, monk of Corvey and historian of the Continental Saxons (c. 967), does not hesitate to do so. He borrows Rudolf of Fulda's account of pagan institutions and shapes the heathen past of his nation into a carefully contoured whole. He develops a single thread of historical tradition into a complex narrative, incorporating heroic dialogue, vivid details, and dramatic scenes, in much the same way that the Beowulf poet seems to have worked.[6] Widukind saw his efforts in recording the deeds of the Saxon leaders (principum nostrorum res gestae litteris . . . commendare [to praise the deeds of our leaders in writing]) as equal in value to the service he earlier performed with his two lives of saints. He wrote his history, he said, partly by virtue of his monastic calling, partly as a member of gens Saxonum [race of Saxons].[7] One historical sense seems to beget another:

---

1. The reference is to Eormenric of heroic legend and Beowulf (1201). Flodoard, Historia Remensis Ecclesiae, IV.5, ed. J. Heller and G. Waitz, MGH, Scriptores Rerum Germanicarum (in folio), 13 (Hanover, 1881), pp. 564, 574.
2. Carl Erdmann, Studien zur Briefliteratur Deutschlands im elften Jahrhundert, Schriften des Reichsinstituts für ältere deutsche Geschichtskunde (=MGH), 1 (Leipzig, 1938), p. 102; K. Leyser, "The German Aristocracy from the Ninth to the Early Twelfth Centuries: A Social and Cultural Survey," Past and Present 41 (1968), 25–53. [Attila was king of the Huns from 434 to 453; Theodoric was king of the Ostrogoths from 490 to 526 (Editor).]
3. On the poet's featuring of pagan elements, see Benson, "Pagan Coloring," pp. 193–213.
4. Rudolf of Fulda, Translatio Sancti Alexandri, ed. B. Krusch, Nachrichten von der Gesellschaft der Wissenschaften zu Göttingen, Phil.-Hist. Klasse, 1933, pp. 405–36.
5. See Wormald, "Bede, Beowulf, and the Conversion of the Anglo-Saxon Aristocracy," pp. 58–63.
6. Larry D. Benson, "The Originality of Beowulf" in The Interpretation of Narrative: Theory and Practice, Harvard English Studies, 1 (Cambridge, Mass., 1970), pp. 1–43.
7. Widukindi Monachi Corbeiensis Rerum Gestarum Saxonicarum Libri Tres, ed. H.-E. Lohmann and P. Hirsch, 5th ed., MGH, Scriptores Rerum Germanicarum in usum scholarum (Hanover, 1935), Bk. I, chs. 1–15. On Widukind, see especially Helmut Beumann, Widukind von Korvei

Widukind, like the *Beowulf* poet, learned much from classical historians, including the art of depicting people whose behavior made sense within the framework of their age and culture.

The *Beowulf* poet's attribution of monotheism to his good heathens is sometimes taken as revealing his ignorance of Germanic paganism, sometimes as a sign of his inability to see the past as anything other than the present. Like Widukind, he mentions pagan error, briefly and in passing (175–88), before depicting noble pagan monotheists for some three thousand lines. In the Alfredian *Orosius*, as in the fifth-century original, God is shown to have always guided the world, even in pagan times. But the paraphraser adds a few touches of his own: the pagan Leonidas places his trust in God; even Hannibal is heard to lament that God would not allow him domination over Rome.[8] The *Beowulf* poet, too, makes his heroes refer again and again to the power and providence of a single God, and he takes Beowulf's victory as a sign that "God has always ruled mankind, as he still does" (700–02, 1057–58). The Danes' hymn in Heorot to a single Almighty (90–98) expresses a Boethian wonder at seeing an invisible God through his creation. Wiglaf's contention that the fallen Beowulf shall for a long time "abide in the Lord's keeping" (3109) suggests a Boethian philosophy of salvation, of individuals ascending by reason alone to a knowledge of one God. It was probably Remigius of Auxerre who around 900 compiled a short treatise on the gods of classical antiquity, announcing—in the final paragraph of his prologue—that a single divine being lay behind the multiplicity of Greek and Roman names for the gods.[9] Renewed contact with the texts of late antiquity, especially Macrobius, Martianus Capella, and Boethius, ended by making some men at least think in a less narrowly religious way.[1] The *Beowulf* poet allows glimpses of a *paradiso terrestre* [earthly paradise] in the distant past— brief, transitory but glowing moments whose thrust is to remind his hearers of all the unfulfilled potential of their pre-Christian heritage.

What emerges from a sufficiently intense concern for history in any literary work is a series of projections inevitably focused by the particular anxieties of the writer. Alfred's *Boethius* reveals that king's fascination with the psychology of the tyrant, his concern for the proper uses of power and wealth, and his insistence, against Boethius, that temporal possessions can be put to good ends.[2] The *Beowulf* poet seems especially con-

(Weimar, 1950), and "Historiographische Konzeption und politische Ziele Widukinds von Korvei," *Settimane di studio del Centro Italiano di Studi sull'alto medioevo* 17 (Spoleto, 1970), 857–94.

8. *The Old English Orosius*, 49.1–3; 103.27–29.
9. *Scriptores Rerum Mythicarum Latini Tres*, ed. G. H. Bode (Cellis, 1834), 1:74. See Ursula and Peter Dronke, "The Prologue of the Prose *Edda*," p. 166.
1. John Scotus Eriugena, whose teaching is reflected in the school of Auxerre, wrote commentaries on all three authors. On his life, see E. Jeauneau, *Jean Scot, Homélie sur le Prologue de Jean*, SC, 151 (Paris, 1969), pp. 9–50, and *Jean Scot, Commentaire sur l'Évangile de Jean*, SC, 180 (Paris, 1972), pp. 11–21.
2. Otten, *König Alfreds Boethius*, pp. 99–118.

cerned to distinguish between justifiable and unjustifiable aggression, to place the warlike activities of his pagan hero in an ethical context. Beowulf resorts to arms out of concern for the defenseless and for the common good, not exclusively out of lust for conquest, ambition, or vengefulness. He is heroic and pious, a pagan prince of peace.[3] Christianity in the early barbarian West may have thought it was being assimilated by a warrior aristocracy, but it ended up—even before the Crusades—accommodating itself to the heroic values of the nobility. The blending of the two cultures would have begun at the time of conversion, but it was an extended process. At one stage, revelry in the hall, vowing oaths of fidelity to a lord, ambushes and plundering and slaughter, all the duties and responsibilities of heroic society were seen as demonic and damnable, as in the eighth-century *Life of Guthlac* by Felix of Crowland.[4] In the Old English *Guthlac A*, the poet even sends in devils to remind the royal saint and hermit his secular obligations, to tempt him with the hall-delights long abandoned after a warlike youth (191–99). The heroic life is the opposite of the life that leads to salvation.

The synthesis of religious and heroic idealism present in *Beowulf* was probably not available to monastic authors at an early date. In the 930s, Odo of Cluny wrote his *Life of St. Gerald of Aurillac* in order to demonstrate for his own aristocratic circle how a layman and noble lord, a man out in the world, could lead a holy existence.[5] Odo gives moral and religious dimensions to Gerald's lifelong martial career. The warrior soothes the suspicious, squelches the malicious, and puts down the violent who refuse to come to terms; he does this not for personal gain but in order to achieve peace for his society. So Beowulf restrains, one after the other, coastguard, Unferth, and Grendel, making friends of two potential foes and ridding Denmark of monsters who pay no wergild. Ottonian Saxony as portrayed by Widukind is—in the heroic cast of its values and the ferocity of its feuds—very close to the world of *Beowulf*.[6] Tenth-century monastic narratives seem, like *Beowulf*, able to find a place for heroic values—even fighting and the bonds of kinship—within a Christian framework. In Hrotsvitha's *Gongolfus* the ideals of a warrior's life are fused with

---

3. See especially Levin L. Schücking, "Das Königsideal im Beowulf" in *MHRA Bulletin* 3 (1929), 143–54; rpt. *EStn* 67 (1932), 1–14. English trans. as "The Ideal of Kingship in *Beowulf*" in *An Anthology of Beowulf Criticism*, ed. Nicholson, pp. 35–49. Robert E. Kaske, "*Sapientia et Fortitudo* as the Controlling Theme of *Beowulf*," *SP* 55 (1958), 423–56; rpt. in *An Anthology of Beowulf Criticism*, pp. 269–310.

4. *Felix's Life of Saint Guthlac*, ed. and trans. Bertram Colgrave (Cambridge, Eng., 1956), pp. 81–83. See E. G. Stanley, "Hæthenra Hyht in *Beowulf*" in *Studies in Old English Literature in Honor of Arthur G. Brodeur*, ed. Stanley B. Greenfield (Eugene, Ore., 1963), pp. 136–51, and Colin Chase, "Saints' Lives, Royal Lives, and the Date of *Beowulf*" in *The Dating of Beowulf*, pp. 161–71.

5. Odo, *Vita S. Geraldi Aureliacensis Comitis*, *PL* 133:639–703. See Carl Erdmann (*Die Entstehung des Kreuzzugsgedankens* [Stuttgart, 1935]), trans. M. W. Baldwin and W. Goffart, *The Origin of the Idea of Crusade* (Princeton, 1977), pp. 87–89. Odo was among Remigius' students at Paris (*Vita Odonis Abbatis Cluniacensis*, ch. 19, in J. Mabillon and L. d'Achery, *Acta Sanctorum Ordanis S. Benedicti* [Paris, 1668–1701], VII.124).

6. Leyser, passim.

the Christian goal of *caritas*, [charity, or the soul's desire for God], while Ruotger's *Life of Bruno*, archbishop of Cologne and brother of Otto the Great, reports with some understatement that "priestly religion and royal determination united their strength" in him.[7] Like these works, the Old English poems that we can date to the tenth century set up no unresolvable contradictions between piety and the heroic life. *The Battle of Maldon*, composed after 991 and regarded as the finest utterance of the Anglo-Saxon heroic age (and most "Germanic" since Tacitus), contains a prayer by a warlord soon to be venerated by the monks of Ely.[8] *The Battle of Brunanburh*, from around 937, is red with blood, God's rising and setting sun, and a historical perspective reminiscent of manifest destiny. *Judith*, probably from the same century, focuses on a prayerful heroine who chops off heads with only slightly less savoir-faire than Beowulf. Between *Bede's Death Song* and *Maldon* something happened to Old English poetry, whether we call this something rebarbarization or adapting Christian models for a new and only partly literate secular aristocracy. New syntheses were becoming possible. Unlike Anglian stone crosses of the eighth century, English religious sculpture after the Danish invasions was able to draw, like *Beowulf*, on pagan myth and heroic legend.[9]

In still another area, the vision of the *Beowulf* poet seems to derive from contemporary concerns, from a need to establish in the present an ideological basis for national unity. I suggested in an earlier paper that the *Beowulf* poet's incentive for composing an epic about sixth-century Scyldings may have had something to do with the fact that, by the 890s at least, Heremod, Scyld, Healfdene, and the rest, were taken to be the common ancestors both of the Anglo-Saxon royal family and of the ninth-century Danish immigrants, the *Scaldingi*.[1] The *Beowulf* poet admires kings who, like Hrothgar, have regional overlordship of surrounding tribes and who, like Beowulf, are powerful enough to keep neighbors in check. A key political catchword—"þeodcyning" ("great" or "national king")—is prominently displayed by the poet in his opening sentence. He depicts the Danish nation's former glory in a time when powerful kings had been able to unite the various peoples of the land, something that did not occur with any permanence in Denmark or England until the tenth century.[2] The *Beowulf* poet does his best to attach his pagan champion

7. *Hrotsvithae Opera*, ed. P. Winterfeld, MGH, Scriptores Rerum Germanicarum in usum scholarum (Berlin, 1902), pp. 35–51; *Ruotgeri Vita Brunonis Archiepiscopi Coloniensis*, ed. Irene Schmale-Ott, MGH, Scriptores Rerum Germanicarum, n. s. 10 (Weimar, 1951), p. 19.
8. See Rosemary Woolf, "The Ideal of Men Dying with their Lord in the *Germania* and in *The Battle of Maldon*," *ASE* 5 (1976), 63–81.
9. E.g., Wayland in Leeds Parish Church, Thor in Gosforth Church, and Sigemund at Winchester Old Minster. See Richard N. Bailey, *Viking Age Sculpture in Northern England* (London, 1980).
1. "Skaldic Verse and the Date of *Beowulf*" in *The Dating of Beowulf*, pp. 123–39, and Alexander Murray, "*Beowulf*, the Danish Invasions, and Royal Genealogy," pp. 101–11 in the same volume.
2. See discussion in Horst Zettel, *Das Bild der Normannen und der Normanneneinfälle in westfränkischen, ostfränkischen und angelsächsischen Quellen des 8. bis 11. Jahrhunderts* (Munich, 1977), pp. 69–84. On West Saxon hegemonial tendencies during the first half of the tenth cen-

to as many peoples as possible—Danes, Geats, Swedes, Wulfings, and Wægmundings—as if to make him the more authentically representative of the culture and traditions of central Scandinavia: an archetypal Northman. Epics have their propagandist appeal. There is a relationship, however indirect, between Virgil's account of the majesty of Rome's legendary past, the glory of her ancient traditions, and the Augustan program to bring back a "pristine" patriotism and code of morals. Both the *Aeneid and Beowulf* are in some sense historical novels, mythically presented, philosophically committed, and focused on the adventures of a new hero.[3] Both poets project onto the distant past features of the society of their own day, consciously and deliberately, in order to provide a sense of continuity. Virgil's Rome is grounded in an earlier Rome; the *Beowulf* poet anchors the West Saxon *imperium* in a brilliant North Germanic antiquity. By the twelfth century, the Normans were very French; yet the more French they became, the more they stressed their Danish ancestry and the heroic deeds of their founding dynasty.[4] By the first quarter of the tenth century, the Danes in England were working hard to be more Christian and English than the English: at mid-century both archbishops of England, Oda and Oskytel, were of Danish extraction.[5] An Old English poem about northern heathens and northern heroes, opening with the mythical figure of Scyld from whom the ruling houses of both Denmark and England were descended, fits nicely with the efforts of Alfred and his successors to promote an Anglo-Danish brotherhood, to see Dane and Anglo-Saxon as equal partners in a united kingdom.

The sadness, the poignancy, the *lacrimae rerum* we associate with *Beowulf* come from the epic poet's sense of duration, of how "time condemns itself and all human endeavor and hopes."[6] Yet though Heorot is snuffed out by flames and noble pagans and their works perish, the poet does not scorn the heroic fellowship whose passing he has had to tell.

tury, see E. E. Stengel, "Imperator und Imperium bei den Angelsachsen," *DAEM* 16 (1960), 15–72; J. L. Nelson, "Inauguration Rituals" in *Early Medieval Kingship*, ed. P. H. Sawyer and I. N. Wood (Leeds, 1977), pp. 68–70.

3. See Robert W. Hanning, *The Vision of History in Early Britain* (New York, 1966), p. 19. Tom Burns Haber makes one of several attempts to list verbal echoes and narrative parallels between the two poems (A *Comparative Study of the 'Beowulf' and the 'Aeneid'* [Princeton, 1931]). Recent publications demonstrating Virgilian influence on the narrative structure and perspective of *Beowulf* include Theodore M. Andersson, *Early Epic Scenery: Homer, Virgil, and the Medieval Legacy* (Ithaca, N. Y., 1976), pp. 145–59, and Alistair Campbell, "The Use in *Beowulf* of Earlier Heroic Verse" in *England before the Conquest: Studies in Primary Sources Presented to Dorothy Whitelock*, ed. Peter Clemoes and Kathleen Hughes (Cambridge, Eng., 1971), pp. 283–92.

4. R. H. C. Davis, *The Normans and their Myth* (London, 1976), pp. 27, 54.

5. Oda, bishop of Ramsbury under Athelstan and archbishop of Canterbury from 940–958, was the son of a Dane who came to England with the first settlers. Oskytel, kinsman of Oda, was the archbishop of York. Oda's nephew was St. Oswald, prominent founder and renovator of monasteries. See J. Armitage Robinson, *St. Oswald and the Church of Worcester*, British Academy Supplemental Papers, 5 (London, 1919), pp. 38–51. The Danes appear to have been widely accepted in English society from at least 927 onwards; see Jacobs, p. 40, and R. I. Page, "The Audience of *Beowulf* and the Vikings" in *The Dating of Beowulf*, pp. 113–22.

6. Bloomfield, "Chaucer's Sense of History" in *Essays and Explorations*, p. 25. [*Lacrimae rerum*, literally "the tears of things," refers here to the sense of sorrow that pervades the end of *Beowulf (Editor)*.]

There is still something left worth ambition: "The task to be accom-
plished is not the conservation of the past, but the redemption of the
hopes of the past."[7] The last word in the poem is uttered by sixth-century
Geats who commend Beowulf as "lofgeornost" ("most intent on glory").
Lady Philosophy assured Boethius (II, pr. 7) that the praise won even by
noble souls is of slight value: only a small part of a tiny earth is inhabited,
and by nations differing in language, custom, and philosophy; even writ-
ten eulogies fail because time veils them and their authors in obscurity.
King Alfred did not entirely accept her last point. He argued that the fame
of a great man can also fade through a kind of *trahison des clercs*—"þurh
þa heardsælþa þara writera ðæt hi for heora slæwðe 7 for gimeleste 7 eac
for recceleste forleton unwriten þara monna ðeawas 7 hiora dæda, þe
on hiora dagum formæroste 7 weorðgeornuste wæron"[8] ("through the
bad conduct of those writers who—in their sloth and in carelessness and
also in negligence—leave unwritten the virtues and deeds of those men
who in their day were most renowned and most intent on honor"). The
purpose of *Beowulf*, as Morton Bloomfield has often reminded us, is
heroic celebration, to present the deeds of a great man in order "to give
his audience new strength and a model."[9] Those of us who were privi-
leged to be Professor Bloomfield's students at Harvard know what such a
model can be worth.

JOHN D. NILES

Reconceiving *Beowulf*: Poetry as Social Praxis[†]

"Poetry makes nothing happen." People familiar with the marginal status
that poetry enjoys in most quarters today are likely to agree with this blunt
assessment, whether or not they lament it and whether or not they per-
ceive the irony that emerges when Auden's words are read in context, as
part of a poem that celebrates the memory of William Butler Yeats—for
Yeats's cadenced words, like those of Auden himself, have made mo-
mentous things happen in the minds of people from all parts of the globe.

The art of poetry has not always been practiced at the margins of soci-
ety, however. In some times and places, it has been a prized activity con-
ducted close to the centers of social power. In an oral context, what we

---

7. Max Horkeimer and Theodor Adorno, *Dialectic of Enlightenment*, tr. John Cumming (New
   York, 1972), p. xv.
8. *King Alfred's Old English Version of Boethius*, p. 44, lines 1–4. [*Trahison des clercs*, literally "trea-
   son of the clerks," refers here to writers who neglect their duty to record the deeds of famous men
   (*Editor*).]
9. *Speculum* 41 (1966), 369.
† From *College English* 61.2 (1998): 143–66. Footnotes are the author's except where followed by
   [*Editor*].

refer to as poetry could aptly be described as functional speech of a highly wrought, privileged kind. Oral poetic performances are often known for their magnificent displays of technical skill. Perhaps more importantly, however, they constitute a praxis affecting the way people think and act. The occasions of oral poetry provide a site where things happen, where power is declared or invoked, where issues of importance in a society are defined and contested. Oral poetic praxis consists in creative acts whereby a mental order is produced or reaffirmed or one order is substituted for another. By "order," adapting Zygmunt Bauman's formulation (119), I mean to denote what is both intelligible to the intellect and potentially useful in the world. Not until the emergence of nineteenth- and twentieth-century Western political ideologies has poetry, as an aspect of highbrow culture, been marked out as a separate realm empty of social function. This concept of "Art-as-Such," as M. H. Abrams has remarked, has outlived what once may have been its own period-specific usefulness.

The anonymous Old English poem that we call *Beowulf*, written out in a unique manuscript copy in about the year 1000 A.D., has plausibly been called "a most distinguished descendant of a long and skillful oral tradition" (Irving, *Rereading* 2). While the question of the mode of composition of the original poem will probably never be resolved, the text as we have it bears the traces of an oral verse-making technique as well as features typically associated with an oral-traditional mentality.[1] This is not

---

1. The literature on oral poetry and poetics is substantial. Among medievalists, it has developed in counterpoint with studies of textuality in an environment where monastic scribes, too, may have participated in an oral culture. Ruth Finnegan provides an overview of oral poetry with remarks on pp. 170–271 about poets and their types; audience; context; function; and the relation of oral poetry to social institutions. Eric Havelock has done much to clarify the role of oral poetic practice in the emergence of early Greek literary culture. Walter J. Ong, in *Interfaces*, addresses the residual power of oral literary forms in works that have been composed in writing; in *Orality and Literacy* he presents a lucid account of the mentality that is characteristic of oral cultures. Paul Zumthor focuses on questions of voice and audience, with examples from technologically advanced societies as well as early ones. Recent research, following Jack Goody and Brian Stock, has tended to conjoin the study of orality and textuality; see D. H. Green for a review of recent scholarship along these lines in the medieval area, Ursula Schaefer for discussion of Old English poetry along lines developed by Zumthor in regard to Old French, and Doane and Pasternack for a set of new essays by scholars working in Old and Middle English. Scholarship on oral-formulaic aspects of *Beowulf* and other Anglo-Saxon poems can trace a direct line of descent from Milman Parry's and Albert Lord's groundbreaking studies of Homer as a singer of tales. Francis P. Magoun, Jr., following Lord, applied Parry's theories to *Beowulf* and other Old English poetic records. Larry D. Benson and others were quick to point out flaws in Magoun's argument. Since then Jeff Opland has approached Anglo-Saxon oral poetry from a comparative ethnological stance with attention to African traditions and with a valuable appendix on the Old English terms for "song" and "singer"; I have analyzed the art of *Beowulf* in the light of oral poetic theory (*Beowulf*); John Miles Foley has pursued further comparative approaches, has amassed a bibliography of the Parry/Lord school, and has integrated the oral theory with recent developments in reader-response theory and the ethnography of performance; Alain Renoir has used the oral theory as a key to unlock special stylistic features of Old West Germanic poetry; Katherine O'Brien O'Keeffe has investigated the phenomenon of "transitional literacy," whereby manuscript records are thought to yield evidence of oral modes of thought; and Calvin Kendall has analyzed the meter of *Beowulf* as a product of a pre-existing oral tradition. See Paul Sorrell for an overview of scholarship relating to *Beowulf* in particular. In the present essay, quotations from the text of *Beowulf* are from the edition by F. Klaeber. Elsewhere ("Sign and Psyche,") I develop the point that the "environment of images" of poetry provides an entry to basic structures of Anglo-Saxon thought and feeling. In "The Role of the Strong Tradition-Bearer," taking Scot-

to say that we will ever know anything much at all about its unknown author or authors. Most attempts to summon the Anglo-Saxon oral poet from the grave have been based on little more than smoke and mirrors, as Roberta Frank ("Search") has pointed out with scholarship and wit.

Some scholars take *Beowulf* to be a learned departure from a kind of oral poetry that had once circulated widely but that had been superseded by the poet's day. If so the poem wears its learning lightly, for in it one can discern few or none of the gestures toward sources, models, patrons, or dates that are characteristic of works composed pen in hand. Other readers take it as a product of the merging of two traditions: a prized aristocratic habit of oral heroic poetry and a refined clerical habit of literacy. That is the stance I am adopting here. If a line of reasoning that I have developed elsewhere is correct (Niles, "Understanding"; cf. Sorrell 36–38), then the poem as we have it is a special production of the kind that results at the interface of an oral tradition and a textual one. It includes formal features, such as epic amplitude and abundant ornamentation, that result when works that are normally performed orally, often in episodic style, are taken down in writing in an event staged by a collector for the express purpose of generating a fine written text.

Whatever the prehistory of the text of *Beowulf* may be, the same questions regarding function can usefully be posed of it. What purposes were served by the performance or recording of a text of this character? What are the cultural issues to which this text represents a response? My aim here is to suggest some preliminary answers to these questions. But before doing so, I should briefly locate the poem in history, as much as can be done.

Beowulf was composed sometime between the sixth- and seventh-century conversion of the English to Christianity and the date of the manuscript itself, which could be as late as 1025: these are the outer limits within which we must work. To say that this period was one of major change is a colossal understatement. This was the time of Anglo-Saxon

---

tish singer and storyteller Duncan Williamson as an example, I develop the point that it is the exceptionally competent individual who powers an oral tradition and creates new systems of order. Sound recordings and videotapes that pertain to my 1984–88 fieldwork are on deposit in the American Folklife Center, the Library of Congress, Washington, D.C.

A number of scholars have addressed the question of when *Beowulf* was composed. Bjork and Obermeier have provided a skeptical review of the various theories regarding date that have been put forward. Roy Liuzza offers a judicious overview of that controversy as well. Important essays on dating *Beowulf* are gathered together by Colin Chase. A number of these question the earlier consensus that *Beowulf* is an eighth-century poem. Alexander Murray's contribution to the Chase volume calls attention to the relation of the genealogical preface of *Beowulf* to the West Saxon royal pseudo-genealogies. Audrey Meaney has pursued this approach and concludes that the preface to the poem is not likely to have taken shape before c. 925. Equally helpful in defining a period when a historical fiction like *Beowulf* would have met with a receptive audience is Roberta Frank, "The *Beowulf* Poet's Sense of History" [reprinted in this edition, pp. 98–111 (*Editor*)]; she too finds it unlikely that a poem of this character would have emerged until after the reign of Alfred. On the other hand, R. D. Fulk has recently reopened the argument for an earlier date. My essay "Locating" develops an argument regarding dating that can only be raised here in brief; thoughts about the possible role of *Beowulf* in a process of nation-building are also developed there.

cultural ascendancy and the era when both the idea and the reality of England came gradually and somewhat fitfully into being. During these centuries, the inhabitants of the Lowland Zone of Britain consolidated their identity as English-speakers who prized both their Old Germanic heritage and their Mediterranean and continental connections. They discarded pagan rites in favor of Christian faith and discipline, whether of the Irish or the Roman persuasion, and they eventually confirmed their adherence to Benedictine monastic ideals. They absorbed the shock of reiterated Viking attacks in the course of which Norse-speaking raiders first ravaged and then farmed the land, marrying into the native population and becoming acculturated to its ways. By the middle years of the tenth century, thanks to the forceful leadership of the kings of the West Saxon royal line from King Alfred the Great (r. 871–899) to Edgar the Peaceful (r. 959–975), a nation had step by step been formed, *Englaland*, modeled on Carolingian and Ottonian precedents[2] and taking inspiration from the ancestral Germanic past, the classical Mediterranean past, and Biblical antiquity. If the rulers of this nation relied on Latin learning to unite the realm and facilitate its administration, they also cultivated a degree of vernacular literacy that was unprecedented in Europe at this time. Given what is known about the role of vernacular languages and book production in making possible the rise of nations in later times (cf. Anderson 41–49), it is plausible to see this Old English textual culture as a prerequisite for the development of nationhood.

Such momentous changes as I have summarized here with ruthless brevity, and with a falsely teleological vision that is the concomitant of hindsight, could not have occurred in the absence of sharp contention as well as numerous setbacks. The vernacular poetry that formed a valued part of Anglo-Saxon culture during this period served, I would suggest, as one of the grounds on which mental conflicts took place. Following the precedent of Cædmon, the first English-language poet known to us by name, and pursuing that example in ever new directions, poets absorbed the values of Mediterranean Christianity, reinvented the Germanic past in the light of the Christian concept of history and the Viking presence in Britain, and transformed both their religion and their tribal heritage into a new mental order, an amalgam that embodied their most basic thinking about the world and their own place in it.

Like other Anglo-Saxon vernacular literature, *Beowulf* had a role in this process. Since there exists no certainty as to when, where, by whom, or for whom the poem was composed, we must remain ignorant of the full nature of that role. Very possibly, the synthesis that the poem represents came about only after Vikings had settled in the isle of Britain in some numbers. The poet's initial display of a Danish line of kings that in-

---

2. In the seventh through the tenth centuries, the Carolingian and Ottonian dynasties ruled the regions associated with modern Germany [*Editor*].

tersects, through the figure of Scyld Scefing, with a famously factitious West Saxon royal genealogy (lines 4–63) lends weight to this hypothesis, for myths of a common origin are an efficient means of promoting ethnic unity. Cultural arguments like these are unlikely to sway early-daters, including those who base their arguments on what they believe, with perhaps an insufficient degree of scepticism, to be reliable linguistic tests. Still, the idea of a tenth-century *Beowulf* accounts for features of the text that might otherwise seem anomalous, such as its occasional late-sounding rhetoric and its treatment of virtuous pagans. Many scholars writing during the past two decades have seen the poem as implicated in the process of cultural realignment that took place after King Alfred's wars and before the renewed Viking troubles of the reign of Ethelred the Unready (r. 978–1016). This is a guess, but an educated one. Attempts to date the poem precisely are likely to involve special pleading, however, while claims for an eighth-century *Beowulf* are still often heard. Given these uncertainties, it would be foolish to offer a thesis about that poem that stands or falls on the basis of an assumption about dating. Equally foolish, however, would be to ignore the possible role of vernacular poetry in absorbing and articulating, in symbolic form, the changes that were taking place in Britain during the period from the Conversion through the West Saxon ascendancy.

Tradition and the Capacity for Change

Whatever its date and place of origin may be, scholars are accustomed to speaking of *Beowulf* as a product of traditional artistry. Tradition, however, can easily be reified and used as a synonym for inertia. When one looks closely at an oral tradition, what one sees are not the abstractions of literary history but rather a set of flesh-and-blood individuals. Unreflective use of the term "tradition" can obscure the effort that is expended by individual persons in the course of producing a work of literature, not just reproducing one. Fieldworkers such as Albert Lord, in his case study of Balkan singer Avdo Medjedović, and Linda Dégh, in her account of story-telling practices in Hungary, have shown what can be learned by studying the artistry of singers and storytellers whose mastery of a tradition is such that they can urge it into new forms.

Frequently, too, scholars speak of *Beowulf* as a vehicle for wisdom. In a broad sense it surely was; but wisdom, too, can easily be reified. Too often it is treated as if it were something that is kept on the shelf, applied, and then reshelved. A full account of *Beowulf* would have to consider sapiential functions that are less solemn and unchanging than wisdom is generally taken to be. For poetry not only gives voice to a given mentality or worldview, but is also a form of play, a mental theater in which issues of worldview are precisely what are at stake. In a recent study of wisdom literature in Old English, Elaine Tuttle Hansen presents a corrective to static concepts of wisdom. In her view, the gnomic voice in poetry is "open to human experience and hence to conflicting perspectives, . . . simultaneously inviting or demanding interpretation and resisting interpretive closure" (176–77).

From Horace to Sidney and beyond, theorists have repeated the claim that poetry has a twofold purpose: to teach and to entertain. Persuasive as the claim has been, it leaves many questions unanswered. Just what is involved in teaching? Of what exactly does entertainment consist? Particularly if we wish to inquire about works composed in oral-traditional contexts, answers to those questions may not be self-explanatory to scholars whose own chief education has been through the written word. Understandably, perhaps, few studies of *Beowulf* have attempted to account for that poem's social functions, although a short essay by Charles Donahue takes a step in that direction. It is therefore worth inquiring what anthropologists have had to say about works partly analogous to *Beowulf* that have been recorded in the field.

In an influential essay published in 1954, the anthropologist William Bascom addressed the question of the use and purpose of folklore (using that term as an approximate synonym for "traditional oral literature" or "traditional verbal arts"). Bascom, an Africanist by training, defines folklore as satisfying four main functions: (1) It allows human beings to escape in fantasy from repressions imposed upon them by society; (2) It validates a culture, justifying rituals and institutions to those who perform and observe them; (3) It educates those in need of education, children in particular; (4) It maintains social control by encouraging conformity to accepted patterns of behavior. Like any typology, Bascom's can be accused of oversimplification, as he himself is quick to grant. To my mind, its chief drawback is that it promotes a false homeostasis. Bascom speaks on one hand of validation, education, and control, on the other hand of quasi-Freudian escape mechanisms that operate through fantasy. All four functions of folklore, in his view, thus serve a single overarching purpose, that of "maintaining the stability of culture" (297, repeated on 298). What is not clear from his account is the answer to two questions: how does culture change, and what role does oral tradition have in this process?

It is the dynamism of oral literature that has chiefly impressed me in the course of fieldwork I have undertaken with singers and storytellers in Scotland. One of the first things one learns in the field is that virtually all tradition-bearers believe they are expressing wisdom. They naturally like to entertain others, as well. Where they differ is in the specific nature of their wisdom, as well as in the degree and kind of their creativity in refashioning the materials of tradition (see Wolf; Finnegan 170–213). Singers and storytellers respond in distinctive ways to the tensions and tropes of their environment. Just as each tradition-bearer speaks an idiolect, each develops an individual repertory. Within that repertory, each person's style is unique. While one tradition-bearer relies on rote memory, others feel free to adapt and invent. The weird events and murders that are the staples of one person's repertory flee like ghosts at the light of day when another storyteller approaches with his jokes and personal anecdotes. While some performers maintain a stable repertory over many years, others are quick to learn new items and discard old ones.

One of the more creative tradition-bearers whom I have recorded in Scotland, Stanley Robertson of Aberdeen, can serve as an example of the dynamism that is characteristic of oral tradition. Robertson knows a great number of ballads, folktales, and tunes that he acquired during his childhood, especially at the campsites between the rivers Don and Dee where his family customarily stayed during the summer months in the company of other traveling people, or tinkers. A convert to Mormonism who has now traveled more widely in the world, he also relates spellbinding tales of his supernatural encounters on a mountain in Utah. He sings both songs that are well known in his region and songs of his own composition that he has set to familiar tunes. Some of his original materials distance him sharply from what he now regards as the false worldview of people of his parents' generation. Although he considers his schooling in Aberdeen to have been worse than worthless, he has developed literary skills on his own and has written three books of stories in Scots dialect, drawing equally on tradition and his own fertile imagination. Any account of the functions of folklore must take into account the restlessness that people like Robertson may feel at the thought of simply "maintaining the stability of culture."

Departing somewhat from Bascom, then, and mindful also of Finnegan's warning that the functions of oral literature are theoretically "infinite" (243) depending on the conditions of performance, I find it helpful to think of traditional literature as satisfying six main functions: the *ludic*, the *sapiential*, the *normative*, the *constitutive*, the *socially cohesive*, and the *adaptive*. Not all these functions need be satisfied by any one work, but most of them are likely to be. Other functions than these could be specified, as well. There is the spread of information, for example. Spanish-language *corridos* have traditionally served as a vehicle for spreading news, just as street ballads did in England in former times. Then there is remuneration. Buskers today, like the minstrels of former times, have the practical motivation of wishing to make a living from their entertainments. But leaving aside economic gain and the dissemination of news, the six functions that I have named seem to be the ones that count most in practice. It would be foolish to distinguish them sharply from one another, for they tend to reinforce one another's effects. Their existence in an equipoise of tension is the chief phenomenon with which we have to deal if we are to make sense not only of *Beowulf* but of a wide range of literary works that have come down to us from the past.

Some readers might object that not one of these functions is the exclusive property of traditional verse, as opposed to literature in general. I would be the first to agree. That point will not negate my claims, I believe, but rather will reinforce the thesis that literary writing, which from an archaeological perspective has developed rather late on in human affairs, is built on the base of oral storytelling. It sometimes incorporates story patterns of great antiquity. In addition, as Ward Parks has shown to be true of Old English poetry, even works composed pen in hand tend to draw on the rhetoric of orality in their invocation of an imagined face-to-face transaction between speaker and listener. I must look to others, however, for an account of how the same functions that are discernible in oral-traditional contexts operate also in literary works that depend more on individual inspiration than on the collective thought of a people.

Let me then review one by one the functions I have named, concentrating on those that have attracted the least attention in the past.

The Ludic

N. S. F. Grundvig, the pioneering Danish scholar of early Germanic literature, was probably not far wrong when he replied as follows to the question of what the poet's intention was in creating *Beowulf*: "If I know the poets of the past, they were, with such compositions, conscious of no other intention than to entertain themselves and others" (Haarder 88). Entertainment can be a serious matter, however, while it would be a hardy scholar these days who would claim that all the effects of a given work of art are a product of the conscious intentions of its maker. Cultural activities that are keenly expressive of the underlying spirit of an era have commonly been viewed as mere entertainment, and it is paradoxically this ludic quality that enables them to bear effortlessly a heavy cargo of meaning.

Johann Huizinga's classic definition of play has an apt relation to poetry in the form of oral performance:

> It is an activity which proceeds within certain limits of time and space, in a visible order, according to rules freely accepted, and outside the sphere of necessity or material utility. The play-mood is one of rapture and enthusiasm, and is sacred or festive in accordance with the occasion. A feeling of exaltation and tension accompanies the action, mirth and relaxation follow. (120)

There is evidence that the Anglo-Saxons considered poetry to be a quintessential form of play in this sense. In *Beowulf*, the special terms for the lyre with which singers accompanied their songs, *gomenwudu* ("joyful wood") (2108a) and *gleobeam* ("musical wood" or "joyful wood") (2263a), point to the pleasure people took in its sound, just as *gleomann* ("music-man") (1160a), one of the two poetic terms for the singer-musician, denotes someone who brings joy to others through his performances. When the *Beowulf* poet presents images of singers performing in public, common to all these imagined scenes is their association with merriment. Songcraft is first mentioned when the poet tells of a time just after the construction of Heorot when a scop sings a song of Creation. The singer's performance evokes a sacral mood and yet also serves as part of the general *dream* ("noisy merriment") (88b) in Heorot, or communal joy of a kind that the Anglo-Saxons relished and that Grendel bitterly resents. In the festive scene that follows the hero's first night in Heorot, a scop sings in a time of rejoicing, when men both young and old ride home from Grendel's mere on a *gomenwap* ("playful journey") (854b), racing their horses as they go. Later that same day, during a time of relaxation and gift-giving in Heorot, a scop sings of the strife of the legendary heroes Finn and Hengest. His song is called a *healgamen* ("hall entertainment") (1066a), and it seems to fall on rapt ears despite its unhappy theme. It is followed by a new round of mirth and drinking (*gamen eft astah,* "merriment resumed" [1160b]). The last metapoetic passage in *Beowulf* occurs once the hero has returned to his homeland, the land of the Geats. He tells his king Hygelac of the *gidd ond gleo* ("song and music") (2105a) that arose in Heorot when the aged Hrothgar took up the harp and sang. The gloomy content of some of these songs does not seem to have spoiled the festive occasion.

When the poet wishes to give force to the idea of earthly desolation, he does so through the image of a ruined hall deprived of its customary music. In the famous passage known as the "Lament of the Last Survivor" (2247–66), one negation heaped upon another — no harp, no falcon, no horse — conveys with bitter finality the meaning of tribal dissolution. In the "Father's Lament" (2444–62a), the silence of the harp is equated with the absence of all *gomen* ("merriment") (2459a) in a desolate hall that has become a site of suicidal melancholy. Still later, when the speaker of the "Messenger's Prophecy" speaks of Beowulf's death, he remarks that the aged king laid aside *hleahtor . . . gamen ond gleodream* ("laughter, merriment, and the joys of music") (3020b–21a), taking this triad of activities as synecdoches for life itself. If poetry can be regarded as a species of play, as the Anglo-Saxon terms for it imply, as Huizinga has claimed, and as Wolfgang Iser has recently reaffirmed on the basis of reader-response theory (249–61), then the hall, for the Anglo-Saxons, is its playground. With its benches, hearth, tapestries, and other adornments, the hall is the honored place of leisure, freedom, companionship, good beer, and the cultivation of aesthetic beauty. The joy of life in the hall, together with threats to that life, has often been described as a controlling theme in the poem (see e.g. Hume; Haarder 205–18; Irving 133–67). For the *Beowulf* poet and his audience, it seems, there could be no more grievous loss than that of the hall with its related activities, the sum of which represented civilization as they knew it.

Granted this consistent verbal link between poetry and play, the claim that traditional poetry has a ludic function remains only a point of departure. All authors play games with readers. To speak of the ludic qualities of *Beowulf* and other Old English poems, with their texture of kennings and riddle-like constructions, could be a rewarding enterprise but would still defer the main question: "What functions are served by this particular form of play?"

The Sapiential

Morton Bloomfield and Charles W. Dunn are forthright in assigning this function primacy in the poetry of early societies: "We argue that the basic role of the poet has been to serve as a carrier of tribal wisdom" (ix). There are good grounds for this emphasis. In general, as Hayden White has remarked, storytelling is "a solution to a problem of general human concern, namely, the problem of how to translate *knowing* into *telling*" (1).

In early societies the poet is the designated keeper of the memories of the tribe. One insults a poet at one's peril; for just as a king is the giver of material gifts, the poet is the donor of that immaterial quality that the *Beowulf* poet refers to variously as *lof, dom, mærðo, tir, blæd, þrymm, weorðmynd,* and *woroldar,* terms whose basic meaning in each case is "fame" or "good repute." The centrality of this concept in the Anglo-Saxon worldview can be recognized by the number of names by which it is known. The English word "honor" sums up its essence without exhausting the nuances of meaning that are conveyed by each of these near-synonyms. The famous last verse of *Beowulf,* however we choose to translate it, conveys in brief this society's obsession with the man who is resolutely *lofgeorn* ("passionate for praise") (3182b). The person of grand gestures and magnanimous spirit, always poised to play a part on the fields of honor and of war, seems to have inspired just as much fascination among the Anglo-Saxons as his equivalent, the Cypriot villager who is *philotimos* ("aspiring of honor"), has done in recent times, as J. G. Peristiany has remarked.

Scholars have sometimes spoken of the encyclopedic character of early epic poetry (Jaeger 3–76; Havelock, *Preface* 61–96). The Homeric poems encompass such broad plains of knowledge that the rhapsode Ion, in Plato's dialogue of that name, must be hard won from the idea that he can learn from Homer all he needs to know about life. The wisdom of poetry can indeed be bluntly practical, as in Hesiod's *Works and Days,* which includes among its various topics the right time of year to plant crops and the proper age at which to marry. Still, an epic encyclopedia has its limits. One cannot look to it for all the minutiae that are stored in the reference shelves of a library, for the chief function of sapiential discourse is to transmit not knowledge in the abstract, but rather a viable culture that remains "close to the human lifeworld" (Ong, *Orality* 42).

In *Beowulf*, to the annoyance of modern readers who lack the cultural competence that Anglo-Saxon aristocrats took for granted, the poet keeps alive the memory of a great number of kings, heroes, and tribes that figure in the storied past of the peoples of the North. He invokes their potent names—"Eormenric," "Weland," "Sigemund," "Ingeld," "Offa," "Hygelac," "Hengest," and the rest—and alludes to their good or ill character, their happy or tragic fate. He thus presents his main characters in a larger-than-life setting that constituted a time of origins for the Germanic peoples, one that was analogous to the Old Dispensation under which Biblical patriarchs lived.[3] This is not a world of random impulses jostling against one another in anarchic flux. The narrator takes pains to assure his audience that God ruled that grand and savage ancestral world across the sea, just as he rules the world today: *Metod eallum weold / gumena cynnes, swa he nu git deð* ("the Lord ruled over all humankind then, just as he still does now") (1057b–58). Uniting past and present is an unbroken sequence of providential interventions in human affairs on the part of a divine Will whose design is for our good, however inscrutable it may seem.

By telling of Old Germanic heroes and the acts by which God made known his power in former times, *Beowulf* must have played an educative role in a society whose schools were for the ecclesiastical elite. For members of the lay aristocracy, poetry was one chief means of education, as Ong has defined that term: "the process whereby society reviews what it knows about everything while it undertakes to pass what it knows on to its newer members" (*Barbarian* 10). Like the Homeric epics in early Greek times, Anglo-Saxon heroic poetry offered lessons in life to an aristocracy whose interests were not always served by education through the church. Some members of the warrior class seem to have felt that training in letters led to loss of manliness. The indifference or even hostility to literacy that Roman historians ascribed to such a barbarian leader as Theodoric the Ostragoth is "symptomatic of a consistently powerful alternative educational tradition throughout the early Middle Ages" (Wormald 98). In latter-day South Africa, tribal chieftains who were schooled according to the European system of education could be chastised for having lost touch with the values of their people. Included in a poem that one Xhosa poet performed in praise of his chief is a passage that criticizes one of that chief's rivals for having acted as a protegé of the white government. The passage ends with the ringing attack, "You thought you were being educated, and yet you were being brainwashed. / Chieftainship is one course that is not studied in the classroom!" (Opland, *Xhosa* 102). A poem like *Beowulf* would have offered Anglo-Saxon aristocrats memorable profiles in courage. At the same time, some of the

---

3. Old Dispensation refers to the conditions under which the Hebrew patriarchs lived in the Old Testament [*Editor*].

central teachings of that poem concern the need for generosity, modera-
tion, and restraint on the part of rulers. This is the theme of Hrothgar's
great homiletic address to the hero (1700–84), and the same theme is
nobly reiterated in the scenes that describe Beowulf's death and crema-
tion. The final terms offered in praise of the dead king—he is said to have
been *mild* 'kind', *monðwære* 'gracious', and *liðe* 'gentle' (3181–82)—
seem more appropriate to an Augustinian *rex justus*[4] than to a Ger-
manic warlord, as L. L. Schücking noted some years ago. Elsewhere
in Old English literature these same terms are used of benign or holy
people, including Christ himself. If *Beowulf* did have a place in a native
educational tradition that was cultivated alongside Latin letters, then the
poem is of interest for the evidence it presents of how the two value-
systems came to merge.

The Normative

If traditional poetry aims at wisdom and not just an accumulation of
knowledge, then it is a value-laden enterprise that has a direct impact on
morality. In the world of *Beowulf*, where what Stephen Greenblatt has
called "the social fabrication of identity" (143) reigns supreme, it is the
social aspect of morality—morality as the basis of the public interest—
that receives almost exclusive attention.

Most of the gnomic asides of *Beowulf* refer to fields of action in which
an individual can show his mastery of the aristocratic ideal of conduct.
Prominent among these asides are the *swa sceal* 'so should' or *swa bið*
'thus is' formulas that provide the audience with "secure resting-points
which comfortably evoke the ideal norms of their society and their world"
(Burlin 42). Such formulas reinforce the normative force of the poem by
defining, through concrete example and counterexample, such concepts
as the character of heroism and the nature of a good king or queen. *Swa
sceal geong guma gode gewyrcean* ("So should a young man bring it about
through his generosity") (20), the poet declares after telling how Scyld's
son prospers and gains power by showering gifts on his retainers. At the
end of the poem, when Beowulf's twelve chosen thanes ride about his
barrow, lamenting his death and conferring fame on him by singing his
praises, the poet notes that they do so *swa hit gedefe bið* ("as is right and
proper") (3174b). While some of the poet's gnomic asides may have a
complex edge to them when taken in context, these examples are unam-
biguous in their celebration of qualities that hold society together.

Through another kind of validating aside, the summary judgment, the
narrator sets a totalizing stamp of approval on what he admires. *Þæt wæs
god cyning* ("That was a good king!"), he says first of Scyld (11b), then
later of Hrothgar (863b), then finally of the aged Beowulf himself

---

4. The theory of just kingship articulated by Augustine of Hippo (354–430), which held that a king
   was bound by law [*Editor*].

(2390b), encouraging us to equate these three kings in terms of their character and achievement. Ne bið swylc cwenlic þeaw ("That is no custom worthy of a queen") (1940b), the poet states of Offa's queen Thryth or Modthryth, who in her youth had a bad habit of putting her suitors to death. Through contrastive pairs of characters, the poet dramatizes a system of values by projecting it into human form. Edward B. Irving, Jr., has remarked on the role of the poem's main actor in this process ("Heroic" 355): "There should be no doubt whatever—it is amazing that anyone has to state this point explicitly—that . . . Beowulf is always a superb role-model." Such a point seems uncontroversial when we consider the characters who figure as foils to the hero: the bully and fratricide Hunferth, for example, or the violent pre-Scylding king Heremod, whom Hrothgar singles out as a model to avoid. To be precise, however, it is not characters so much as character traits, as expressed in specific actions, that are held up as contrasts. Sigemund had his dark side. Heremod once held bright promise. Hunferth recovers well despite his rude initial manner. Thryth's shrewishness was eventually tamed. Beowulf himself, many readers have thought, shows questionable judgment based on only a limited understanding of the events that constitute his fate.

It is through such modeling of moral behavior that *Beowulf* can in part be ascribed the function of social control. With no trace of self-conscious embarrassment, the poet invites his audience to emulate the positive example and scorn the negative one. In this way the poem could have served the Anglo-Saxon warrior aristocracy as a means of enculturation. Any child or any aspirant to power could have internalized the poem's wisdom and learned from its examples. While gaining competence in the special ludic "language within the language" of poetry, members of the audience simultaneously would have gained competence in social norms. Members of the warrior aristocracy, in particular, could have found their value-system reinforced, with its royalist bias (to use a term favored by Clark 47–48) and its emphasis on hierarchical rule. If uncertain how to play the game of honor, any listener could attend the poet's school.

The Constitutive

Imaginative literature is vastly more than a box for accepted wisdom and a platform for moral certitudes, however. It is also a means by which people represent and structure the world. It not only mirrors reality, with whatever distortion this mirroring process involves; it constitutes a parallel version of reality that helps make the world intelligible and navigable. Its field of existence can be regarded as a heterocosm ("other world"), to use K. K. Ruthven's term (1–15). Like the ludic zones of organized play or the liminal zones of ritual that Victor Turner has so well described, a heterocosm will both resemble ordinary reality and depart from it in ways that may be equally striking. Its validity cannot be gauged in mimetic terms but rather depends on its internal coherence. "What are the rules of this world? What are the principles that make for consistency and predictability within it?" These are the questions that a listener or reader must ask of any narrative work. "Ask," I say, but most of us answer these questions unconsciously while absorbed in the process of listening or reading.

What matters in the heterocosmos is not so much its verisimilitude as its conformity to the laws of its own kind of storytelling. This is what Tolkien means when, in his deft essay on fairy tales, he states that the story-maker "makes a Secondary World which your mind can enter. Inside it, what he relates is 'true': it accords with the laws of that world" (36). This is also what I have found from time to time in Scotland, when a person has concluded an absolutely fantastic narrative with the emphatic remark "And that's a true story." Truth in storytelling is not something to be confused with historical accuracy or mimetic plausibility, nor is it the opposite of falsehood, fantasy, or error. Rather, like truth in a general sense, it is an eminently useful concept, what Hans Vaihinger has called a "system of ideas which enables us to act and to deal with things most rapidly, neatly, and safely" (108). From such a perspective, truth in both oral and literate settings operates as a conceptual tool. It is a means of distinguishing order in the midst of what might otherwise seem like chaos.

A heterocosm is far more than a repository for wisdom or a place to police one's neighbors. It is a way of mapping reality into its most basic constituent features: inside and outside, now and then, here and there, us and them, male and female, young and old, free and non-free, safe and risky, the rulers and the ruled, the public and the private, the holy and the unholy, the clean and the unclean, the just and the unjust, and so on. At the same time, it endows these contrastive features with a high truth-value. As one learns to navigate a heterocosmos, by a series of lightning-fast mental adaptations one also learns to navigate the world of human action.

Such a concept of poetry as a constitutive act, a social praxis, is in accord with current thinking about the nature of language. According to a key metaphor that goes back to the work of Saussure,[5] language is not a window that permits us to gaze on reality with little or no distortion. It is an eye, a highly complex psychoneural mechanism that mysteriously gives rise to ideas as the seer filters and selects external stimuli in accord with pre-established mental capacities. Eyes see the world as a problem to be solved, not as a mass of information. In like manner, there is no way to engage directly with the "real" world in or through poetry, for the language in which poetry is composed can never be transparent. It is a com-

5. Ferdinand de Saussure (1857–1913), a linguist best known for his posthumously published *Course in General Linguistics* (1916) [*Editor*].

plex semi-opaque medium that is the result of innumerable acts of filtering and organizing on the part of countless people. It solves problems in the process of registering them.

An attempt to describe in detail the way that poetry like *Beowulf* helped to constitute a mental world might begin by inspecting the poet's word-hoard, the poetic lexicon itself. It might trace how those elements that were perceived as the basic building-blocks of social order found expression in a wealth of keywords, both synonyms and near-synonyms, that refer to such concepts as the lord and the retainer, weapons and armor, ships and the sea, the body and the hall, gifts and gift-giving, warfare and feuding, women and cupbearing, God and devils, death and the soul, fame and shame. Each of these lexical clusters marks out a primary element of the heroic world. Where we do not find such clusters, the poet expresses his meaning with less fluency; or, perhaps, as when we probe for psychological depths in a character, the mentality that we search for does not exist. Lexical study of this kind would quickly shade into description of what Alvin Lee has called the coherent "environment of images" (231) in *Beowulf* and other Old English verse. Irving's study of the hall as the controlling image of *Beowulf*—not only the radiant hall Heorot, "the vital heart of the heroic world" (142), but also the various absent halls and anti-halls that the poet calls into being—is another step in this direction. Studies of poetic imagery provide an entry to the poem's great theme of communal solidarity, as well as to what has been described as the poem's "overwhelmingly protective, defensive, almost desperately guardianlike tone" (Raffel 33).

The Socially Cohesive

Oral poetry has one key function that distinguishes it from literature meant to be read in isolation. This is its social side, in a literal sense.

When people gather together to hear a work of oral literature, they share a single space. Crowded together, perhaps, they may push against their neighbors, drink the same beer, smell the same scent of smoke, sweat, and wool. In the intervals between songs, people may embrace, trade news, or flirt; fights may break out; friendships may be cemented or business deals brought to a head. In such a setting, the content of a poem is not necessarily its most important property. Instead, people may value the human interchange that the occasions of poetry provide, with their prospect of intimacy and a shared experience to be remembered for months or years to come.

The same is true of any game, of course. The fact of human interchange may be more important than the sum of what is won or lost, and this is why people like to play games and watch them, win or lose. Barring some disastrous falling out, the end result of any form of play is a set of strengthened social ties. A tribe, a group, a family, or a pair of friends finds a greater sense of cohesion, of having a common fate, culture, and values. With luck, at times, what Turner has called "existential" or "spontaneous" *communitas* (*Ritual Process* 131–32) will carry over into spheres of action where group solidarity can make the difference between plenty and want, peace and dissension, survival and death.

Often, though not always, an awareness of community implies a sense of ethnic identity. Sociologists familiar with the subjective nature of ethnic categories have stressed that ethnicity is not simply inherited; it is invented and chosen, sometimes on cultural grounds. Max Weber defines ethnic groups as "those human groups that entertain a subjective belief in their common descent because of similarities of physical type or of customs or of both" (389). George de Vos accepts the stress on subjectivity in this definition, as well as its reliance on culture as an ethnic marker, and in addition he stresses the way that a sense of identity, of "us-ness," can scarcely exist without a contrary sense of "non-us-ness" as well. In his view, an ethnic group is "a self-perceived inclusion of those who hold in common a set of traditions not shared by the others with whom they are in contact" (18). A strong and resilient cultural form such as oral heroic poetry can play a critical role in the invention of ethnicity in this sense. Whether one accepts the historicity of the Anglo-Saxons' Myth of Migration or, like some archaeologists (e.g. Hodges) regards this vision of the past as a largely factitious one that evolved in the rubble of post-colonial Roman Britain, the working of this myth into a heroic poem like *Beowulf* suggests that this poetry served to confirm an ideology of national origin and identity, as Nicholas Howe has argued. Through its initial invocation of the Scylding dynasty (lines 4–63), the poet honors kings who not only ruled over Denmark but also figure in the pseudo-genealogies of the West Saxon royal line. He thus turns ancestry into an instrument of ideology, as Craig Davis has pointed out. Furthermore, by making his fictive hero Beowulf a Geat, the poet ascribes him membership in a tribe whose name *Geatas*, in the Old English vernacular translation of Bede's *Historia Ecclesiastica*, is used as the equivalent to Bede's *Iuti (or Iutae)*, nowadays translated "Jutes"—one of the three founding peoples of Anglo-Saxon England. Both the *Beowulf* poet and the prose translator seem here to be involved in a process of creative ethnicity that serves to glorify the English by stressing their descent from ancestral figures of extraordinary stature. Similarly, by having Hrothgar's scop sing a song about the heroic vengeance taken by the legendary figure Hengest (1063–1159a), here presented as a "half-Dane," the *Beowulf* poet is very likely asserting the stature as well as the Scandinavian connections of a well-known dynastic ancestor, for Hengest, according to a tradition affirmed in Bede and the *Anglo-Saxon Chronicle*, was the founder of the Kentish line of kings. Later, through a tribute to Offa, the renowned king of the Angles during the time that they dwelled in a part of what is now Denmark (lines 1944–62), the poet offers a transparent compliment to Offa II, king of

Mercia (r. 757–796), the most powerful of the Mercian line of kings, which eventually was absorbed into the West Saxon line. In these various ways, *Beowulf* may have helped to promote an ethnic myth that fostered pride in a common Anglo-Scandinavian culture and heritage and that at the same time folded famous kings of the past into the genealogy of the tenth-century West Saxon royal line.

Social cohesion is thus not just a feature of the milieu in which works like *Beowulf* may have been performed. It is also one of the poem's controlling themes. The theme is voiced from the very start: *Hwæt, we . . . gefrunon* ("Lo! We have heard . . .") (1–2). "We" are the ones who know the stories, the fictive narrator assures his fictive audience. We have much in common with our neighbors, who know the same stories, who share the same customs, who appreciate the same poetic language, and (so the fiction asserts) who are listening by our side. As the story then proceeds, the narrator offers image after image of another fictive audience, a dramatic audience within the poem (as Lumiansky has remarked) that responds to the course of events as surrogates for real readers or listeners. When the narrator tells of the funeral of Scyld Scefing (26–52), he invites us in our imaginations to stand shoulder to shoulder with Scyld's companions, gazing as the dead king's ship recedes on the horizon. When he tells of the anxious watch of Beowulf's men as they stare, sick at heart, into the bloody waters of Grendel's mere (1602b–5a), he invites us to participate in their distress. When he tells how twelve chosen Geats circle the dead king's barrow (3169–82), he leaves us free to echo their dignified lament in our minds, *swa hit gedefe bið* ("as is meet and proper") (3174b).

At work in such scenes is a complex psychological process of *Einführlung*[6] and resistance. If *Beowulf* was performed aloud, its listeners could readily have identifed themselves with the dramatic audience within the poem, just as any individual reader today can identify with whichever character occupies the "hero position" at a given moment in the narrative. The possibility of ironic distance is always present, as well. The Danes give up hope for the hero's return. We know, though they do not, that he is alive in the depths of Grendel's mere. The Geats lament their king's death. We know, but they do not, that his soul has previously departed "to seek out the judgment of the righteous" (*secean soðfæstra dom*) (2820). Still, the strong tendency of traditional verse, as opposed to many varieties of recent fiction, is to collapse the walls of time and space so as to create the illusion of continuity between the heterocosmos of the poem and the world in which we live—so much so that singers of tales have been known to slip into the first person narrative voice when describing the actions of the hero, as happens in the *Mwindo Epic* from central Africa, as its collector and editor Daniel Biebuyck has noted (37).

---

6. Empathy, or sympathetic understanding (German) [*Editor*].

One reason why this perception of continuity is so strong is that oral literature has an uncanny power to raise the dead. By this claim I do not just mean the power to evoke an image of Achilles and Hector, Roland and Charlemagne. Any imaginative literature can do this. I mean the way that singers and storytellers sometimes feel themselves in the very presence of people from the past, often the people from whom they heard the song or story in former years. One tradition-bearer with whom I have spent many hours in Scotland, Duncan Williamson, has commented on how strongly this image of the dead can be evoked through the images and cadences of one's own storytelling:

> If I could tell you a tale the memory just floods back as a picture — I can see him [my father] sittin there by the fire and my mother there and all the children gatherin around the fire — . . . just a open fire in the ground — and I can remember my father, his short, short mustache, and he was sittin there, in his, in his late thirties. And I can visualize him the minute I tell a story. (Linda Williamson 73).

Williamson's powers of association are not unique. During one of my field trips, when a traveler from Montrose responded to my request that she sing the ballad known widely as "The Two Sisters," I noticed her husband leave the room for no apparent reason. Later a third person well acquainted with the couple drew me aside to tell me that the man associated the song so strongly with his dead brother — "That was Johnny's song!" — that he could not bear to hear his wife sing it even for my academic purposes.

Examples like these could be multiplied. They point to one of the best-kept secrets of literary studies: that one of the primary functions of oral literature is to keep alive the memory of people who have gone before. By this phrase I mean to refer not to the fictive people in the narratives in question, but rather to the flesh-and-blood human beings who are indelibly associated with a song or story in one's mind. The fellowship of song that sustains a viable oral tradition and is invoked by it, in turn, consists not only of the men and women who gather together at one another's elbows, mug in hand. It includes the spirits of the dead, who may temporarily reside with the living as long as the singer or storyteller holds forth. Scholars have long noted this connection between the dead and the living. In the Fiji Islands, for example, the dead are literally believed to sing the epic songs that are the most valued form of oral literature: "the ancestors themselves chant the songs as they teach them to the poet, and it is in their name that they are delivered" (Finnegan 171, drawing on the research of B. H. Quain).

In the many societies of the world that anthropologists have opened up for our inspection, we see well-documented examples of the kind of human situation that we can only imagine as a context for Anglo-Saxon literature. While it would be a mistake to extrapolate blindly from these examples to the past, they serve as reminders that beyond the worn or burned manuscripts that are our precious link to the past, there were such contexts peopled by men and women who found their group allegiance cemented through the interchange of song.

The Adaptive

If traditional verse had no other function than maintaining the stability of culture, then it would be a static medium of use only in a world where ripe fruit never falls. Apart from random error in transmission, there would be no reason for it to change over time. Oral tradition not only serves as a charter for existing social structures, however; it can also express the conflicting claims of different social groups. In Edmund Leach's words, myth and tradition constitute "a language of argument, not a chorus of harmony" (278). Despite a conservatism that is sometimes startling, the verse traditions of the world do change, and they change in a directed way, as part of shifts involving a culture as a whole. Sometimes, when momentous events exert intolerable pressure on a poetic tradition, it is displaced altogether, as happened with the discourse of English heroic poetry after the Norman Conquest. Traditional heroic poetry continued to be made and recorded in England after the Conquest—it may even have flourished more brilliantly than before—but this poetry was composed in the French language on topics of interest to the Norman ruling class. Barring conquest and catastrophe, a dynamic and even subversive capacity within the tradition encourages an impressive degree of adaptation. To invoke Auden again, the words of the dead are ceaselessly modified in the guts of the living.

In the preceding section of this essay, I noted some examples of how *Beowulf* may have promoted social cohesion through its fictions of an antique world. It is important to stress that the mental world that the poem invoked was not "handed down from time immemorial," as people routinely remark of oral tradition. It had to be fashioned at a particular historical moment, or in a series of historical moments that were linked together by individual poets each of whose actions constituted a social praxis. Such a mental world could not have been sustained in the absence of an ideology supportive of it—in its mature form, an ideology of enlightened Christian nationhood, I would claim. While a poem like *Beowulf* may well have been regarded as a "useless fiction" by some members of the clergy, the fact that it was preserved in writing, almost surely in a monastic setting, suggests that at least some members of the clergy not only shared the interest of laymen in tales set in the ancestral Germanic past, but also had some awareness of the capacity of poetry to encode ideology. In Anglo-Saxon society, poetry could enhance the power of ideology by allowing it to speak aloud in the special language and measured cadences of verse. For whatever reasons, the poem was preserved, and in its extant copy it testifies to the cultural adaptations that characterized the time when it was made.

Although traditional verse can be partisan, as for example the *Song of Roland* was in the context of the Crusades and was made to be during the period of national rivalries that preceded World War I, it is normally not so much a tool of social conflict as it is the terrain on which large-scale intellectual interchange takes place. As a collective representation of an imagined world, oral heroic poetry can be a means by which a shift to new values is effected. Like any social drama, it can serve to integrate a social group that has been broken apart by factional interests so as "to rearticulate opposing values and goals in a meaningful structure, the plot of which makes cultural sense" (Turner, "Social Dramas" 164). The regional rivalries that, to judge from available evidence, were the bane of Anglo-Saxon society during the period known as the Heptarchy are scarcely discernible within the narrative of *Beowulf.*[7] Instead, the poet offers a vision of what can be achieved when a king of quasi-imperial stature, such as the aged Beowulf, rules over his people with wisdom and with what can only be called a kind of Christian forbearance. No matter that Beowulf never heard of Christ; he still acts with saint-like fortitude. That the ideal of kingship articulated in *Beowulf* represented a change from the period of warring chieftains scarcely needs belaboring.

The reason for the inherent capacity for change in oral poetic tradition may be a basic one having to do with the nature of language itself. Language is naïvely regarded as a way of imitating or describing the world. As George Steiner has maintained, it also fulfills a precisely opposite function:

> *Language is the main instrument of man's refusal to accept the world as it is.* Without that refusal, without the unceasing generation by the mind of 'counter-worlds'—a generation which cannot be divorced from the grammar of counter-factual and optative forms— we would turn forever on the treadmill of the present. Reality would be . . . 'all that is the case' and nothing more. Ours is the ability, the need, to gainsay or 'un-say' the world, to image and speak it otherwise. (218)

Whether we regard the life of art as one version of the *vita contemplativa*—a love affair with the Other, the absent object of bemused imaginings—or as one version of the *vita activa,* "a form of resistance to the imperfection of reality" (Brodsky 221), it is a species-specific human activity.[8] By their power to generate counter-worlds peopled by men and

---

7. Heptarchy designates the organization of early Anglo-Saxon England into the seven kingdoms of Kent, Sussex, Wessex, Essex, East Anglia, Mercia, and Northumbria [*Editor*].

8. In Christian thought, *vita contemplativa* refers to the contemplative life in which one withdraws from society and *vita activa* refers to the active life in which one engages directly with society [*Editor*].

women of extraordinary courage, strength, ruthlessness, magnanimity, and ferocity, historical fictions like *Beowulf* can be a means of expressing social imperatives, charting moral errors, and sculpting systems of order. Although only *fabulae*, or "lies" in medieval parlance, such fictions can serve as the intellectual basis of emergent institutions and practices that, in the course of events, will in turn be displaced.

Poetry and Transformation

In this essay I have advanced the view that major works of orally grounded literature, works like the Homeric poems or *Beowulf*, are not just cultural items to stuff into one's suitcase, "great books" to be checked off a list of things to know. They are the result of a series of significant adaptations. In their manifold reiterations, whether in public performance or private reading, whether they are granted patronage by the great or find a more humble welcome, they constitute a social praxis involving the collaboration of many individuals. Even after their first reasons for existence have evaporated, such works continue to help constitute the historical present as they are appropriated into the consciousness of people in subsequent generations. What they are not, most emphatically, are boxes containing wisdom, mere objects for antiquarian display. They are rather the result of a collective, even restive, engagement with the question of what wisdom is, in a world that may seem stable or may seem in risk of spinning out of control.

When we look upon *Beowulf* as a representative of an honored type of poetry—one that served the Anglo-Saxons as a discourse, in Foucault's sense of a corporate means for dealing with a subject and authorizing views of it—we can see it as both the result of a set of cultural transformations and a means by which such transformations took place. If the concepts set forth in this essay are valid, then that poem's synthesis of the Germanic and Biblical pasts, of Danish and English interests, and of heroic and Christian values illuminates the role that traditional verse played in the development of a new mentality during what might fittingly be called, in the Anglo-Saxon context, the renaissance of the tenth century. *Beowulf* is not only a splendid poem that satisfied an Anglo-Saxon taste for wild adventure set in a dreamland of the past. It also served as a vehicle for political and cultural work in a time of nation-building. Whoever was responsible for making it achieved a remarkable synthesis. The poem speaks to the role that traditional verse can play in the consolidation of new mentalities. If we are to cross the threshold of understanding that research into the interface of literacy and orality have opened to our eyes, then we will enter a realm of critical inquiry where issues of meaning and literary value will dovetail with the question of what work the poem did in its time.

Works Cited

Abrams, M. H. "Art-as-Such: The Sociology of Modern Aesthetics." *Bulletin of the American Academy of Arts and Sciences* 38 (1985): 8–33. Rpt. with additional references in his *Doing Things with Texts: Essays in Criticism and Critical Theory.* Ed. Michael Fischer. New York: Norton, 1989. 135–58.

Anderson, Benedict. *Imagined Communities: Reflections on the Origin and Spread of Nationalism.* London: Verso, 1983.

Auden, W. H. *Collected Poems.* Ed. Edward Mendelson. London: Faber and Faber, 1991.

Bascom, William R. "Four Functions of Folklore." *Journal of American Folklore* 67 (1954): 333–49. Rpt. in *The Study of Folklore.* Ed. Alan Dundes. Englewood Cliffs, NJ: Prentice-Hall, 1965. 279–98.

Bauman, Zygmunt. *Culture as Praxis.* London: Routledge, 1973.

Benson, Larry D. "The Literary Character of Anglo-Saxon Formulaic Poetry." *PMLA* 81 (1966): 334–41.

Biebuyck, Daniel, and Kahombo C. Mateene, ed. and trans. *The Mwindo Epic from the Banyanga.* Berkeley: U of California P, 1971.

Bjork, Robert E., and Anita Obermeier. "Date, Provenance, Author, Audiences." *A Beowulf Handbook.* Ed. Robert E. Bjork and John D. Niles. Lincoln: U of Nebraska P, 1997. 13–34.

Bloomfield, Morton W., and Charles W. Dunn. *The Role of the Poet in Early Societies.* Cambridge: D. S. Brewer, 1989.

Brodsky, Joseph. "Poetry as a Form of Resistance to Reality." Trans. Alexander Sumerkin and Jamey Gambrell. *PMLA* 107 (1992): 220–25.

Burlin, Robert B. "Gnomic Indirection in *Beowulf.*" *Anglo-Saxon Poetry: Essays in Appreciation for John C. McGalliard.* Ed. Lewis E. Nicholson and Dolores Warwick Frese. Notre Dame: U of Notre Dame P, 1975. 41–49.

Chase, Colin, ed. *The Dating of Beowulf.* Toronto: U of Toronto P, 1981.

Clark, George. *Beowulf.* Boston: Twayne, 1990.

Davis, Craig. "Cultural Assimilation in the West Saxon Royal Genealogies." *Anglo-Saxon England* 21 (1992): 23–36.

Dégh, Linda. *Folktales and Society: Storytelling in a Hungarian Peasant Community.* Trans. Emily M. Schossberger. Bloomington: Indiana UP, 1969.

De Vos, George A. "Ethnic Pluralism: Conflict and Accommodation." *Ethnic Identity: Creation, Conflict, and Accommodation.* Ed. Lola Romanucci-Ross and George De Vos. 3d ed. Walnut Creek, CA: AltaMira, 1995. 15–47.

Doane, A. N., and Carol Braun Pasternack, eds. *Vox Intexta: Orality and Textuality in the Middle Ages.* Madison: U of Wisconsin P, 1991.

Donahue, Charles J. "Social Function and Literary Value in *Beowulf.*" *The Epic in Medieval Society: Aesthetic and Moral Values.* Ed. Harold Scholler. Tübingen: Niemeyer, 1977. 382–90.

Finnegan, Ruth. *Oral Poetry: Its Nature, Significance, and Social Context.* Cambridge: Cambridge UP, 1977.

Foley, John Miles. *Immanent Art: From Structure to Meaning in Traditional Oral Epic.* Bloomington: Indiana UP, 1991.

———. *Oral-Formulaic Theory and Research: An Introduction and Annotated Bibliography.* New York: Garland, 1985.

———. *The Singer of Tales in Performance.* Bloomington: Indiana UP, 1995.

———. *Traditional Oral Epic: The Odyssey, Beowulf, and the Serbo-Croatian Return Song.* Berkeley: U of California P, 1990.

Frank, Roberta. "The *Beowulf* Poet's Sense of History." *The Wisdom of Poetry: Essays in Early English Literature in Honor of Morton W. Bloomfield.* Ed. Larry D. Benson and Siegfried Wenzel. Kalamazoo: Medieval Institute Publications, 1982. 53–65 and 271–77.

———. "The Search for the Anglo-Saxon Oral Poet." *Bulletin of the John Rylands University Library of Manchester* 75 (1993): 11–36.

Fulk, R. D. *A History of Old English Meter.* Philadelphia: U of Pennsylvania P, 1992.

Goody, Jack. *The Interface Between the Written and the Oral.* Cambridge: Cambridge UP, 1987.

Green, D. H. "Orality and Reading: The State of Research in Medieval Studies." *Speculum* 65 (1990): 267–80.

Greenblatt, Stephen. *Learning to Curse.* New York: Routledge, 1990.

Haarder, Andreas. *Beowulf: The Appeal of a Poem.* Viborg: Akademisk Forlag, 1975.

Hansen, Elaine Tuttle. *The Solomon Complex: Reading Wisdom in Old English Poetry.* Toronto: U of Toronto P, 1988.

Havelock, Eric A. *The Muse Learns to Write: Reflections on Orality and Literacy from Antiquity to the Present.* New Haven: Yale UP, 1986.

———. *Preface to Plato.* Cambridge: Harvard UP, 1963.

Hodges, Richard. *The Anglo-Saxon Achievement: Archaeology and the Beginnings of English Society.* Ithaca: Cornell UP, 1989.

Howe, Nicholas. *Migration and Mythmaking in Anglo-Saxon England*. New Haven: Yale UP, 1989.

Huizinga, J. *Homo Ludens: A Study of the Play-Element in Culture*. London: Routledge, 1949.

Hume, Kathryn. "The Concept of the Hall in Old English Poetry." *Anglo-Saxon England* 3 (1974): 63–74.

Irving, Edward B., Jr. "Heroic Role-Models: Beowulf and Others." *Heroic Poetry in the Anglo-Saxon Period*. Ed. Helen Damico and John Leyerle. Kalamazoo: Medieval Institute Publications, 1993. 347–72.

——. *Rereading Beowulf*. Philadelphia: U of Pennsylvania P, 1989.

Iser, Wolfgang. *Prospecting: From Reader Response to Literary Anthropology*. Baltimore: Johns Hopkins UP, 1989.

Jaeger, Werner. *Paideia: The Ideals of Greek Culture*. Trans. Gilbert Highet. Vol. 1.2d ed. New York: Oxford UP, 1975.

Kendall, Calvin B. *The Metrical Grammar of Beowulf*. Cambridge: Cambridge UP, 1991.

Klaeber, F., ed. *Beowulf and the Fight at Finnsburg*. 3d ed. Lexington: Heath, 1950.

Leach, E. R. *Political Systems of Highland Burma*. 1954. Boston: Beacon P, 1964.

Lee, Alvin A. *The Guest-Hall of Eden: Four Essays on the Design of Old English Poetry*. New Haven: Yale UP, 1972.

Liuzza, Roy Michael. "On the Dating of *Beowulf*." *Beowulf: Basic Readings*. Ed. Peter S. Baker. Garland: New York, 1995. 281–302.

Lord, Albert Bates. "Avdo Medjedović, *Guslar*." *Journal of American Folklore* 69 (1956): 320–30. Rpt. in his *Epic Singers and Oral Tradition* 57–71.

——. *Epic Singers and Oral Tradition*. Ithaca: Cornell UP, 1991.

——. *The Singer of Tales*. Cambridge: Harvard UP, 1960.

Lumiansky, R. E. "The Dramatic Audience in *Beowulf*." *JEGP* 51 (1952): 445–50.

Magoun, Francis P., Jr. "The Oral-Formulaic Character of Anglo-Saxon Narrative Poetry." *Speculum* 28 (1953): 446–67.

Meaney, Audrey L. "Scyld Scefing and the Dating of *Beowulf*—Again." *Bulletin of the John Rylands University Library of Manchester* 71 (1989): 7–40.

Mitchell, W. J. T., ed. *On Narrative*. Chicago: U of Chicago P, 1981.

Murray, Alexander Callander. "*Beowulf*, the Danish Invasions, and Royal Genealogy." Chase 101–11.

Niles, John D. *Beowulf: The Poem and Its Tradition*. Cambridge: Harvard UP, 1983.

——. "Locating *Beowulf* in Literary History." *Exemplaria* 5 (1993): 79–109.

——. "The Role of the Strong Tradition-Bearer in the Making of an Oral Culture." *Ballads and Boundaries: Narrative Singing in an Intercultural Context*. Ed. James Porter. Los Angeles: Department of Ethnomusicology and Systematic Musicology, 1995. 231–40.

——. "Sign and Psyche in Old English Literature." *American Journal of Semiotics* 9 (1992): 11–25.

——. "Understanding *Beowulf*: Oral Poetry Acts." *Journal of American Folklore* 106 (1993): 131–55.

O'Keeffe, Katherine O'Brien. *Visible Song: Transitional Literacy in Old English Verse*. Cambridge: Cambridge UP, 1990.

Ong, Walter J. *The Barbarian Within*. New York: Macmillan, 1968.

——. *Interfaces of the Word: Studies in the Evolution of Consciousness and Culture*. Ithaca: Cornell UP, 1977.

——. *Orality and Literacy: The Technologizing of the Word*. London: Methuen, 1982.

Opland, Jeff. *Anglo-Saxon Oral Poetry: A Study of the Traditions*. New Haven: Yale UP, 1980.

——. *Xhosa Oral Poetry: Aspects of a Black South African Tradition*. Cambridge: Cambridge UP, 1983.

Parks, Ward. "The Traditional Narrator and the 'I Heard' Formulas in Old English Poetry." *Anglo-Saxon England* 16 (1987): 45–66.

Parry, Milman. *The Making of Homeric Verse*. Ed. Adam Parry. Oxford: Clarendon, 1971.

Peristiany, J. G. "Honour and Shame in a Cypriot Highland Village." *Honour and Shame: The Values of Mediterranean Society*. Ed. J. G. Peristiany. London: Weidenfeld and Nicolson, 1965. 171–90.

Quain, B. H. *The Flight of the Chiefs: Epic Poetry of Fiji*. New York: Augustin, 1942.

Raffel, Burton. "Translating Medieval European Poetry." *The Craft of Translation*. Ed. John Biguenet and Rainer Schulte. Chicago: U of Chicago P, 1989. 28–53.

Renoir, Alain. *A Key to Old Poems: The Oral-Formulaic Approach to the Interpretation of West-Germanic Verse*. University Park: Pennsylvania State UP, 1989.

Robertson, Stanley. *Exodus to Alford*. Nairn: Balnain, 1988.

——. *Fish-Hooses: Tales from an Aberdeen Filleter*. Nairn: Balnain, 1990.

——. *Nyakim's Windows*. Nairn: Balnain, 1989.

Ruthven, K. K. *Critical Assumptions*. Cambridge: Cambridge UP, 1964.

Schaefer, Ursula. *Vocalität: Altenglische Dichtung zwischen Mündlichkeit und Schriftlichkeit*. ScriptOralia 39. Tübingen: Gunter Narr Verlag, 1992.

Schücking, L. L. "Das Königsideal im *Beowulf.*" *Modern Humanities Research Association Bulletin*
    3 (1929): 143–54. Trans. as "The Ideal of Kingship in *Beowulf.*" *An Anthology of Beowulf Crit-
    icism.* Ed. Lewis E. Nicholson. Notre Dame: U of Notre Dame P, 1963. 35–49.
Sorrell, Paul. "Oral Poetry and the World of *Beowulf.*" *Oral Tradition* 7 (1992): 28–65.
Steiner, George. *After Babel: Aspects of Language and Translation.* New York: Oxford UP, 1975.
Stock, Brian. *The Implications of Literacy: Written Language and Models of Interpretation in the
    Eleventh and Twelfth Centuries.* Princeton: Princeton UP, 1983.
——. *Listening for the Text: On the Uses of the Past.* Baltimore: Johns Hopkins UP, 1990.
Tolkien, J. R. R. "On Fairy-Stories." *Tree and Leaf.* London: Allen and Unwin, 1964. 11–70.
Turner, Victor. *The Ritual Process: Structure and Anti-Structure.* Ithaca: Cornell UP, 1977.
——. "Social Dramas and Stories about Them." Mitchell 137–64.
Vaihinger, Hans. *The Philosophy of "As If."* Trans. C. K. Ogden. New York: Harcourt Brace, 1935.
Weber, Max. *Economy and Society.* Vol. 1. New York: Bedminster, 1968.
White, Hayden. "The Value of Narrativity in the Representation of Reality." Mitchell 1–24.
Williamson, Linda. "What Storytelling Means to a Traveller." *Arv* 37 (1981): 69–76.
Wolf, John Quincy. "Folksingers and the Re-Creation of Folksong." *Western Folklore* 32 (1973):
    225–36.
Wormald, C. P. "The Uses of Literacy in Anglo-Saxon England and Its Neighbours." *Transactions
    of the Royal Historical Society,* 5th series 27 (1977): 95–114.
Zumthor, Paul. *Introduction à la poésie orale.* Paris: du Seuil, 1983. Trans. by Kathy Murphy-Judy
    as *Oral Poetry: An Introduction.* Minneapolis: U of Minnesota P, 1990.

MICHAEL LAPIDGE

Beowulf and the Psychology of Terror[†]

It is a commonplace of literary criticism that *Beowulf* is a heroic poem.[1]
The commonplace has been stated so often that it has lost any precision
it might once have had. For what do we mean by "heroic poetry"? Here
is the definition, in plain words, given by Sir Maurice Bowra in his book
Heroic Poetry:

> The first concern of heroic poetry is to tell of action, and this affects
> its character both negatively and positively. Negatively it means that
> bards avoid much that is common to other kinds of poetry, includ-
> ing narrative — not merely moralising comments and description of
> things and place for description's sake, but anything that smacks of

---

[†] From *Heroic Poetry in the Anglo-Saxon Period: Studies in Honor of Jess B. Bessinger, Jr.,* ed. Helen
   Damico and John Leyerle (Kalamazoo, MI: Medieval Institute Publications, 1993): 373–402.
   Translations appearing in brackets are the editor's.
1. There would be little point in providing a complete conspectus of secondary literature in which
   Beowulf is referred to as a heroic poem. Note simply that the notion is pervasive in the Intro-
   duction to what is the standard edition of the poem, that by Fr. Klaeber, *Beowulf and The Fight
   at Finnsburgh,* 3rd ed. (Lexington, Mass.: Heath, 1950), esp. p. lviii; and that it informs the two
   standard literary histories of Old English: C. L. Wrenn, *A Study of Old English Literature* (Lon-
   don: Harrap & Co., 1967), esp. p. 107 ("*Beowulf* is the editorial title of the long heroic poem
   which is the supreme monument of the Anglo-Saxon poetic genius"); and S. B. Greenfield and
   D. G. Calder, *A New Critical History of Old English Literature* (New York: New York Univ. Press,
   1986), esp. p. 136, where *Beowulf* is treated in a chapter devoted to "Secular Heroic Poetry." See
   also K. Sisam, *The Structure of Beowulf* (Oxford: Clarendon, 1965), p. 1: "I start from the posi-
   tion that, though it contains historical, elegiac, gnomic, and didactic elements, *Beowulf* is an
   heroic narrative poem. . . ." In what follows I cite *Beowulf* from the Klaeber edition (see above);
   other Old English verse is cited from *The Anglo-Saxon Poetic Records,* ed. G. P. Krapp and E. V.
   K. Dobbie, 6 vols. (New York: Columbia Univ. Press, 1931–53).

ulterior or symbolical intentions. Positively it means that heroic po-
etry makes its first and strongest appeal through its story.[2]

If it is the first concern of heroic poetry to tell of action, to make its pri-
mary appeal through story, and to avoid symbolic language, then I sub-
mit that *Beowulf* is in no sense a heroic poem. It is true that some of the
characters mentioned in the poem figure elsewhere in heroic poetry,
properly defined; but the *Beowulf*-poet's primary concern could scarcely
be said to lie solely in action, or in his characters' involvement in it. On
the contrary, *Beowulf* is very much taken up with reflection—on human
activity and conduct, on the transience of human life—and it is couched
throughout in language that is characteristically oblique and allusive.
Calvin Kendall has recently described the nature of the poem, and his
description strikes me as a valuable antidote to earlier notions concern-
ing its heroic nature:

> . . . even though *Beowulf* is a poem about a hero who engages
> monsters and a dragon in mortal combat, it is extraordinarily lack-
> ing in action. The poet spends most of his time circling about a few
> moments of intense activity. He meditates, and his characters med-
> itate, on the meaning of the events which occur or which have oc-
> curred or which are likely to occur.[3]

A central concern of the *Beowulf*-poet, in other words, is with human per-
ception of the external world and with the workings of the human mind,
as he himself states at one point:

> Forþan bið andgit   ǣghwǣr sēlest,
> ferhðes foreþanc.   (1059–60a)

[Therefore discernment, mental anticipation, is best in everything.]

I should like here to explore one facet of the *Beowulf*-poet's concern with
the workings of the human mind, namely his portrayal of the monster
Grendel and his description of the monster's approach to Heorot.

Once we have read *Beowulf* (several times), we have a moderately clear
notion of Grendel's nature: what (roughly) he looked like, how he be-
haved, where he lived, who his mother was, and so on. He looked like a
man, except he was bigger (*nǣfne hē wæs māra   þonne ǣnig man ōðer*;
line 1353); indeed he was so big that it took four men to carry his head
back from the mere on a stake (lines 1634–39). He had real joints, like a
man, which cracked (line 760). His fingers had nails like steel (line 985),
and a terrifying light shone from his eyes (*him of ēagum stōd / ligge gelī-
cost   lēoht unfǣger*; lines 726b–27). He was invulnerable to iron
weapons (lines 802–03, 987–89). He carried with him a bag or *glōf* into

2. C. M. Bowra, *Heroic Poetry* (London: Macmillan, 1952), p. 48.
3. C. B. Kendall, *The Metrical Grammar of Beowulf*, Cambridge Studies in Anglo-Saxon England,
   5 (Cambridge: Cambridge Univ. Press, 1991), p. 5.

which he stuffed his victims (line 2085). He bit off their heads and drank their blood (lines 742–45), like a vampire. He stalked the moors at night, sometimes alone, sometimes with his mother, with whom he lived in a cave under a mere (lines 1345–72).

All these details emerge once we have read the entire poem—I stress this fact—and allow us to see what sort of creature the *Beowulf*-poet had in mind. That is to say, the details suggest that Grendel is analogous to certain monsters in other Germanic literatures, particularly Old Norse sagas.[4] What emerges from consideration of these analogues is that the *Beowulf*-poet must in the first instance have conceived Grendel in terms of an Old Norse *draugr*, an "undead man" or "ghost" or "zombi," a dead man who had not been properly buried and therefore became an animated corpse able to haunt the living by walking about, usually at night and in the mist.[5] Such *draugar* are frequently encountered in the Old Norse sagas: thus there is one named Agnarr in the *Hálfdanar Saga Eysteinssonar*, and another of the same name in *Gullþóris Saga*. More pertinent to *Beowulf* is the *draugr* called Ögmundr in *Örvar-Odds Saga*, who is invulnerable to iron weapons and who lives beneath a waterfall with his mother, a troll-woman or *gýgr*, who is said to be human on top but beast (claws included) beneath. However, the *draugr* that most closely resembles Grendel is Glámr in *Grettis Saga*. The character of Glámr provides so striking and instructive a contrast with Grendel that it is worthwhile briefly to summarize the outlines of the story, even though they may be well known to students of *Beowulf*. The story in question is found in chapters thirty-two to thirty-five of *Grettis Saga*:[6]

> Thorhall of Vatnsdal acquired a Swedish shepherd named Glámr to
> look after his flocks in winter. Glámr was a surly and difficult man
> with wolf-grey hair who was irreligious (he never went to mass) and

---

4. See especially two studies by N. K. Chadwick: "Norse Ghosts: A Study in the *Draugr* and the *Haugbúi*," *Folk-Lore* 57 (1946): 50–65 and 106–27, and "The Monsters and *Beowulf*," in *The Anglo-Saxons: Studies in some Aspects of their History and Culture presented to Bruce Dickins*, ed. P. Clemoes (London: Bowes & Bowes, 1959), pp. 171–203. A more recent essay by K. Hume ("From Saga to Romance: The Use of Monsters in Old Norse Literature," *Studies in Philology* 77 [1980]: 1–25, esp. 9–15) is concerned with monsters in the context of social reality. See also the brief but helpful discussion by J. D. Niles, *Beowulf: The Poem and its Tradition* (Cambridge, Mass.: Harvard Univ. Press, 1983), pp. 10–11.

5. The *Beowulf*-poet nowhere says explicitly that Grendel is a living dead man (he seldom says anything explicitly), though that is probably the implication of the terrifying light in his eyes. Note that there appears to be no Old English cognate of ON *draugr*; such a cognate, if it ever existed, would have been **dréah*. However, it would seem that ON *draugr* originally meant something like "tree-stump," and its use to mean "living dead" may therefore be metaphorical; see J. de Vries, *Altnordisches etymologisches Wörterbuch* (Leiden: Brill, 1961), pp. 81–82, who points to Finnish *raukka* (*verstorbener, böser Geist*) and Lappish *rauk* (*Seegespenst*), as well as to various uncertain Indo-European analogues, without arriving at certainty (I am grateful to Paul Bibire for advice on this matter). If *draugr* is in origin a metaphorical usage, it is perhaps not surprising that there is no Old English cognate.

6. See *Grettis saga Ásmundarsonar*, ed. G. Jónsson, Íslenzk Fornrit 7 (Reykjavik: Hið Íslenzka Fornritafélag, 1936), pp. 107–23; the episode is translated in *Beowulf and Its Analogues*, trans. G. N. Garmonsway and J. Simpson (London: J.M. Dent & Sons, 1968), pp. 302–12.

was hated by everyone. At Yuletide Glámr appeared at Thorhall's farmstead demanding food (even though the farmstead was fasting for Christmas). He was given food, and then went out into a blizzard, his breath smelling abominably. The following day they found him dead, his body swollen to the size of an ox. They tried to drag the body back to the church for burial, but unsuccessfully; when they took a priest out to find the body so as to perform the last rites, they became lost, and did not find it until after the priest had departed. Accordingly, they simply build a cairn of stones over the body and left it at that.

This form of unconsecrated burial was clearly insufficient, and Glámr duly became a *draugr*: he walked over houses, breaking them up, and assaulted men. A shepherd appointed to replace Glámr was found dead at Glámr's cairn, "his neck broken and every bone in his body wrenched from its place" (chap. 33). Thorhall's cowherd was then killed in a similar way, leaving only Thorhall and his wife alive at the farmstead. At this point Grettir, the principal character of the saga, heard about the *draugr* and determined to challenge it. The story of the encounter is well known and provides a particularly striking parallel to Beowulf's encounter with Grendel: Grettir waits alone in the hall, seated on a bench; Glámr seizes him; a violent wrestling match ensues during which all the furniture is broken up; eventually the two tumble outside, Grettir on top of Glámr; Glámr's eyes catch the moonlight, and "Grettir himself related that that sight was the only one which ever made him tremble" (chap. 35). Grettir eventually kills Glámr by cutting off his head.

The terrifying light emitted by Glámr's eyes is reminiscent of the *lēoht unfǣger* that stood out from Grendel's eyes, as many commentators have observed. I do not wish to press these parallels: my point is simply that the *Beowulf*-poet's starting-point for his conception of Grendel must have been a *draugr* like Ögmundr in *Örvar-Odds Saga* or like Glámr in *Grettis Saga*, though these sagas are of course several centuries later than *Beowulf*. But what a difference there is in presentation and conception! Whereas the author of *Grettis Saga* gives us a case history of how his *draugr* came to haunt Thorhall's farmstead, and gives us at the outset a moderately detailed account of his appearance (wolf-grey hair, abominable breath), such details as we have concerning the appearance of Grendel only emerge after the confrontation with Beowulf (and indeed in certain cases—the *glōf*, for example—only after Beowulf himself is back in Geatland). In my view, the *Beowulf*-poet's oblique and allusive presentation of Grendel is a crucial feature of his art.[7] In order to appreciate this art, it is necessary to put ourselves in the position of someone

---

7. The same point is made tellingly by Niles, *Beowulf: The Poem and its Tradition* (n. 4 above), p. 8, who remarks that "Such vagueness [in the description of Grendel] is calculated" and goes on to draw an instructive contrast with the detailed description of the Green Knight in *Gawain and the Green Knight*.

hearing or reading the poem for the first time and to eliminate any pre-
conceptions we might have about the monster's nature or appearance.

(1) The first mention of the monster occurs immediately after Heorot
has been completed:

> Ðā se ellengæst   earfoðlīce
> þrāge geþolode,   sē þe in þ̄ystrum bād.   (lines 86–87)

[Then the fierce spirit painfully endured hardship for a time, he who
dwelt in the darkness.]

The first noun used in the poem to describe the monster, *ellengæst*, is not
a precise, defining term:[8] it is a compound formed from *ellen* (strength
[or] power) and *gǣst*. This second element is probably intentionally am-
bivalent, insofar as *gǣst* (with long *æ*) means "demon" or "spirit" (cf.
ModE *ghost*), whereas *gæst* (short *æ*) means "visitor" (cf. ModE *guest*).[9]
Grendel is both ghost and guest. So at the first mention of the monster,
the audience learns only that it was a powerful ghost/guest that dwelt in
darkness.

(2) The next time it is mentioned the monster is a *fēond on helle*
(line 101b), an "enemy in hell," and we are told both its name and
habitat:

> wæs se grimma gǣst   Grendel hāten,
> mǣre mearcstapa,   sē þe mōras hēold,
> fen ond fæsten. . . .   (lines 102–04a)

[The grim spirit was called Grendel, known as a rover of the borders,
one who held the moors, fen and fastness.]

Again it is a *gǣst*, a grim one this time, which inhabits moors, fens, and
fastnesses (inaccessible places).[1] It is also a *mǣre mearcstapa* (notorious
wanderer in march-lands).[2] More important, its name is Grendel. The
naming of the monster implies familiarity, a process of identification, and
hence, a demystification of what it is or might be. Yet I suspect (as will
become clear) that this ready familiarity is something that the poet

---

8. The word *ellengǣst* occurs uniquely in line 86. Should one emend to read *ellorgǣst* (alien spirit)
[with Grein and Riegel; cf. lines 807, 1349, 1617, and 1621]? See discussion by J. Hoops, *Kom-
mentar zum Beowulf* (Heidelberg: Carl Winter, 1932), p. 26.
9. See Hoops, *Kommentar*, pp. 29–30.
1. On the medieval association of fenlands with hell, see R. D. Cornelius, "Palus inamabilis,"
Speculum 2 (1927): 321–25.
2. It has been suggested by N. Kiessling ("Grendel: A New Aspect," *Modern Philology* 65 [1968]:
191–201) that *mǣre* in line 103 is not the adjective meaning "famous, notorious" but rather the
noun *mǣre* (night-monster, incubus), as in ModE night*mare*. According to Kiessling the same
meaning is intended in line 762, *Mynte se mǣra*. There are serious difficulties with this inter-
pretation, however, serious enough to render it impossible: in the first place, *mǣre* meaning
night*mare* has a short syllable, whereas the metrical position of *mǣre* in line 103 requires a long
syllable; and, more importantly, the Old English word *mǣre* meaning night*mare* is elsewhere in
Old English and the Germanic languages invariably a feminine noun (see J. D. Pheifer, ed., *Old
English Glosses in the Epinal-Erfurt Glossary* [Oxford: Oxford Univ. Press, 1974], p. 95). I return
to the question of Grendel and the nightmare below.

wished to avoid,[3] and the use of such a name freed him from the need to use any further defining or descriptive nouns. The proper name, in other words, identifies without describing. In any case, if the poet wished to avoid communicating anything of the monster's nature, he chose an ideal name for it, for the etymology and meaning of the name *Grendel* are unknown. Various etymological explanations were proposed in the nineteenth century, and these were carefully catalogued by E. G. T. Rooth:[4] the opinion of Jacob Grimm, that the word was related to OHG *grintil* (bolt, bar); that of Karl Weinhold, that it was a derivative of OE *grindan* (to grind, shatter, crush), hence *Grendel* meant "the crusher," a derivation that was endorsed by W. W. Skeat; that of Thomas Arnold, that it was an early form of ME *gryndel* (angry); and that of Gregor Sarrazin, that it was cognate with ON *grindill* (violent wind or gale). To these Rooth added his own explanation, namely, that it was cognate with ON *grandi* (a sandbank beneath the water), whence **grandil* would be a creature from the bottom of the sea (cf. ModE *grindle*, a "mudfish"); hence *Grendel*, according to Rooth, meant *Seegrundmann* or "Sandmann," a metaphor for death (*Grendel ist der Tod*).[5] A few years later, A. Pogatscher proposed that the name was derived ultimately from the word *gram*, which in all early Germanic languages means "angry" or "filled with hatred," whence the Germanic etymon for Grendel's name, **grandilaz*, meant "hostile pursuer."[6] It will be clear even from this brief review of etymological explanations of Grendel's name that the meanings are derived more from a sense of how Grendel behaves in *Beowulf* than from any conviction about what the elements of the name might be. It is at least possible that the poet consciously chose for his monster a name that defied explanation and lacked precise denotation or connotation.

(3) The next lines offer some explanation of the monster's former habitat:

> fīfelcynnes eard
> wonsǣlī wer   weardode hwīle.   (lines 104b–05)

[Unhappy creature, he lived for a time in the home of the monsters' race.]

---

3. The capitalization of Grendel's name is a modern editorial device and one that obviously contributes to our sense of familiarity. But no such capitalization is found in the manuscript, and I have often wondered if the name should be left uncapitalized in order to accentuate the feeling of strange unfamiliarity that the monster provokes: "the grim ghost/guest was called a grendel (whatever that is)." However, I realize that the construction *wæs haten* implies a personal name and that, if a common noun *grendel* was intended throughout, we should expect that it would at some point be qualified with a definite article.

4. E. G. T. Rooth, "Der Name Grendel in der Beowulfsage," *Anglia Beiblatt* 28 (1917): 335–40; Rooth's information is summarized by R. W. Chambers, *Beowulf: An Introduction to the Study of the Poem*, with a supplement by C. L. Wrenn (Cambridge: Cambridge Univ. Press, 1959), p. 309.

5. Rooth, "Der Name Grendel" (n. 4 above), p. 340.

6. A. Pogatscher, "Altenglische *Grendel*," in *Neusprachliche Studien: Festgabe Karl Luick zu seinem sechzigsten Geburtstage* (Marburg: N. G. Elwert'sche Verlagsbuchhandlung, 1925), p. 151.

Interesting here is the fact that, for the first time, we are given some impression of the monster's shape: he is referred to as a *wonsæli wer* (wretched *man*). The "land of the *fifel*-kin" where this wretched man dwelled is presumably water, since elsewhere in Old English poetry the noun *fifel* (sea-monster) is used in compounds as a term for the sea or ocean: for example, the *fifelwæg* in *Elene* (line 237), the *fifeldor* in *Widsith* (line 43), or the *fifelstream* in the *Metres of Boethius* (line 26).[7] The implication is that Grendel was at some point a denizen of water (possibly the reference here is simply an anticipation of the mere about which we are subsequently told: lines 820 and, esp., 845–49). Immediately thereafter we are told that the Creator had condemned this race of (sea)monsters as being progeny of Cain, and, by way of further explanation, the poet gives a list of *other* monstrous races sprung from Cain— *eotenas ond ylfe ond orcneas, / swylce gigantas* ["trolls and elves and monsters—likewise the giants"] (lines 112–13a). These monsters are associated with Grendel only insofar as he once dwelled in the land of *fifel*-kin: note that the poet does *not* say that Grendel *was* any of these monsters. They are named to evoke an atmosphere of ancestral evil, not to give precision to Grendel's genealogy.

(4) The monster is next mentioned when it launches its first attack on Heorot—when it enters the hall, grim and greedy, and seizes thirty thegns. At this point it is described as a *Wiht unhælo, / grim ond grædig, . . .* ["The creature of evil, grim and fierce"] (lines 120b–21a). A *wiht* is a "creature," no more, no less; whether it carried a connotation of the supernatural, as Mary Serjeantson suggested by reference to phrases such as *unfæle wiht* [bad creature] or *yfel wiht,* [evil creature],[8] is unclear to me. I suspect rather that the poet has deliberately chosen an imprecise term in order to mask the nature of his monster.

(5) During the monster's ensuing attacks on Heorot, it is referred to as a *gāst* ["demon", "spirit"] (line 133), a *healðegn* ["hall-thane"] (line 142), and a *fēond* ["enemy"] yet again (line 143); but no further specification of its appearance is given.

(6) The monster's depredations continue for a period of twelve years, during which time it goes on persecuting:

> (ac se) æglæca   ēhtende wæs,
> deorc dēaþscua. . . .   (lines 159–60a)

[for the monster was relentless, the dark death-shadow]

That the monster is a "dark death-shadow" is anything but a precise description. More precision seems promised from the qualification that it was an *āglæca* ["adversary"] (for the spelling, cf. lines 732, 739, 1000, and

---

7. Cf. M. S. Serjeantson, "The Vocabulary of Folklore in Old and Middle English," *Folk-Lore* 47 (1936): 51.
8. Ibid., p. 46.

1269; the spelling *ǣglǣca*, as here, presumably represents the effects of i-mutation on the *a*-). Unfortunately the precise meaning of this term is disputed, and the matter is complicated by the fact that elsewhere in the poem it is used of Sigemund (line 893) and jointly of Beowulf and his adversary the dragon (line 2592).[9] Etymology might help to throw light on the meaning of the word, but there is as yet no consensus about what that etymology might be. F. Holthausen concluded that it was unknown.[1] In 1931 F. A. Wood suggested that it was formed from a prothetic vowel *a* plus an element *glac*,[2] but more recently it has been derived from the elements *ag-* and *-lǣc*. C. M. Lotspeich in 1941 derived the second element from OE *lacan* (to jump, move rapidly) and suggested that the first was cognate with Lithuanian *eiga* (a going, a march) and Greek οἴχομαι (to go away), whence the word *aglǣca* had a fundamental sense of "pursuing" or "stalking."[3] It might seem curious that no closer cognates for *ag-* can be found than Lithuanian and Greek, and a more plausible (in my view) etymology was proposed by F. Mezger in 1946, who suggested that *ag-* was cognate with Gothic *agis* (terror, fright), OHG *egiso* and hence OE *ege* and *egesa* (terror).[4] Thus, following Mezger's etymology, an *aglǣca* is a "demon [or] monster striking terror into the heart of men."[5] This latter explanation is evidently more appropriate to the atmosphere of the poem; but, whatever its meaning, it in no way contributes to the visual definition of the monster.

(7) The poet next pauses briefly to sum up the dire effects of the monster's depredations:

> Swā fela fyrena   fēond mancynnes,
> atol āngengea   oft gefremede.   (lines 164–65)

---

9. The meaning of *aglǣca* is normally derived contextually, as by Klaeber in the glossary to his edition, or (at greater length) by D. M. E. Gillam, "The Use of the Term *ǣglǣca* in *Beowulf* at lines 893 and 2592," *Studia Germanica Gandensia* 3 (1961): 145–69. There is an excellent (but incomplete) survey of proposed explanations of the word by S. M. Kuhn, "Old English *aglǣca*— Middle Irish *ochlach*," in *Linguistic Method: Essays in Honor of Herbert Penzl*, ed. I. Rauch and G. F. Carr, Janua linguarum series maior, vol. 79 (The Hague: Mouton, 1979), pp. 213–30, at 214–20.

1. F. Holthausen, *Altenglisches etymologisches Wörterbuch* (Heidelberg: Carl Winter, 1934), p. 3.

2. F. A. Wood, "Prothetic Vowels in Sanskrit, Greek, Latin and Germanic," *American Journal of Philology* 52 (1931): 137: ". . . in the meaning 'warrior, hero' the prefix has its more common perfective or intensive force."

3. C. M. Lotspeich, "Old English Etymologies," *Journal of English and Germanic Philology* 40 (1941): 1: "This fundamental meaning of OE *ag-* as 'pursuing,' 'stalking' explains the twofold use of *aglǣca* as 'monster' and 'hero,' because a pursuer can be either detested or admired."

4. F. Mezger, "Goth. Aglaiti 'Unchastity,' OE Aglǣc 'Distress'," *Word* 2 (1946): 69. The same etymology was proposed (independently) by M. L. Huffines, "OE *aglǣce*. Magic and Moral Decline of Monsters and Men," *Semasia* 1 (1974): 71–81. I confess myself unable, however, to follow the logic of Huffines's argument by which OE *lacan* is associated with "the type of movement and dance which accompanied sacrificial rites" (p. 72), whence an *aglǣca* "can be defined as a being who inspires fear by magical powers" (p. 74).

5. Huffines, "OE *aglǣce*" (n. 4 above [p. 141]; cf. Mezger, "Goth. Aglaiti," p. 70: "The deeds of the *aglǣca* Grendel are so terrible that horrible fright strikes the hearts of the Norþ-Dene (*Norþ-Denum stod atelic egesa*) when they hear Grendel sing a 'song causing terror.' . . ." It is with the terms *ege, egesa, gryre, brōga* that the actions of the *aglǣcan* and their effect on human beings are characterized. It is, accordingly, with good reason that one connects *ag-* in *aglǣca* with *ege, egesa* (fear, horror, terror, monster). On *egesa* see also below.

[Thus many crimes the enemy of mankind committed, the terrible walker-alone, cruel injuries one after another.]

We know already that the monster is the enemy of mankind; that it is *atol āngengea* (dire solitary) is a new, but not visual, descriptive detail. The word *āngenga* is relatively rare in Old English, being used twice of the monster (here and in line 449) and elsewhere only by Ælfric.[6] The solitary nature of the monster serves to accentuate the sense of mystery but, once again, does nothing to clarify our visual perception of it.

(8) Thus far we, the audience, have no clear visual impression of the monster's appearance: it is a dark death-shadow in the shape of a man. After twelve years of attacks, the Danes have presumably formed some visual impression of Grendel. But the poet is careful always to present Grendel from the Geats' point of view: to them, as to us the audience, the monster is unknown. When in due course Beowulf arrives in Denmark to challenge this monster, he has no clearer perception of its appearance than we do, as he states specifically:

> Þū wāst,   gif hit is
> swā wē sōþlīce   secgan hȳrdon,
> þæt mid Scyldingum   sceaðona ic nāt hwylc,
> dēogol dǣdhata   deorcum nihtum
> eaweð þurh egsan   uncūðne nīð.   (lines 272b–76)

[You know whether it is so, as we have indeed heard, that among the Scyldings I know not what foe, what dark doer of hateful deeds in the black nights, shows in terrible manner strange malice.]

Although he has gone to the trouble of crossing the sea with a company of chosen men, Beowulf himself has evidently acquired only the vaguest of information concerning the opponent he has come to Denmark to confront: he knows only that it is *sceaðona ic nāt hwylc* (some kind of destroyer, I know not what), that it is a furtive persecutor (*dēogol dǣdhata*), and that in its campaign of terror it wreaks incomprehensible hostility (*uncūðne nīð*). The poet is careful to protract our (and Beowulf's) sense of the monster's incomprehensible nature. Nor does the coastguard trouble to supply details to Beowulf's lacunose knowledge of his future opponent, and indeed at no time does anyone at Hrothgar's court brief Beowulf properly about what he is about to undertake.[7] Beowulf presents

---

6. Ælfric used the word in *Catholic Homilies* I.vii to refer to the solitary star seen by the Three Wise Men (ed. B. Thorpe. *The Homilies of the Anglo-Saxon Church*, 2 vols. [London: The Ælfric Society, 1844–46], 1:106) and again in *CH* I.xxxiv to describe the miraculous bull seen on Mt. Garganus (ibid., p. 502). These usages by Ælfric rule out the suggestion by Serjeantson ("The Vocabulary of Folklore," n. 7 above [p. 140], p. 45) that *angenga* might connote the Devil. Serjeantson was unaware of Ælfric's usages, however. Here and elsewhere I have had the benefit of drawing on A. diP. Healey and R. L. Venezky, *A Microfiche Concordance to Old English* (Toronto: Univ. of Toronto Press, 1980).

7. One might compare the somewhat fuller briefing given by Hrothgar *after* Beowulf has defeated Grendel, and after Grendel's mother has attacked Heorot for the first time: at that point Hrothgar deems it appropriate to give Beowulf an account of what his countrymen have seen, namely

Hrothgar with his credentials for dealing with *fēondas* [enemies] and then outlines elaborate arrangements for the disposal of his corpse if he should fail in his challenge of the monster. During the course of this speech, Beowulf refers to the monster as a *þyrs* (line 426),[8] an *æglæca* again (line 433), a *fēond* again (line 439), an *āngenga* again (line 449), and yet again an *atol æglæca* (line 592). Hrothgar and the court then go to bed, and Beowulf sits awaiting the approach of the monster. The point is simply that, when the monster does approach Heorot, neither the audience nor Beowulf has the slightest notion of what it is or what it looks like. The poet has carefully created an impression of the monster's dire impact but has avoided giving any indication of its appearance;[9] the emphasis has rather been on the incomprehensible aspect of the monster (*sceaðona ic nāt hwylc, . . . uncūðne nīð*; lines 274b, 276b). It is because the monster lies beyond our comprehension, because we cannot visualize it at all, that its approach is one of the most terrifying moments in English literature:

> Cōm on wanre niht
> scrīðan sceadugenga.   Scēotend swæfon,
> þā þæt hornreced   healdan scoldon,
> ealle būton ānum.   Þæt wæs yldum cūþ,
> þæt hīe ne mōste,   þā Metod nolde,
> se s[c]ynscaþa   under sceadu bregdan;—
> ac hē wæccende   wrāþum on andan
> bād bolgenmōd   beadwa geþinges.
> Ðā cōm of mōre   under misthleoþum
> Grendel gongan,   Godes yrre bær;
> mynte se mānscaða   manna cynnes

---

that *two* prowlers had often appeared, one in the likeness of a woman, the other like a man only larger, etc. (lines 1345–72). One might think that Beowulf would have been grateful for such information at the outset. The details are withheld because the *Beowulf*-poet was trying to create an atmosphere of terror, not to describe the antagonists with military precision.

8. A *þyrs*, as we learn from *Maxims II*, is a solitary fen-dweller: *þyrs sceal on fenne gewunian, / ana innan lande* (lines 43–44). See also R. Jente, *Die mythologischen Ausdrücke im altenglischen Wortschatz*, Anglistische Forschungen 56 (Heidelberg: Carl Winter, 1921), pp. 187–89, as well as E. G. Stanley, "Two Old English Phrases Insufficiently Understood for Literary Criticism: *þing gehegan* and *seonoþ gehegan*," in *Old English Poetry: Essays on Style*, ed. D. G. Calder (Berkeley and Los Angeles: Univ. of California Press, 1979), pp. 69–71.

9. In a brief article J. R. Hulbert ("A Note on the Psychology of the *Beowulf* Poet," in *Studies in English Philology: A Miscellany in Honor of Frederick Klaeber*, ed. K. Malone and M. B. Ruud [Minneapolis, Minn.: Univ. of Minnesota Press, 1929], pp. 189–95) speculated intelligently on the *Beowulf*-poet's persistent avoidance of graphic visual detail. Hulbert was concerned especially with replying to W. W. Lawrence ("The Haunted Mere in *Beowulf*," *Publications of the Modern Language Association* 27 [1912]: 208–45), who had pointed to a series of inconsistencies in the poet's description of the mere, namely that it appeared to be situated both in fenland as well as on high and rocky land. Hulbert argued that these inconsistencies were irrelevant: "the poet did not visualize the scene because he was not accustomed to visualizing anything" (p. 192). By the same token the appearance of Grendel is left vague (p. 194) because the poet's concern was rather with suggesting moods and states of mind (p. 195). See also Stanley, "Two Old English Phrases" (n. 8 above [p. 143]), p. 69: "Part of the obscurity of the poem as far as a literary understanding is concerned is that we do not know what criteria to adopt for visualizing monsters." I am suggesting that the poet, far from wishing us to adopt criteria for visualizing Grendel, exercised great care in choosing language that would prevent such visualization.

> sumne besyrwan   in sele þām hēan.
> Wōd under wolcnum   tō þæs þe hē wīnreced,
> goldsele gumena   gearwost wisse
> fættum fāhne. . . .
> Cōm þā tō recede   rinc sīðian
> drēamum bedæled.   (lines 702b–21a)

[There came gliding in the black night the walker in darkness. The warriors slept who should hold the horned house — all but one. It was known to men that when the Ruler did not wish it the hostile creature might not drag them away beneath the shadows. But he, lying awake for the fierce foe, with heart swollen in anger awaited the outcome of the fight. Then from the moor under the mist-hills Grendel came walking, bearing God's anger. The foul ravager thought to catch some one of mankind there in the high hall. Under the clouds he moved until he could see most clearly the wine-hall, treasure-house of men, shining with gold. . . . The creature deprived of joy came walking to the hall.]

The emotional effect of this passage has been brilliantly analyzed by Arthur Brodeur, who showed how the threefold repetition of *cōm*, each time with a different infinitive, marks distinct stages in Grendel's advance and in the audience's mounting sense of horror; it is, as he rightly noted, a "hair-raising depiction of death on the march."[1] Subsequent commentators have amplified Brodeur's analysis in interesting ways,[2] and there is no need here for further analysis, save to mention that the reason why this moment is so terrifying is precisely that what approaches Heorot is a creature of completely unknown aspect or dimension.[3] It advances not in precise, definite footsteps but with a muffled, gliding movement (*scrīðan*). As it draws closer and closer and closer (the advance marked by the threefold repetition of *cōm*), the terror grows and becomes stifling, almost as in a nightmare.

I shall return to the nightmare sensation in a moment; for now it is enough to stress that the poet was demonstrably interested in the nature and mechanism of fear. Throughout the poem is a recurrent vocabulary used to describe sensations of fear and terror, much of it unique to *Beowulf*. Three words in particular require discussion: *brōga*, *egesa*, and *gryre*.

---

1. A. G. Brodeur, *The Art of Beowulf* (Berkeley and Los Angeles: Univ. of California Press, 1959), esp. pp. 89–91 (quotation from p. 90).
2. A. Renoir, "Point of View and Design for Terror in *Beowulf*," *Neuphilologische Mitteilungen* 63 (1962): 154–67; S. B. Greenfield, "Grendel's Approach to Heorot: Syntax and Poetry," in *Old English Poetry: Fifteen Essays*, ed. Robert P. Creed (Providence: Brown Univ. Press, 1967), pp. 275–84; G. Storms, "Grendel the Terrible," *Neuphilologische Mitteilungen* 73 (1972): 427–36; and K. O'B. O'Keeffe, "*Beowulf*, Lines 702b–836: Transformations and the Limits of the Human," *Texas Studies in Literature and Language* 23 (1981): 484–94.
3. Cf. Niles, *Beowulf: The Poem and its Tradition* (n.4 above [p. 136]), p. 8: "It is as if the poet were deliberately exploiting the power that the unknown, the half-known, the dark, and the shapeless can exert over the imaginations of adults who have not lost the child's ability to fantasize."

(a) *brōga* (terror [or] horror).[4] When Grendel's mother attacks Heorot
in revenge for the death of her son the attack is one of pure horror: none
of the warriors had time even to think of helmet or spear, *þā hine se brōga
angeat* [when the terror seized him] (line 1291b). Later in the poem,
when the dragon attacks the Geats, the horror of the attack (*brōga*) was
made quickly known to Beowulf (line 2324); and when Beowulf confronts
the dragon each adversary was horrific to the other: *ǣghwæðrum wæs /
bealohycgendra   brōga fram ōðrum* [To each of them as they threatened
destruction there was terror of the other] (lines 2564b–65). The horror of
warfare is conveyed by a compound, *herebrōga* (line 462). That *brōga* con-
notes a sense of indescribable horror is clear from a passage in *Guthlac A*
that describes the hellish fiends who assaulted the saint in his hermitage:

<blockquote>
Oft þær broga cwom
egeslic ond uncuð,   ealdfeonda nið.   (lines 140–41)
</blockquote>

[Often the terror came there, appalling, incomprehensible, the mal-
ice of ancient foes.]

The sense here that *brōga* connotes a sensation of horror not previously
experienced (*uncūð*) is clear from the fact that it is used eschatologically
to describe the horrors of Judgement Day and hell (*Judgement Day II*,
line 123), and may give point to the chronicler's observation that in A.D.
991 tribute was first paid to the Vikings *for ðam miclan brōgan þe hi
worhton* [for their campaign of terror].

(b) *egesa*, also meaning "terror," "horror,"[5] is more generally used than
brōga but has a similar semantic range. We have already seen that, accord-
ing to the reports that had reached Beowulf in Geatland, the monster on dark
nights was revealing previously unexperienced hostility (*uncūðne nið*)
through its campaign of terror, *þurh egsan* (line 276), and, when Beowulf
and the monster are locked in deadly combat, the noise of their struggle
caused *atelīc egesa* (dire terror; line 784), among the Danes.[6] The word con-
veys perhaps less intensity than *brōga*—it is used by old Beowulf when he
says that for fifty years no-one had threatened his kingdom with *egesa* (line
2736), meaning simply "provoked fear"—but like *brōga* it is used to refer to
the terrors of the Last Judgement. Interestingly, it is used in *Daniel* to de-
scribe the terror that filled Nebuchadnezzar when he awoke from his dream:

<blockquote>
þa of slæpe onwoc,   (swefn wæs æt ende),
eorðlic æðeling,   him þæs egesa stod,
gryre from ðam gaste.   (lines 523–25a)
</blockquote>

4. For discussion of this word in Old English, see L. L. Schücking, *Untersuchungen zur Bedeu-
tungslehre der angelsächsischen Dichtersprache*, Germanische Bibliothek 11 (Heidelberg: Carl
Winter, 1915), pp. 30–31.
5. Ibid., pp. 33–37.
6. The *Beowulf*-poet frequently uses compounds of *egesa*, such as *egesfull* (line 2929) or *egeslīc*
(lines 1649, 2309, 2825), or *glēdegesa* (line 2650) and *līgegesa* (line 2780, the terror of fire), or
wæteregesa (line 1260, the terror of water).

[then the earthly prince awoke from sleep, (his rest was at an end), fear arose in him, terror of that spirit.]

The terror caused by dreams, especially nightmares, will occupy us in a moment; note here only that *egesa* is used synonymously with *gryre*.

(c) *gryre* also means "terror" or "horror."[7] It is used frequently in the earlier part of *Beowulf* to describe the terror inflicted by the monster: *Grendles gryre* in line 384, and again in 478. At another point Beowulf retorts to Unferth that the monster would never have committed *swā fela gryra* (so many deeds of terror; line 591) if Unferth were as tough as he says he is. The terror of Grendel's mother is said to be only so much less than his, as a woman's strength is less than a man's: *Wæs se gryre læssa . . . swā bið mægþa cræft* (lines 1282b–83b). Outside of *Beowulf*, the word is used frequently by the poet of *Daniel*, nearly always in combination with *egesa*, to describe (for example) the terror of the flames faced by the Three Youths in the furnace (line 466) or the terror inspired by the God of the Israelites (line 592). What distinguishes the *Beowulf*-poet from all other Old English poets in this respect, however, is the frequency and nature of the poetic compounds that he employed, and sometimes coined, having *gryre* as a constituent element: note *fǣrgryre* (a horror-attack; line 174), *(gryre)brōga* (horrific horror; line 2227), *gryrefāh* (terrifying in adornment), a word unique to *Beowulf* (lines 2576 and 3041); *gryregiest* (horrific stranger; line 2560), *gryregeatwe* (horrific armament; line 324), *gryrelēoð* (a song of horror; line 786), *gryrelic* (horrifying; lines 1441, 2136), *gryresīð* (a horrific expedition; line 1462), *wīggryre* (the horror of battle; line 1284), and so on.

The entire semantic field of fear and terror would make an interesting subject for study in its own right. My point is simply that *Beowulf* is permeated with it. It is essential to ask why, and in what ways, the *Beowulf*-poet was so interested in the representation of terror.

Fear of the unknown is one of the most innate and primeval of all human instincts, and it is one that has been well studied by modern psychologists (who refer to it as fear of "the novel").[8] Even from the very beginnings of the modern discipline, psychologists have been interested in the mechanism of fear. Thus William James, in *The Principles of Psychology* (1890), described the "peculiar kind of horror" associated with the supernatural:

> To bring the ghostly terror to its maximum, many usual elements of the dreadful must combine, such as loneliness, darkness, inexplicable sounds, especially of a dismal character, moving figures half dis-

7. See Schücking, *Untersuchungen zur Bedeutungslehre* (n. 4 above [p. 145]), pp. 48–49.
8. For general orientation, see I. M. Marks, *Fears and Phobias* (London: Heinemann, 1969), pp. 13–35 ("Aetiology of Fear"), esp. 26–28 on the fear of novelty, and S. Rachman, *The Meanings of Fear* (Harmondsworth: Penguin, 1974), pp. 40–44.

cerned (or, if discerned, of dreadful aspect), and a vertiginous baffling of the expectation.[9]

These words could serve, *mutatis mutandis*, as an accurate description of the emotional effect of the monster's approach to Heorot (note, in particular, "moving characters half discerned"). Whereas James identified and described this instinctual fear, it was left to others to analyze more deeply its causes and mechanisms. In an influential article published in 1946, for example, Donald Hebb analyzed fear of the novel in animals, in terms of visual patterns that differ from those familiar to the animal;[1] subsequent researchers have noted the mechanism of fear in reactions by animals to objects moving towards them, where the reaction is clearly not dependent on previous visual experience.[2] This phenomenon is referred to by psychologists as "looming." Once again, it would be possible to describe the audience's reaction to the approach of Grendel in terms of the instinctual fear caused by the "looming" of something unknown.

A different, but parallel, avenue of analysis was broached by Sigmund Freud, who in 1919 published his influential essay on *Das Unheimliche (The Uncanny)*. In this essay Freud identified the most terrifying example of "the uncanny" as follows:

> Many people experience the feeling [of fright] in the highest degree in relation to death and dead bodies, to the return of the dead, and to spirits and ghosts. . . . There is scarcely any other matter . . . upon which our thoughts and feelings have changed so little since the very earliest times, and in which discarded forms have been so completely preserved under a thin disguise, as our relation to death.[3]

Freud tended to see the reaction to the uncanny in terms of tension between what has been "repressed" and what has been "surmounted" (*der Gegensatz zwischen Verdrängtem und Überwundenem*), a distinction that is analogous to Hebb's analysis of instinctual reactions in animals to the unknown.[4]

One characteristic way in which deep instinctual fears and repressed anxieties find expression is in nightmares. Freud himself did not devote

---

9. W. James, *The Principles of Psychology*, 2 vols. (London: Macmillan, 1890), 2:419.
1. D. O. Hebb, "On the Nature of Fear," *Psychological Review* 53 (1946): 259–76, esp. 268–72; Hebb notes (p. 268) that "fear occurs when an object is seen which is like familiar objects in enough respects to arouse habitual processes of perception, but in other respects arouses incompatible processes," and observes that the effective condition for fear of the strange or novel is a "perceptual deficit" (p. 272).
2. See G. W. Bronson, "The Fear of Novelty," *Psychological Bulletin* 69 (1968): 350–58, esp. 352–53.
3. *Sigmund Freud: Studienausgabe IV, Psychologische Schriften* (Frankfurt: Fischer Taschenbuch Verlag, 1982), p. 264; trans. *The Pelican Freud Library*, vol. 14, *Art and Literature* (Harmondsworth: Penguin, 1985), p. 364. I am grateful to my colleague Stephen Heath for advice on Freud.
4. *Sigmund Freud: Studienausgabe IV*, p. 271; trans. *The Pelican Freud Library*, 14:372; on Hebb's analysis, see n. 1 above [p. 147].

detailed attention to nightmares,[5] and it was left to one of his followers, Ernest Jones, to explore the mechanisms and manifestations of night-mares. In his classic study, *On the Nightmare* (1931), Jones applied Freudian principles to the analysis of nightmares and deduced that the nightmare "is a form of anxiety attack . . . essentially due to an intense mental conflict centreing [*sic*] around [*sic*] some repressed component of the psycho-sexual instinct."[6] Modern psychologists are less inclined than Jones to stress the sexual nature of the impulses lying behind night-mares;[7] Jones's great merit was to have assembled a mass of evidence, mostly literary, much of it from earlier centuries, illustrating the forms that nightmares characteristically take. From his work it became clear that (to quote the words of J. A. Hadfield): "The distinctive feature of a nightmare in the more restricted sense of the term is that of a monster, whether animal or sub-human, which visits us during sleep and produces a sense of dread."[8] It is the intense feeling of dread and horror created by the monster's approach that, in the view of modern psychiatrists, does in-deed constitute the distinctive feature of the nightmare.[9] Modern med-ical techniques of measurement, such as electroencephalographic and electromyographic tracings, have made it possible to define the mecha-nism of nightmares more accurately, and psychologists are now able to distinguish, for example, between the most explosive kinds of terror-attack, or nightmare proper, which occur during the phase of non-REM (= non–Rapid Eye Movement) or slow-wave sleep, and severe anxiety dreams, which occur during the phase of REM (= fast or paradoxical) sleep.[1] The details of modern psychiatric analysis need not concern us here; our concern is with the nature of the nightmares themselves.

The nightmare dream image, as we have seen, is characteristically a monster in animal or sub-human form, which approaches the dreamer in a threatening manner; as Mack has observed, all nightmares follow this common pattern: "Inevitably the dreamer, whether child or adult, is about to become the victim of a murderous or devouring attack or is threatened with death by a destructive creature."[2] It is probably not pos-sible to define the appearance of the destructive creature of nightmares more specifically, but certain features do tend to recur in the reports

5. Two of Freud's most famous case-histories involved nightmares: "Analysis of a Phobia in a Five-Year-Old Boy" (1909) and "From the History of an Infantile Neurosis" (1918). However, as J. E. Mack has noted (*Nightmares and Human Conflict* [Boston: Little, Brown & Co., 1970], pp. 24–25), Freud's concern here was more with neuroses than with nightmares *per se*.
6. E. Jones, *On the Nightmare* (London: Leonard and Virginia Woolf at the Hogarth Press, 1931), p. 75.
7. See, for example, the remarks of Mack, *Nightmares and Human Conflict* (n. 5 above [p. 148]), pp. 9, 16.
8. J. A. Hadfield, *Dreams and Nightmares* (Harmondsworth: Penguin, 1954), p. 176.
9. See R. L. Verteuil, "A Psychiatric Approach to the Study of the Nightmare," *Canadian Psychiatric Association Journal* 7 (1962): 151–58, as well as Mack, *Nightmares and Human Conflict* (n. 5 above [p. 148]), p. 2.
1. Mack, *Nightmares and Human Conflict* (n. 5 above [p. 148]), pp. 60–61.
2. Ibid., p. 147.

of subjects. For example, one report quoted by Mack referred to the "terrifying muffled sound of the haunter's step,"[3] whereas other reports from Germany speak of a more or less formless (*gestaltlos*) monster having a large head and uncanny bulging eyes (*unheimliche Glotzaugen*).[4] The relevance of these descriptions to Grendel will be obvious: a destructive creature, more or less formless, launching a devouring attack, approaching by terrifying muffled steps, having a large head and unusual eyes (if not precisely *Glotzaugen*) that emit a terrifying light. It is as if the *Beowulf*-poet was attempting to evoke the creature of nightmares in his description of Grendel.

For twentieth-century psychologists, building on the work of Freud and Jones, the monsters of our nightmares are merely our own impulses and anxieties projected and objectified and personalized into creatures of the external world.[5] What is striking, however, is the objective reality that people of earlier centuries attributed to such monsters. The causes of such projection are convincingly explained by psychologists in terms of differentiation between intrapsychic phenomena and the external world (I quote the opinion of Mack for convenience):

> The deepest anxieties of the nightmare relate to a time in early childhood when the ability to differentiate between what is inside and what is outside is a fragile or developing capacity, easily upset under the conditions of sleep. It is the time before age five when dream experiences are accepted as real and when the malevolent agents the small child confronts in the nightmare cannot be put aside by his own corrective powers. . . . Only in the past century . . . has it been possible to approach nightmares and other dreams as having primarily a psychological or physiological reality or as reflecting man's struggle to integrate internal and external realities, rather than as possessing objective validity in the surrounding environment.[6]

The point is simply that, in centuries before our own, the monsters of nightmares were perceived to have an external, objective reality and were not simply figments of a tortured imagination.

How did the Anglo-Saxons perceive their nightmares? Anglo-Saxon physicians were evidently aware that the nightmare was both a (diseased) mental state and an external, objective phenomenon. This much is implicit in the normal Old English word for "nightmare,"[7] namely *niht-*

---

3. Ibid., p. 7.
4. See the detailed account of nightmares in the *Handwörterbuch des deutschen Aberglaubens*, ed. E. Hoffmann-Krayer and H. Bächtold-Stäubli, 10 vols. (Berlin-Leipzig: W. de Gruyter, 1927–42), vol. 1, cols. 281–305, s.v. *Alptraum*); see esp. col. 285 for the formless monster with large head and bulging eyes.
5. Hadfield, *Dreams and Nightmares* (n. 8 above [p. 148]), p. 189.
6. Mack, *Nightmares and Human Conflict* (n. 5 above [p. 148]), pp. 9, 11.
7. The compound *nihtmare* is (oddly perhaps) not attested in surviving Old English records; it first occurs as a compound in the late thirteenth century in the *South English Legendary* (see *NED*, s.v. *nightmare*). The simplex *mare* occurs in the Épinal-Erfurt Glossary (spelled in eWS

genga, which means "night-goer" or "night-stalker." Several recipes or prescriptions against *nihtgengan* are found in Old English medical writings, and these give us a sense of how Anglo-Saxon physicians classified and treated the nightmare. Thus in the so-called *Third Leechbook,* an anonymous compilation that accompanies Bald's *Leechbook* in the unique surviving manuscript (a mid tenth-century manuscript perhaps from Winchester, now London, British Library, Royal 12. D. XVII), there is a recipe for various mental afflictions. The medication is decidedly odd. The physician is instructed to:

> seek in the crop of young swallows for some little stones, and mind that they touch neither earth nor water nor other stones. Look out three of them; they are good against headache and eye-suffering and the foe's afflictions and night-goers (*nihtgengan*) and . . . nightmares (*hi beoþ gode wiþ heafodece ond wiþ eagwærce and wiþ feondes costunga and nihtgengan and . . . maran* [III.I]).[8]

It would be helpful to know what precisely was meant by the "foe's afflictions"; but leaving these aside, and with the possible exception of *eagwærc,* the other disorders in this list are mental states. Elsewhere in the *Third Leechbook* there is a recipe for a salve to be used specifically against *nihtgengan: Wyrc sealfe wið nihtgengan, wyl on buteran elehtran, hegerifan, bisceopwyrt, reade magþan, cropleac, sealt; smire mid him, bið sona sel* (III.54).[9] In yet another Anglo-Saxon medicinal recipe, this time in the *Herbarium pseudo-Apulei,* the plant betony is prescribed as a remedy against various mental afflictions: *hie hyne scyldeþ wið unhyrum nihtgengum ond wiþ egeslicum gesihðum ond swefnum.*[1] It emerges from these various recipes that the external, objectified form of a nightmare, the *nihtgenga,* was treated by Anglo-Saxon physicians as a mental disorder, in the same category as headaches and other kinds of terrifying nocturnal vision.

We have seen that there are close similarities between the *Beowulf-*poet's description of Grendel and the monsters of nightmares as known to modern psychologists. The poet was, it seems to me, attempting to evoke in his audience the sensation of terror that is experienced in nightmares. This is not tantamount to saying, crudely, that Grendel is a nightmare. The poet does not explicitly describe Grendel as a *nihtgenga;* yet the diction of the poem plays on this suggestion. Grendel's afflictions are

---

as *mera* or *merae*), where it glosses Latin *incuba;* see Pheifer, *Old English Glosses in the Epinal-Erfurt Glossary* (n. 2 above [p. 138]), p. 30, line 558, with commentary at p. 95.

8. O. Cockayne, *Leechdoms, Wortcunning, and Starcraft of Early England,* Rolls Series 35, 3 vols. (London: Longman, et al., 1864–66), 2:306.

9. Ibid., 2:342: "Work up a salve against *nightgengan:* boil in butter lupins, hedgerife, bishopwort, red maythe, cropleek, salt; smear the patient with this, he will soon be well."

1. *The Old English Herbarium and Medicina de Quadrupedibus,* ed. H. J. de Vriend, Early English Text Society, o.s. vol. 286 (Oxford: Oxford Univ. Press, 1984), p. 30: "it shields him [the patient] from uncanny night-goers [*nihtgengan*] and from terrifying visions and dreams."

described as the *nihtbealwa mǣst* (worst of night-horrors; line 193).[2] The monster is twice referred to as an *āngenga* (lines 165, 449). More pointedly still, the monster is a *sceadugenga* that advances *on wanre niht* (lines 702–03) to a place where nearly everyone is sleeping (*scēotend swǣfon*). The configuration of these various terms—*nihtgenga, nihtbealu, āngenga, sceadugenga on niht*—can scarcely be coincidental. Without explicitly saying so, the *Beowulf*-poet was drawing his Grendel in terms of the *nihtgengan* of terrifying nocturnal visions.

It may be worthwhile, finally, to reflect briefly on the descriptive techniques by which the poet evoked his nightmarish monster. In certain interesting respects, these techniques are similar to those used by modern writers of horror fiction, and indeed by makers of horror films; in short, by the creators of what is called "art-horror." Because there has been a massive burgeoning of "art-horror" during the past generation the form has begun to attract the attention of scholars and critics,[3] and some critical discussion of "art-horror" is relevant to *Beowulf*. Particularly relevant is the analysis by Noel Carroll in his recent study, *The Philosophy of Horror*.[4] Carroll begins from the premise that monsters are the distinguishing mark of "art-horror" and then attempts to define the nature of these monsters by reference to various categories of unnatural beings:

> Boreads, griffins, chimeras, baselisks, dragons, satyrs, and such are bothersome and fearsome creatures in the world of myth, but they are not unnatural; they can be accommodated by the metaphysics of the cosmology that produced them. The monsters of horror, however, breach the norms of ontological propriety presumed by the positive human characters in the story.[5]

The distinction drawn here is a crucial one. The monsters that were depicted in Anglo-Saxon illustrated manuscripts of works such as the

---

2. As we have seen, Grendel is referred to constantly as a *feond* (lines 101, 143, 164, 439, 725, 748, etc.). For this reason it would be especially interesting to know what kind of medical disorder the compiler of the *Third Leechbook* was referring to by the term *feondes costunga* (see above): was it, too, a sort of terrifying nocturnal vision? If so, the *Beowulf*-poet's repeated reference to Grendel as a *feond* would heighten the impression of a nightmare, which the poet was (in my view) trying to create.

3. The bibliography is too extensive to be listed here. Some notable recent studies include: J. Briggs, *Night Visitors: The Rise and Fall of the English Ghost Story* (London: Faber & Faber, 1977); L. Daniels, *Fear: A History of Horror in the Mass Media* (London: Paladin Books, 1977); G. St. J. Barclay, *Anatomy of Horror: The Masters of Occult Fiction* (London: Weidenfeld & Nicolson, 1978); D. Punter, *The Literature of Terror: A History of Gothic Fictions from 1765 to the Present Day* (London: Longman, 1980); M. B. Tymn, *Horror Literature: A Core Collection and Reference Guide* (New York and London: Bowker, 1981; J. B. Twitchell, *The Living Dead: A Study of the Vampire in Romantic Literature* (Durham, N.C.: Duke Univ. Press, 1981); idem, *Dreadful Pleasures: An Anatomy of Modern Horror* (Oxford: Clarendon Press, 1985), D. J. Hufford, *The Terror that Comes in the Night: An Experience-Centered Study of Supernatural Assault Traditions* (Philadelphia, Pa.: Univ. of Pennsylvania Press, 1982); and M. Aguirre, *The Closed Space: Horror Literature and Western Symbolism* (Manchester: Univ. of Manchester Press, 1990).

4. N. Carroll, *The Philosophy of Horror or Paradoxes of the Heart* (New York and London: Routledge, Chapman and Hall, 1990).

5. Ibid., p. 16.

Mirabilia Orientis[6] are like Carroll's "boreads, griffins" etc.: they are fear-some enough, but consist essentially of startling combinations of animal and human members and can be easily visualized as such. For this rea-son I am not persuaded by the imaginative attempt by J. D. Niles to vi-sualize Grendel in terms of the hellish monster in human form with ape-like features and steely claws depicted in one English manuscript of the *Mirabilia Orientis* (London, British Library, Cotton Tiberius B. v, fol. 81[V]), which serves as the frontispiece of his book.[7] As we have seen, in the first seven hundred or so lines of the poem (before Grendel's confronta-tion with Beowulf), the *Beowulf*-poet carefully avoided giving his readers any descriptive details concerning Grendel that would enable them to vi-sualize him within categories familiar from their external world. (After the confrontation, of course, Grendel's nature is well known to Beowulf and the Geats, so the sense of suspense and terror is dissipated.) The mon-ster Grendel provokes a sensation of horror precisely because it lies *out-side* perceived cultural or scientific categories and is, therefore, frighteningly unfamiliar.[8] It is the purpose of a horror story to make cred-ible the existence, usually by gradual means, of something that is in prin-ciple *unknowable:* in Carroll's words, "something which, ex hypothesi, cannot, given the structure of our conceptual scheme, exist, and that can-not have the properties it has."[9] As Freud recognized long ago,[1] and as modern philosophers have reaffirmed,[2] the most successful authors of horror fiction aim to exploit the instinctual human fear of the unknown.

The *Beowulf*-poet clearly realized that instinctual human fear results from the perception of monstrous creatures that lie outside familiar con-ceptual categories (and hence are unknowable, or "uncanny" in Freud's term). That is why he carefully avoided supplying any kind of precise vi-sual description of his monster, so that what eventually approached Heo-rot would be sensed as something truly horrific because totally unfamiliar. The horror resulting from the threatening approach of unfa-

---

6. See R. Wittkower, "Marvels of the East: A Study in the History of Monsters," *Journal of the War-burg and Courtauld Institutes* 5 (1942): 159–97, and J. B. Friedman, *The Monstrous Races in Medieval Art and Thought* (Cambridge, Mass.: Harvard Univ. Press, 1981).
7. Niles, *Beowulf: The Poem and its Tradition* (n. 4 above [p. 136]), pp. 14–15.
8. Carroll, *The Philosophy of Horror* (n. 4 [p. 151] above), p. 35: "it is tempting to interpret the ge-ography of horror as a figurative spatialization or literalization of the notion that what horrifies is that which lies *outside* cultural categories and is, perforce, unknown."
9. Ibid., p. 182.
1. *Sigmund Freud: Studienausgabe IV*, pp. 271–72; trans. *The Pelican Freud Library* (n. 3 above [p. 147]), 14:372–73; "The Contrast between what has been repressed and what has been sur-mounted cannot be transposed on the uncanny in fiction without profound modification; for the realm of phantasy depends for its effect on the fact that its content is not submitted to reality-testing . . . there are many more means of creating uncanny effects in fiction than there are in real life."
2. See especially K. L. Walton, *Mimesis as Make-Believe: On the Foundations of the Representa-tional Arts* (Cambridge, Mass.: Harvard Univ. Press, 1990), pp. 195–204 ("Fearing Fictions"). Walton explores the mechanism of fear that is experienced by a subject watching a horror film (which he defines as "quasi-fear") in distinction to "real" fear. I am grateful to Neil Malcolm for drawing my attention to Walton's discussion, and for much helpful advice on the nature of fear.

miliar monsters is experienced most intensely in nightmares, and it is no coincidence that the poet described his monster in terms evocative of the *nihtgengan* of nightmares. His evocation of terror is unique in Old English literature and, indeed, has no real parallel in narrative fiction until the nineteenth century; even the Old Norse sagas, with their monstrous *draugar*, bear no resemblance to *Beowulf*, insofar as these are presented in clearly defined visual terms. The *Beowulf*-poet's presentation of Grendel, in other words, betrays his fascination with the workings of the human mind and the mechanism of fear. And here, not in the narrative action of heroic poetry, where known heroes fight with known adversaries, is where the poet's primary interests lay.

JOYCE HILL

"Þæt Wæs Geomuru Ides!"
A Female Stereotype Examined[†]

In her recent book on the king's wife in the early Middle Ages, Pauline Stafford observes that "women have usually stood half hidden in the wings of the historical pageant."[1] For the period with which Stafford is concerned, A.D. 500 to the mid-eleventh century, the task of rescuing royal women from this sometimes unwarranted obscurity is made particularly difficult by the nature of the surviving historical record, which means that at times the activities of the men of the royal house are almost as obscure as those of the women. Even so, women consistently fare worse. To quote Stafford once again: "When the doings of the kings were retailed, the activities of their queens were normally considered unimportant" (p. 2), and when, for some reason, they did attract the attention of clerical chroniclers and biographers, the information recorded about them was subject to the distortions of anti-feminism and a political partisanship which often tended to make them scapegoats for the king's actions. The resulting historical stereotype can hinder our perception of the nature and significance of the woman's role within the royal circle almost as much as the straightforward lack of information. But the stereotypes are not totally unyielding, as a number of sensitive historical interpretations have recently shown,[2] with the result that a more rounded picture

† From *New Readings on Women in Old English Literature*, ed. Helen Damico and Alexandra Hennessey Olsen (Bloomington: Indiana UP, 1990) 235–47. The author's abbreviations for the titles of Old English poems have been silently spelled out. Translations appearing in square brackets are the editor's. Footnotes are the author's except where followed by [*Editor*].
1. Pauline Stafford, *Queens, Concubines and Dowagers: The King's Wife in the Early Middle Ages* (London: Batsford, 1983), p. 1.
2. There is a full bibliography in Stafford's *Queens, Concubines and Dowagers*, pp. 216–26. In my comments on the position of royal women in early medieval history I am particularly indebted

is now emerging which gives the royal women of this period the importance that they undoubtedly deserve.

As for history, so for heroic poetry. There too women stand half-hidden in the wings of the legendary pageant. On one level the comparison can be made directly, since many legend-cycles evolve from the events of history and all present themselves as the stories of kings, princes, and noble warriors. The aristocratic milieu within which the legendary events take place is thus, in social terms, equivalent to those most fully recorded in the annals and biographies of early medieval history, and if they, in various ways and for various complex reasons, underplay or distort the significance of the female role, so too does heroic legend, for reasons which are not dissimilar. Yet the comparison between history and heroic poetry is not a straightforward one, since heroic legend-cycles are history transformed into poetry or, in some cases, mythology or folktale re-presented as heroic legend. From the time when the majority of legend cycles originated, in the fourth, fifth, and sixth centuries, to the date of their surviving written form in late Anglo-Saxon manuscripts, a given narrative was subjected to the transforming effects first of oral and then of written transmission, which filtered in through the stylizing and stereotyping processes of mnemonic patterning and the formulaic structures of Germanic verse. Thus, on one level the new insights into the role of early medieval royal women can directly advance our understanding of the role of the aristocratic women in heroic legend, but on another they must be exploited indirectly, as a model of the historical reality from which the legendary stereotypes have emerged. Both kinds of comparison will be used in this paper, in an attempt to define how far the female figures in Old English heroic poetry are given roles which are plausible in historical terms, and to assess the effect upon their presentation of the transforming power of heroic legend. In the historical record of the early Middle Ages, the stereotyped images of royal women veered between "incarnation of evil or unattainable perfection, great ascetic or materfamilias, mistress of the household or Jewish warrior, seductress or virgin, Queen of Heaven or Byzantine empress,"[3] each, of course, developed and exploited for a particular purpose which is open to historical analysis and which, in turn, leads to an understanding of the reality behind the role. In heroic poetry, as will be shown, the dominant stereotype is that of the *geomuru ides* [sad or mournful woman]. The discussion of how and why it evolved leads into a discussion of its central importance in articulating the tragedy of heroic life.

---

to Stafford's book and, to a lesser extent, to her article "Sons and mothers: family politics in the early middle ages," in *Medieval Women*, ed. Derek Baker, Studies in Church History, Subsidia I (Oxford: Basil Blackwell, 1978), pp. 79–100, and to the articles by Christopher N. L. Brooke, " 'Both small and great beasts': an introductory study," and Janet L. Nelson, "Queens as Jezebels: the careers of Brunhild and Balthild in Merovingian history," on pp. 1–14 and 31–78 respectively of the same collection.
3. Stafford, *Queens, Concubines and Dowagers*, p. 31.

The historical reality that is of fundamental importance in understanding the role of royal women, both in early medieval history and in heroic legend, is the fact that "the household was not only the center of government but a model for it."⁴ That being so, no lines can be drawn within the royal family dividing public from private life; kings governed by personal rule and the consequence of this for royal women is that their domestic position in the royal court put them not on one side of dynastic politics, but at the heart of it. The sources of their power were, of course, informal, depending on their importance, as childbearers, for the maintenance of the dynastic line, their capacity to influence the king and those around him, their acquisition of privileged information, and their access to wealth, but the possibilities for exploitation were formidable and never more so than when the succession was at stake. As Stafford has reminded us: "The idea that royal blood in male veins carried claims to the throne died hard, and opened throneworthiness to a wide group,"⁵ and, in a situation of such relative uncertainty, the queen could play the part of king-maker by using her informal but effective power-base to support one male claimant against all the rest. There were even times, if the dynasty were strong enough, when her support might ensure the acceptance of a minor as king with the queen holding power, to a greater or lesser extent, as regent, although it was always the case that "minorities were dangerous, even intolerable, at a date when kings ruled in more than name and especially if the need for military leadership was pressing."⁶ The risks presented themselves as vividly to the imagination of the heroic poet as they did to the leaders of early medieval societies.

The exercise of power, particularly if it is through informal channels, is, of course, liable to abuse, and there were queens in history who were accused not only of incest and adultery but also of malevolence and murder. The one example of the wicked queen which Old English heroic poetry gives us is the problematic Modþryðo, or Þryðo, in *Beowulf*.⁷ Against this, however, and despite all the political and ecclesiastical biases of chroniclers and biographers, there emerges a strongly delineated picture of royal women exercising power in an acceptable if "domestic" manner, contributing to dynastic stability, offering counsel, and upholding the

4. Ibid., p. 28.
5. Ibid., p. 152.
6. Ibid., pp. 153–54.
7. *Beowulf* 1931–62. For a summary of the textual problems, including the difficulty of determining the woman's name, see *Beowulf, with the Finnesburg Fragment*, ed. C. L. Wrenn, rev. W. F. Bolton (London: Harrap, 1973), p. 168. For a recent study of the episode, see Constance B. Hieatt, "Modþryðo and Heremod: Intertwined Threads in the *Beowulf*-poet's Web of Words," *Journal of English and Germanic Philology* 83 (1984): 173–82. The text of *Beowulf* which is cited throughout is that of *Beowulf and the Fight at Finnsburg*, ed. Fr. Klaeber, 3rd ed. (Boston: D. C. Heath and Co., 1950). For all other Old English poems the text cited is that of *The Anglo-Saxon Poetic Records*, ed. George Philip Krapp and Elliott Van Kirk Dobbie, 6 vols. (New York: Columbia University Press, 1931–42).

dignity and status of the king through participation in the important prac-
tices of gift-exchange which cemented the system of personal rule.

Such was the power available to the queen temperamentally suited to
make use of it. But not all women in the royal house had these possibili-
ties, at least in the early years of their life. In an age when, as Andreas Fis-
cher has recently reminded us, marriage was a contract between two
men, guardian and suitor,[8] arranged marriages between ruling families
often served the needs of dynastic policy and the woman became a pawn
in the political game. The arrangement was often a success—aristocratic
women did not, in any case, expect a free choice of husband for reasons
of love—but where it was not a success, perhaps because the alliance that
the marriage was meant to stabilize broke down, the woman might face
repudiation or even death. The historian's observation that "when
women sealed alliances made by the sword, they became forcible re-
minders of defeat"[9] is equally apt for heroic poetry.

Ealhhild in *Widsið* and Wealhþeow, Hygd, and Freawaru in *Beowulf*
demonstrate how closely allied to historical reality as we now understand
it heroic legend can sometimes be, although we have no certain knowl-
edge that any of them as named is derived, unlike Eormanric, for exam-
ple, from an actual historical figure.[1] The advantages of re-examining
them in the light of modern assessments of the role of women in early
medieval society as outlined above are that we are more alert to the im-
plications of the often allusive details which are provided, and we can see
that, despite the stylization of their presentation, they have a recognizable
reality which, like the recognizable reality of the material objects of
heroic poetry, establishes a relationship between the temporally impre-
cise world of legend and the world of the Anglo-Saxon audience.

Ealhhild, Wealhþeow, and Hygd all participate in the public cere-
monies of gift-exchange which are so bound up, in heroic poetry as in
early medieval history, with loyalty, status, and honour. In *Widsið* the
scop, who is as much a preserver of the king's or hero's reputation as any
warrior-þegn [warrior-retainer], portrays himself in his imagination as re-
ceiving from Eormanric a great torque, which he later surrenders to his
own lord Eadgils, who gives him in return the land which is his patri-
mony. But he receives also, as part of the gift-exchange pattern, another

---

8. Andreas Fischer, *Engagement, Wedding and Marriage in Old English*, Anglistische Forschun-
   gen 176 (Heidelberg: C. Winter, 1986), p. 19.
9. Stafford, *Queens, Concubines and Dowagers*, p. 44.
1. For Ealhhild, see below n. 5 [p. 164] and 6 [p. 164]. As for the women of *Beowulf* I am not, of
   course, suggesting that the Scandinavian kings did not have wives, merely that we do not have
   an historical record of them as named in the poem. There is no reason why we should: our his-
   torical evidence for the origin of legend cycles concerns only those leaders and tribes who were
   noticed by late antique historians and the Scandinavians were not, apart from the time when
   Hygelac made his raid on the Frisians, which was recorded by Gregory of Tours because it in-
   volved the Franks. In any case, the interaction between Wealhþeow and Beowulf and that be-
   tween Hygd and Beowulf cannot have an historical basis, even though they are presented as
   "history," because Beowulf himself is unhistorical. [*Widsith* (*Widsið*) is an Old English poem
   that lists numerous characters, some legendary and some historical (*Editor*).]

torque from Ealhhild, which by implication he keeps. Her reward is that she is praised by him as a giver of gifts:

> Hyre lof lengde   geond londa fela,
> þonne ic be songe   secgan sceolde
> hwær ic under swegle   selast wisse
> goldhrodene cwen   giefe bryttian.
>
> (*Widsith* 99–102)

(Her praise lingered throughout many lands when I had to tell in song where I knew the best of gold-adorned queens dispensing gifts under the sky.)

The centrality of the act to the value-system of the heroic world is confirmed by the language and nature of the poet's response: *giefe bryttian* recalls the treasure-giver formulas (*beaga brytta* 'dispenser of rings', *sinces brytta* 'dispenser of treasure') which serve as kennings for the heroic king. In referring to the reputation that she (like kings) earns by treasure-giving, the poet uses *lof*, a word rich in connotations of male heroic glory; and the poet's reward, fame in poetic legends which will spread through many lands, is identical with that for the mighty kings and heroes. A similar pattern is found in *Beowulf*. The hero, rewarded with treasure by Hroðgar, surrenders that treasure to his own lord, Hygelac, in Geatland, and receives a sword, land, and rank in return, but a formal part of the same public ceremonies is Wealhþeow's gift of a neck-torque and horses to Beowulf and his presentation of them to Hygd. We recall Stafford's observations, based on the evidence of history, that "royal women in general and queens in particular cannot be divorced from ideas of wealth and status,"[2] and we set it alongside the approving comments of the *Beowulf*-poet that although Hygd was as yet a young queen:

> næs hio hnah swa þeah,
> ne to gneað gifa   Geata leodum,
> maþmgestreona.
>
> (*Beowulf* 1929–31)

(nevertheless she was not mean, nor too niggardly of gifts, of precious treasures, to the people of the Geats.)

Hygd is also described as *wis welþungen* 'wise and accomplished' (1927), just as Wealhþeow, at the moment when she too is first introduced, is said to be *wisfæst wordum* 'wise in words' (626). The recurrence of the detail might well suggest that wisdom is a formal element in a stylized and idealized description and so, of course, on one level it is. But we have been made more aware recently of the practicalities that it points to: the participation of royal women in the exercise of per-

---

2. Stafford, *Queens, Concubines and Dowagers*, p. 109.

sonal rule, the frequency with which their advice influenced the
course of events, and the acceptability of this kind of contribution
to theorists such as Sedulius Scottus who, in his *Liber de rectoribus
Christianis*, commented on the appropriateness of kings plucking the
fruits of their wives' good counsels.[3] Wealhþeow, realistically enough,
offers advice to Hroðgar about his conduct as a treasure-dispensing
king, about his response to Beowulf, and about the problems of suc-
cession, alluding obliquely in the process to the risks of rival claimants
when primogeniture is not the exclusive hereditary principle (*Beowulf*
1169–87). Her support of her own sons against the possibly older
Hroþulf,[4] who could thus be seen by himself and others as a more
promising candidate if Hroðgar's sons were still minors when he died,
finds parallels in history, but the realities of history also help us under-
stand the response of Hygd in passing over her own son when faced
with the risks of minority rule in the face of external military threat.
After Hygelac's death on the Frisian raid, she is in the position of many
a queen dowager of history and takes direct action in arranging the suc-
cession, offering the throne to the elder and militarily more effective
Beowulf, Hygelac's nephew, in an attempt to avoid the problems inher-
ent in the succession of a child (*Beowulf* 2369–72). Beowulf's refusal,
which in any case has no historical foundation since he is a figure
drawn into the Geatish dynasty from Germanic mythology,[5] makes
sense in poetic rather than political terms.

In this survey of the correspondences between the royal women of his-
tory and the royal women of heroic legend, we turn finally to Freawaru,
whose fate as a political pawn is graphically described by Beowulf
(2024–69). It is clear from the outset that the marriage, to establish an al-
liance between the hostile tribes of Danes and Heathobards, is a matter
of policy only. Hroðgar

3. Sedulius Scottus, *Liber de rectoribus Christianis*, ed. S. Hellmann, Quellen und Untersuchun-
gen zur lateinischen Philologie des Mittelalters (Munich: Beck, 1906), cap. V. An English ver-
sion is available as *Sedulius Scottus: "On Christian Rulers" and "The Poems,"* translated with
Introduction by Edward Gerard Doyle, Medieval and Renaissance Texts and Studies 17 (Bing-
hamton: Medieval and Renaissance Texts and Studies, 1983).
4. Hroþulf is the son of Hroðgar's younger brother Halga. A possible scenario for the struggle for
the throne, which includes the supposition that Hroþulf is older than Hroðgar's sons and is fa-
vored by Hroðgar more than his own offspring, is given by R. W. Chambers, *Beowulf: An Intro-
duction to the Study of the Poem with a Discussion of the Stories of Offa and Finn*, 3rd ed. with
supplement by C. L. Wrenn (Cambridge: Cambridge University Press, 1963), pp. 13–16. For a
translation of the texts relating to Hroþulf, see G. N. Garmonsway and Jacqueline Simpson, *Be-
owulf and its Analogues* (London: J. M. Dent and Sons, 1968), pp. 155–206.
5. For the analogues to Beowulf's adventures, see Garmonsway and Simpson, *Beowulf and its Ana-
logues*, pp. 301–39, and for a discussion of their mythological and folktale origins, see G. V.
Smithers, *The Making of "Beowulf,"* Inaugural Lecture (Durham: Durham University Press,
1961). For further extensive discussion, including the theories about Beowulf's mythological ori-
gins which are not now generally accepted, see Chambers, *Introduction*, pp. 41–97. Beowulf's
genealogical incorporation into the Scandinavian royal circle is discussed by R. T. Farrell, "Be-
owulf, Swedes and Geats," *Saga Book of the Viking Society* 18 (1972): 225–86, and by Norman
E. Eliason, "Beowulf, Wiglaf and the Wægmundings," *Anglo-Saxon England* 7 (1978): 95–105.

> þæt ræd talað,
> þæt he mid ðy wife   wælfæhða dæl,
> sæcca gesette.
>
> (*Beowulf* 2027–29)

(considers it good counsel, that he should with the woman settle a part of his deadly feuds, of his battles.)

But it is a policy which, as Beowulf's immediately following aphorism makes clear, is carried out in the light of the universal perception that such an alliance is almost certain to fail:

> Oft seldan hwær
> æfter leodhryre   lytle hwile
> bongar bugeð,   þeah seo bryd duge!
>
> (*Beowulf* 2029–31)

(Very rarely after the fall of a prince does the deadly spear remain quiet for a little while, although the bride may be of worth!)

Some kings in history felt uneasy about marrying their daughters far from the protection of their own kingroup, but marriages for purposes of allegiance were a political reality. On the one hand they point to the importance of women in dynastic matters, but on the other they highlight their vulnerability and their inferior status as formally defined. The poetic expression of this insignificance in Freawaru's case is the absence of any comment on her own reactions and her consequent reduction in the imagination to a mere cipher; for all her importance in the arrangement of the alliance, the initiative and action in the episode rest entirely with the men.

There is, then, a fundamental historical reality in the roles that are attributed to royal women in Old English heroic poetry. It is reflected, we notice, in the details of what they do and what is done to them which, as in history, show them to be central figures in royal government. But it is reflected also, again as in the historical record, in the imbalance between the attention given to them and the attention given to the men. In the gift-exchange ceremonies involving Eormanric, Eadgils, Widsið, and Ealhhild, the exchange with Ealhhild comes after the complete cycle of male gift-giving and receiving has been detailed, although admittedly, as we have seen, careful attention is paid to it. In *Beowulf* the gift-exchange involving the two queens is again subordinate to the male exchanges, both in its position in the narrative and in the noticeably small amount of space devoted to it. Wealhþeow's comments about the future of the Danish kingdom are clear but indirect and deferential, as if there are limits to a woman's public intervention; Hygd's momentous offer of the throne to Beowulf, even including the importuning of the people as a whole and Beowulf's refusal, is covered in eight lines; and the treatment of Freawaru, as noted above, puts her firmly on the sidelines, highlighting the difference between male and female roles. Women act or are acted upon within their blood or marriage family, and whilst this domestic focus is in no way demeaning, since family, dynasty, and rule are not separable, they are undeniably limited in their sphere of activity, operating through and on behalf of the royal men, whose power is initially won and then sustained on the battlefield.

The distinctions of role which constitute the historical ideal[6] and which were usually, if not always, observed, are sharpened by the processes of transformation which change history into heroic legend. I have examined elsewhere some of the patterns of transformation which occur insofar as they affect the development of the overall narrative and the presentation of the male heroes: the shedding of minor characters, the reassignment of events, the adjustments to chronology, and the blurring of the intrigues and manipulations of the sometimes unattractive political circumstances in which the original events were played out.[7] The resulting legends, which may be seen as stylizations of history, present us with a relatively uncomplicated and to some extent idealized view of male power, in which events are clearly shown to be motivated by the decision of individual heroes responding to immediate personal pressures and the demands of their own heroic code. It is far harder to specify how women are affected by these patterns of transformation, not least because the direct historical evidence for the start of the legend, which we sometimes have and which we can use in identifying patterns and developing analogies, gives little or no information about women. In a more general way, however, the recent work on the role of royal women in early medieval history provides a basis for some suggestions about what the nature and cause of the transformations might have been. If we now recognize that royal women in history often had considerable power, but that they exercised it through informal channels within the royal household by intrigue and personal influence, it follows that in any context where the warlike activity of men is emphasized and their political maneuverings played down, women will tend to appear less effective than the historical models lead us to expect. A polarization of this kind is a likely product of the circumstantial simplifications which are part and parcel of the transformation from history into legend: the highlighting and stereotyping of an idealized male heroism has as its counterpart the highlighting and stereotyping of female helplessness.

6. In addition to the ideal presented by Sedulius Scottus (for which, see note 3 above [p. 158]), there is, for example, the tract *De ordine palatii*, written by Archbishop Hincmar of Rheims, whose comments on the role of royal women are summarized by Stafford, *Queens, Concubines and Dowagers*, p. 99.
7. *Old English Minor Heroic Poems*, ed. Joyce Hill, Durham and St Andrews Medieval Texts 4 (Durham and St. Andrews, 1983), pp. 6–11, with further details in the Glossary of Proper Names, pp. 78–104. A valuable, broadly based study of the patterns of heroic legend is Jan de Vries, *Heroic Song and Heroic Legend*, trans. B. J. Timmer (London: Oxford University Press, 1963).

There are many examples of the stereotype in Old English heroic poetry, but the most developed is Hildeburh, who dominates the Finnsburh Episode in *Beowulf* (1063–1159). Parallels from history and from heroic poetry suggest that she might have been married to Finn as a *freoðuwebbe* [peace-weaver], to cement an alliance between Danes and Frisians, but the poet does not tell us; the contrast with the presentation of Freawaru is striking. Instead Hildeburh is presented from the start as a stereotype of the sorrowing woman, the victim of a situation not of her own making, in which she is the inevitable loser as the Frisians and the Danes act against each other according to the dictates of their code of honor. They are the initiators, making and breaking oaths, giving and receiving treasure, concerning themselves with the formal symbols of public power and esteem in the temporary peace, and finally being galvanized into brutally destructive activity by the shame of being thought unwarlike and disloyal. She, on the other hand, gains in imaginative stature from her still dignity in mourning. The only initiatory act attributed to her is the command to place her brother and her sons shoulder to shoulder on the funeral pyre. But even this one act contrasts with the many acts of the male warriors, for it has only a backward-looking symbolic value in emphasizing the intertribal loyalties that could have been and which are now felt in a purely personal capacity by Hildeburh alone. The powerful but ultimately futile gesture highlights the polarization of male and female roles, which is further highlighted in the final scene, when the Danes, after the bloody massacre of Finn and his men, plunder the Frisian treasurehoards and carry Hildeburh back to Denmark as the supreme victim, reduced to the status of an object, as if she were part of the booty of war.

The poet, speaking with the voice of the *scop* in Heorot, knew that in Hildeburh he was presenting and defining a stereotype and signaled this fact by the curiously approving assessment *þæt wæs geomuru ides!* 'that was a sad lady!' (*Beowulf* 1075), just as he established Scyld Scefing as the stereotypical king by the half-line *þæt wæs god cyning!* 'that was a good king!' (*Beowulf* 11). Both stereotypes function in similar ways to serve the larger purposes of the poem: Scyld to define the essentials of kingliness and Hildeburh to define the essentials of heroic tragedy. The polarization is again apparent: the male figure being an opportunity to present in their ideal form concepts of success in war, decisive action, integration into a comitatus,[8] the status-enhancing values of treasure, a loyalty that transcends death, and the refounding of an illustrious dynasty; the female being a figure of inaction and isolation, a victim of the destructive forces of "heroism," and a witness to the degradation of treasure—and of human (female) life—to the level of mere plunder. There is no difficulty in identifying in Hildeburh some of the ways in which the *geomuru ides* stereo-

---

8. In Germanic culture, a band of retainers who owed allegiance and military service to a lord and in exchange received protection and treasure [*Editor*].

type could be exploited by a poet responsive to the tragic implications of heroic life.[9]

Later, in underlining the epic scale of the hero's death, which brings a dynasty to an end and with it the security of the whole people, mourning women are used again. One, a *mægð scyne* 'beautiful maiden', figures in the Messenger's vivid prediction of Geatish exile. No longer will she wear a torque around her neck:

> ac sceal geomormod,   golde bereafod
> oft nalles æne   elland tredan,
> nu se herewisa   hleahtor alegde,
> gamen ond gleodream.
>
> (*Beowulf* 3018–21)

(but she will, sad-minded, deprived of gold, often, not once only, tread the foreign land, now the army leader has laid aside laughter, joy, and convivial mirth.)

The other, perhaps an older woman,[1] at Beowulf's funeral pyre:

> (song) sorgcearig,   sæde geneahhe,
> þæt hio hyre (hearmda)gas   hearde (ondre)de,
> wælfylla worn,   (wigen)des egesan,
> hy[n]ðo (ond) h(æftny)d.
>
> (*Beowulf* 3152–55)

(the sorrowful one sang, said often, that she feared for herself harsh days of harm, a great number of slaughters, terror of warriors, humiliation and captivity.)

Outside *Beowulf* the stereotype is exemplified by such figures as Beadohild and Mæðhild in *Deor* and by the women of *The Wife's Lament* and *Wulf and Eadwacer*. It is true that we cannot locate the anonymous women with any confidence, if at all, in known legend-cycles[2] and that the disputed attempts to identify Mæðhild take us only

---

9. For a more extensive discussion of the relationship of this "digression" and others to the poem as a whole, see Adrien Bonjour, *The Digressions in "Beowulf,"* Medium Ævum Monographs 5 (Oxford: Blackwell, 1950).

1. The manuscript is in such a poor state at this point that much depends on editorial reconstruction, although the general situation is clear enough. Klaeber's edition, from which the quoted lines are taken, reconstructs line 3150b as *(s)io g(eo)meowle* 'the old woman/wife', although this produces a *hapax legomenon* in *geomeowle*. Wrenn's edition as revised by Bolton reconstructs the quoted passage differently, although it is still a woman mourning, and makes *Geatisc meowle* '(a) Geatish maiden/woman', out of the scanty manuscript evidence for line 3150b.

2. An attempt was made by R. Imelmann, *Forschungen zur Altenglischen Poesie* (Berlin: Weidmann, 1920), pp. 1–38, to link *The Wife's Lament, Wulf and Eadwacer, The Husband's Message, The Wanderer,* and *The Seafarer* in an Odoacer legend. More recently A. C. Bouman, *Patterns in Old English and Old Icelandic Literature* (Leyden: Universitaire Pers, 1962), pp. 41–91, has proposed a connection between *The Wife's Lament* and the Sigurðr cycle. But such solutions to the enigmas of the "plot" are unsatisfactory and have met with little acceptance. Indeed, for *The Wife's Lament* arguments have been put forward that the speaker is the Church expressing her separation from and longing for Christ, the Synagogue, or a displaced pagan god, and even that the speaker is in fact a man. For one example of each approach, see respectively: M. J. Swanton,

as far back as seventeenth-century Scandinavian ballads.[3] It is also true that Beadohild is a figure whose story, like that of Beowulf, is not history transformed into legend, but mythology re-presented in heroic form.[4] But none of these problems of origin and identification diminish the contribution that these female figures make to the perception that the stereotype of the woman-as-victim, as *geomuru ides*, was a dominant one in Old English and that it carried considerable emotional weight, akin to that of the exile, to which it is often close in circumstance and language.

In all these cases the stereotype is presented to us directly. Admittedly Deor, with the benefit of hindsight, knows that the troubles of Beadohild and Mæðhild passed away, but this statement stands apart from each allusion, just as the anticipation of the end of sorrow was beyond the power of either woman to conceive. The vignette captures each at the moment of helpless grief and makes its impact as much because we recognize the force of the image as because we know or can guess the story that surrounds it.

Recognition of the *geomuru ides* as the dominant female stereotype in Old English heroic poetry is also a factor in our response to the other women discussed earlier and, through them, a factor in our response to the heroic world at large. Of these, Freawaru is an obvious case in point, being in a position similar to that of Hildeburh. Her grief is not articulated, as we have seen, but the effectiveness of Beowulf's account depends in part on the extra-textual perceptions relating to the *geomuru ides* stereotype that we bring to bear upon the suggestive underplaying of her presentation. The circumstances by which Freawaru comes to be in this vulnerable position are all too clear and put none of the male figures in a good light. In the case of Wealhþeow, Hygd, and Ealhhild, the circumstances leading up to their marriages are unexplained, but again we

"*The Wife's Lament* and *The Husband's Message*: A Reconsideration," *Anglia* 82 (1964): 269–90; R. E. Kaske, "A Poem of the Cross in the Exeter Book: *Riddle 60* and *The Husband's Message*," *Traditio* 23 (1967): 47–71 (p. 71); A. N. Doane, "Heathen Form and Christian Function in *The Wife's Lament*," *Mediaeval Studies* 28 (1966): 77–91; Rudolph C. Bambas, "Another View of the Old English *Wife's Lament*," *Journal of English and Germanic Philology* 62 (1963): 303–309. In the case of *Wulf and Eadwacer* a detailed argument has recently been put forward for returning to the idea that it is a poem about wolves: Peter Orton, "An Approach to *Wulf and Eadwacer*," *Proceedings of the Irish Royal Academy* 85(C) (1985): 223–58. By far the most widely accepted reading of each, however, is that the speaker is a sorrowing woman, victimized by male-dominated social circumstances.

3. For the identification of Mæðhild, see *Deor*, ed. Kemp Malone (London: Methuen and Co., Ltd., 1933; 4th rev. ed., Exeter: University of Exeter, 1977), pp. 8–9. The serious difficulties with Malone's identification are pointed out by F. Norman, "*Deor*: A Criticism and an Interpretation," *Modern Language Review* 32 (1937): 374–81.

4. Beadohild, as daughter of Niðhad, is raped by the mythological smith, Welund, as part of his revenge against Niðhad. In the Eddic poem *Vǫlundarkviða*, the smith is already married to someone else, but in *Þiðreks saga* there is a happier ending: she marries Velent (Welund) and their son Viðga (the Wudga of *Widsið* 124, 130, and the Widia of *Waldere* II, 4, 9) is drawn into the legend cycles that grew up around Þeodric and Eormanric. For a summary, see my *Old English Minor Heroic Poems*, pp. 79, 95, 101–104, under the names Beadohild, Niðhad, Wada, Welund, Wudga.

have to admit that they are thereby made vulnerable and are thus drawn
into the stereotypical pattern as potential victims.

Wealhþeow, despite her evident security when Beowulf visits Den-
mark, is likely to have been married to Hroðgar from another tribe, if her
name "foreign slave" may be taken as an indicator that she was a captive
in war. But even if we are inclined not to put much weight on extrapola-
tion of this kind, we can still be in no doubt that her present happiness is
precarious, since her comments on the succession cast a shadow over the
celebrations by reminding us of the dynastic struggles which so thor-
oughly expose the woman's vulnerability. Hygd likewise anticipates trou-
ble when Hygelac is dead if the young Heardred should succeed, which
he does, and we know that the Geatish tragedy also is eventually played
out. Heardred is killed by the Swedes, and although the end is postponed
by Beowulf's rule, the dynasty ends with his death, when the conquest
and exile of the Geats seems assured. Precisely how Hygd fares in all this
we. do not know, but she cannot escape being caught up in the destruc-
tion of the tribe. Like Wealhþeow, she can attempt to stave off trouble
but, unlike the men, she cannot make the grand gesture of confronting
fate directly and so achieve the freedom of heroic success that can be won
either through victory or a glorious death.

Ealhhild is an altogether more problematic case. The most likely in-
terpretation of the somewhat confusing information that we are given
about her is that the Widsið-poet knew her in legend as the wife of Eor-
manric,[5] but there is little doubt that she is a woman married out of her
own tribe and as a freoþuwebbe 'peace-weaver' (Widsith 6), with all the
risks that this entailed, both in legend and in life. If we go further and ac-
cept her identification with Eormanric's wife as known in Old Norse,
where she is called Svanhildr, we can anticipate her later cruel death at
the hands of her husband, a tyrannical figure who, for all his generosity,
which is admitted in Widsið and in medieval German texts, has a well-
deserved reputation for violence.[6] In any event, the predictable expecta-
tions are aroused by lines 5–9, when the stereotypes of female
peace-weaver and oath-breaking king are brought together.[7]

What draws these women towards the model of the geomuru ides, then,
is our recognition of patterns: our knowledge of the legends themselves,

5. For a summary of the problem, see my Old English Minor Heroic Poems, pp. 81–82.
6. The development of the Eormanric cycle is examined in detail by Caroline Brady, The Legends
   of Ermanaric (Berkeley: University of California Press, 1943). The traditions about Eormanric's
   wife and the possibility of identifying her with Ealhhild are discussed in Widsith: A Study in Old
   English Heroic Legend, ed. R. W. Chambers (Cambridge: Cambridge University Press, 1912),
   pp. 15–28.
7. Fælre freoþuwebban is used of Ealhhild in line 6 and wraþes wærlogan of Eormanric in line 9.
   In Widsith, ed. Malone, Anglistica 13 (Copenhagen: Rosenkilde and Bagger, 1962), pp. 29–35,
   the editor argues strongly for "hostile to treaty-breakers" as the interpretation of wraþes wærlogan,
   but this is a forced interpretation inspired by Malone's wish to rectify what he sees as being an
   otherwise inconsistent portrait. The effort is unwarranted, however, since the presentation of
   Eormanric in Widsið as both treacherous and generous is paralleled elsewhere. See my Old Eng-
   lish Minor Heroic Poems, pp. 83–84.

which exist outside the text as well as in it and which, in specific cases, may predict the woman's final sorrow; our perception of the general patterns of heroic narrative, in which there is always the risk, if not the realization, of tragedy; and the particular awareness, conditioned by the dominant stereotype, that the noble woman is, in the end, essentially helpless.

The patterns can be recognized even in the figure of *Hildegyð in *Waldere*.[8] She encourages the hero, she articulates as well as any male figure ever does the choice of absolutes that the hero must face, and she describes with great clarity the element of imprudence which impels the hero forward to fight on the enemy's terms. Alongside her

> [∴] is se dæg cumen
> þæt ðu scealt aninga oðer twega,
> life forleosan   oððe l . . . gne dom
> agan mid eldum,   Ælfheres sunu
> (*Waldere* I, 8–11)

(the day is come that you, son of Ælfhere, must do one of two things, lose your life or earn lasting glory among men)

we can place the *Maldon*-poet's:

> hi woldon þa ealle   oðer twega,
> lif forlætan   oððe leofne gewrecan
> (*Maldon* 207–208)

(then they all wanted one of two things, to lose their lives or avenge their beloved one)

or the absolutes offered by Sigeferð in *The Battle of Finnsburh*:[9]

> Ðe is gyt her witod
> swæþer ðu sylf to me   secean wylle.
> (*Finnsburh* 26–27)

(Furthermore, it is decreed for you here which of two things you will gain from me.)

And in Hildegyð's reference to Waldere's rash bravery (I, 12–19), we are reminded of the recurring pattern of heroic legend which dictates that the heroes seek out their opponents, fight on their ground, and in various ways allow the enemy to set the terms of the encounter.[1] In sum, her

---

8. The convention among critics is to assign the first speech in the *Waldere* fragment to Hildegyð although her name does not appear in the manuscript. [*Waldere* is a fragmentary Old English poem concerning Walter of Acquitaine, in which Hildegyð (though unnamed) is believed to appear (*Editor*).]
9. An Old English poem about the same episode in *Beowulf*, lines 1063–1159 [*Editor*].
1. Beowulf goes *to* Denmark, *into* Grendel's mere, and *to* the dragon's lair. His initial proof of his heroic stature also observes this pattern since he fights the sea-monsters in the water, and it is very effectively exploited in lines 677–87, when Beowulf refuses to use a sword against Grendel. That this encounter is a wrestling match is integral to the given (mythological) plot, but in the

speech is as comprehensive an evocation of the determinants of male heroism as one could hope to find in so short a dramatic address. And yet, she speaks *as a woman* and her encouragements therefore—and I use therefore advisedly—contain within themselves the awareness that heroic risk, so often accepted as gloriously elevating, brings with it fear of loss:

> ðy ic ðe metod ondred,
> þæt ðu to fyrenlice   feohtan sohtest
> æt ðam ætstealle   oðres monnes,
> wigrædenne.

(Waldere I, 19–22)

(therefore I feared for your fate, in that you sought the fight too rashly at the other man's position, according to his plan of battle.)

If the outcome of the story is close to that in the Latin *Waltharius*,[2] as seems probable, it is, for once, a story with a happy ending, so that Hildegyð is not drawn towards the stereotype to the same extent as other participatory figures are, such as Wealhþeow, Hygd, or Ealhhild. But even Hildegyð does not stand completely outside it, for we recognize and accept the ambiguities in her speech because we recognize and accept that the woman is always potentially, if not actually, the victim.

To recognize this fact, to acknowledge the force of the stereotype, is not, however, to conclude that for women the patterns of heroic poetry are necessarily reductive. The heroic code puts a premium on action and physical aggression and takes as indicators of power success in war and the acquisition of treasure, often by brutal means. But in the Old English tradition the consequences of such a code also stand revealed and it is partly through the female figures that this revelation is achieved. If the processes which transform history into legend tend to marginalize the women of the heroic world, judged from the viewpoint of "story," the sophistication of certain Anglo-Saxon poets' responses to that legendary material give women a position of ethical and imaginative importance.

Old English poem the hero had to be presented as conventionally armed. The common "pattern of imprudence" is used to explain, in heroic terms, how the hero comes to be in the position of fighting hand to hand. The same "pattern of imprudence" may be what justifies Byrhtnoð's heroic stature in *The Battle of Maldon*. For further discussion of this aspect of heroism, see N. F. Blake, "The Genesis of *The Battle of Maldon*," *Anglo-Saxon England* 7 (1978): 119–29, and T. A. Shippey, "Boar and Badger: An Old English Heroic Antithesis?" *Leeds Studies in English* n.s. 16 (1985): 220–39. *Waldere* I, 12–19, presents some problems of interpretation, although the general sense is unmistakable. For a detailed discussion, see my *Old English Minor Heroic Poems*, pp. 44–45, and the further comment by Shippey.

2. Summarized in my *Old English Minor Heroic Poems*, pp. 20–23. For the whole text in translation, see H. M. Smyser and F. P. Magoun, Jr., *Survivals in Old Norwegian of Medieval English, French and German Literature, together with the Latin versions of the heroic legend of Walter of Acquitaine*, Connecticut College Monograph, vol. 1 (Baltimore: Waverly Press, Inc., 1941). [*Waltharius* is a Latin poem concerning Walter of Acquitaine (*Editor*).]

HELEN BENNETT

The Female Mourner at Beowulf's Funeral: Filling in the Blanks/Hearing the Spaces[†]

The passage in *Beowulf* dealing with the female mourner, lines 3150–5, does not actually exist. The manuscript leaf is full of holes, tears and stains, and the missing text cannot be recovered. Only the first half-line, the last on folio 201r, is virtually intact and legible without some textual manufacturing. The rest of the passage (dis)appears at the top of folio 201v. Line 3151a is entirely missing, and all the other half-lines lack at least parts of words. The scholarly tradition has been to use the latest technology and the most informed conjectures to reconstruct lost letters and words. In one sense, then, *Beowulf* 3150–5 is the dream of patriarchal scholars: the holes in the text allow them to insert their own inverted reflection to fulfill the supposed desire of the text while confirming their own ideologies. These reconstructions have yielded another example of the passive female victim in Old English poetry. Traditional techniques of reconstructing and interpreting a text through analogues, however, can produce a quite opposite picture of the female mourner as strong and enduring. In the common Germanic heritage manifested in extant Old English and Old Norse poetry, the female is an active and powerful presence. But even this feminist reading participates in the patriarchal drive for a complete, closed, authorized text, with all of its holes filled. Contemporary psychoanalytic and feminist theory examining woman's relation to language and the symbolic order gives greater attention to silences and spaces, enabling us to accept the *Beowulf* passage as meaningful in its very incompleteness.

What exists in the manuscript is itself subject to debate. Letters have faded since the manuscript was first transcribed, but examination under high-intensity and ultraviolet lighting has enabled scholars to see previously invisible letters.[1] A conservative version of the passage is

swylce giomorgyd   . . . at meowle   3150
                      . . . unden heor . . .
    . . . sorgcearig   . . . ðe g . . . neah . . .
    Þ(æt) hio hyre . . . gas   hearde . . . de

[†] From *Exemplaria* 4.1 (1992): 35–50. Translations appearing in brackets are the editor's. Footnotes are the author's except where followed by [*Editor*]. This article developed from work begun at an NEH Summer Seminar "*Beowulf* and the Reception of Germanic Antiquity," held at Harvard University in 1987 and directed by Joseph Harris, Harvard University, and Thomas Hill, Cornell University.

1. For a thorough history of the emendations and readings proposed for the passage, see Tilman Westphalen, *Beowulf 3150–55: TextKritik und Editionsgeschichte*, Bochumer Arbeiten zur Sprach und Literaturwissenschaft 1 (Munich: Fink, 1967).

wa . . . ylla wonn   . . . des egesan
hyðo ha . . . d²   3155

Scholars agree that *Beowulf* 3150–5 contains references to a sad song [*giomorgyd* 3150a], a woman [*meowle* 3150b], sorrows [*sorgcearig* 3152a], slaughter [*wælfylla* 3153a], and terror [*egesan* 3153b]. Beyond that consensus, speculations diverge on textual reconstruction and the identity of the mourner. The version long accepted, the one adopted in Frederick Klaeber's influential edition, is that proposed by Sophus Bugge in 1887:

Swylce giomorgyd   [s]io g[eo]meowle   3150
[æfter Biowulfe   b]undenheorde
[song] sorgcearig   sæde geneahhe,
þæt hio hyre [hearmda]gas   hearde [ondr]ede,
wælfylla worn   [wigen]des egesan,
hy[n]ðo [ond] h[æftny]d.   3155

Likewise a sorrowful song the old woman
with bound up hair sang about Beowulf,
said that she severely dreaded days of evil,
many slaughters, the terror of warriors,
harm and captivity.[3]

Examination of the manuscript under ultraviolet light by A. H. Smith in 1938 revealed an *iat* in the second half-line (3150b), which led to John Pope's widely accepted 3150b *Geatisc meowle*, "Geatish woman" instead of "old woman." But this development did not settle her identity or the reconstruction of the text. Pope, identifying the Geatish woman as Hygd, suggests for line 3151

[Wedercwen awræc   w]undenheorde

the queen of the Weders, with wound hair, recited,

despite Smith's confirmation of an initial *b* for 3151b *bundenheorde*. Pope thus changes the alliterative pattern of the line, as well as the identity of the mourner.[4]

---

2. This version is based on Westphalen's photographs of folio 201v (Tafeln V and VI) and Julius Zupitza's facsimile (*Beowulf*, 2nd ed. EETS, no. 245 [New York: Oxford University Press, 1967]); Westphalen's *Beowulf 3150–55 Falttafel-Anhang*, a compilation of all editions and translations of the passage from Thorkelin A (1767) through 1967; and Howell D. Chickering, Jr., ed. and trans., *Beowulf: A Dual-Language Edition* (Garden City: Anchor Books, 1977).

3. Frederick Klaeber, ed., *Beowulf and The Fight at Finnsburg*, 3rd ed. (Lexington: D. C. Heath and Company, 1950). All translations of passages from *Beowulf* and other Old English poems are mine, unless otherwise indicated.

4. Smith's findings are recorded in "The Photography of Manuscripts," *London Mediaeval Studies* 1 (1938) [1937–9]: 179–207. Pope originally proposed the emendation *Geatisc meowle* in *The Rhythm of Beowulf: An Interpretation of the Normal and Hypermetric Verse-Forms in Old English Poetry* (New Haven: Yale University Press, 1942), 232 ff. His mention of Smith's discovery of the *b* in 3151b appears in "Three Notes on the Text of *Beowulf*," *MLN* 67 (1952): 509. And his reading for line 3151 that I have cited appears in "*Beowulf* 3150–51: Queen Hygd and the Word 'Geomeowle'," *MLN* 70 (1955): 83. The issue of "bound" or "wound" hair is significant

In fact, Tilan Westphalen's exhaustive, book-length study of the passage documents seven scholarly proposals for the woman's identity, proposals which fall into the two main categories "Beowulf's wife" and "not Beowulf's wife." Under "Beowulf's wife," the two choices are 1) an unknown, previously unmentioned woman, or 2) Hygd. Under "not Beowulf's wife" are five possibilities: 1) a woman of indeterminate age (an old matron or a young maiden), who, in the name of the Geatish people and especially her immediate companions, leads the lament; 2) a (young) woman who is to be burned with Beowulf as a companion in death (perhaps a concubine of Beowulf's); 3) an (old) woman participating in such a sacrifice; 4) a professional *Klageweib* [hired mourner] (with prophetic inclinations?); and 5) a highly-ranked lament leader (the old, widowed Queen Hygd, who did not remarry?).[5]

Weighing all the arguments, Westphalen opts for the highly speculative reading of Hygd as Beowulf's wife, and uses circular reasoning to support his interpretation with textual reconstruction, while supporting his reconstruction with the interpretation. His reconstruction follows:

> Swylce giomorgyd   (Ge)at(isc) meowle,
> (Biowulfes cwen)   (b)undenheorde,
> (song) sorgcearig   (sæl)ðe g(e)neahl(eas),
> þæt hio hyre (here)g(eon)gas   hearde ond(r)ede,
> wælfylla worn,   (w)erudes egesan,
> hyðo ond hæf(t)nyd.   Heofon rece s[w]ealg.[6]

> Likewise a mournful song the Geatish woman,
> Beowulf's queen, with hair bound up, sang sorrowfully,
> in misfortune (with insufficient luck), that she
> raiding attacks feared severely, many slaughters,
> the terrors of troops, shame and captivity.
> Heaven swallowed up the smoke.

He says the assumption of Hygd as referent reinforces the proposed 3151a *Biowulfes cwen*, while Hygd can be construed as the referent without being named because of the presence of 3150b *(Ge)at(isc)-meowle* and 3151a *Biowulfes cwen*; then he adds the qualification "if this or a similar expression should have been present in the text" (324). Of course, it will only ever again be present in the text if he or other editors put it there.

---

since mourners wore their hair loose or disheveled as a standard part of their appearance; see Carol J. Clover, "Hildigunnr's Lament," in *Structure and Meaning in Old Norse Literature: New Approaches to Textual Analysis and Literary Criticism*, eds. John Lindow, Lars Lonnroth, and Gerd Wolfgang Weber (Odense: Odense University Press, 1986), 162–3; and Theresa C. Blakeley, "Mourning Songs," *Funk and Wagnall's Standard Dictionary of Folklore, Mythology, and Legend*, 2:755–7. Clover tries to argue that "'wound-[=wavy-] haired' accords better with this picture" (167).
5. Westphalen, 289. My translation from German.
6. Ibid., 286.

Furthermore, both Westphalen and Pope defend the identification of Hygd on the basis of tradition:

> there is a general tendency in heroic poetry, especially when it is also as strongly aristocratic as *Beowulf* or the *Iliad*, to prefer such individuals, if any are available, to nameless types.[7]

Several tendencies emerge from the scholarly positions surveyed: no emendations have gained universal and definitive acceptance; different editions indicate different letters as actually in the manuscript; many of the interpretations rest on broader, non-Germanic stereotypes of female roles in society; and all see the mourner's position as weak. But tradition may be used equally effectively to demonstrate the strength of the mourner.

The inclination to see lamentation as weak derives from the conception of the heroic world as "a world of action and of public recognition for deeds performed, not of brooding and soul searching."[8] This world of action is almost exclusively a man's world, and so men have an obligation to act rather than to brood.[9] Beowulf himself says,

> Selre bið æghwæm,
> þæt he his freond wrece, þonne he fela murne.
> Ure æghwylc sceal   ende gebidan
> worolde lifes;   wyrce se þe mote
> domes ær deaþe;   þaet bið drihtguman
> unlifigendum   æfter selest.   1384b–1389[1]

> It is better for every person that he his friend avenges than that he mourns greatly. Each of

---

7. Pope, "*Beowulf* 3150–51," 79. However, Tauno Mustanoja, in "The Unnamed Woman's Song of Mourning over Beowulf and the Tradition of Lamentation," NM 68 (1967): 1–27, uses the woman's namelessness to argue for her membership in a Germanic, and, more broadly, an Indo-European tradition of female mourners.
   Howell D. Chickering's reading links the Geatish woman to the female practice of weaving:

> swylce giomor-gyd   [Ge]at[isc] meowle 3150
> [Biowulfe brægd,]   bunden-heorde.

> Likewise a sad song the Geatish woman
> with bound up hair wove for Beowulf.
>   (Chickering's translation)

Christine Fell suggests that *wifmann* is etymologically related to words for "weaving" (*Women in Anglo-Saxon England* [Oxford: Basil Blackwell, 1984], 39), and Freud names weaving as women's only contribution to culture, their affinity for the craft deriving from an instinctual desire to imitate the way pubic hair covers their genitals (in Luce Irigaray, *Speculum of the Other Woman*, trans. Gillian C. Gill [Ithaca: Cornell University Press, 1985], 112). Thus, Chickering's reconstruction draws on and reinforces traditional views of woman and her attributes.
8. Fred Robinson, "History, Religion, Culture," in *Approaches to Teaching Beowulf*, eds. Jess B. Bessinger, Jr. and Robert F. Yeager (New York: MLA, 1984), 119.
9. In "Maiden Warriors and Other Sons," *JEGP* 85 (1986): 35–49, Carol Clover discusses the Norse tradition of female warriors who, under certain conditions, renounced their femininity and took on male roles in blood feuds.
1. Passages from Old English poetry are taken from George Philip Krapp and Elliott Van Kirk Dobbie, eds., *The Exeter Book*, vol. III, and *Beowulf and Judith*, vol. IV of *The Anglo-Saxon Poetic Records* (New York: Columbia University Press, 1936, 1953).

> us shall endure the end of life in the world;
> let him who may perform works of glory before
> death; that is the best afterwards for the
> lifeless warrior.

When a man cannot fight, he has failed in his world, and when he utters a lament, he is generally acknowledging the limitations of the male world structure. "The Lament of the Last Survivor" (lines 2247–66) and "The Father's Lament" (lines 2444–62a) in *Beowulf* reflect the failure of the *comitatus* and of the wergild/revenge system.[2] The speaker in *The Wanderer* mourns the loss of his lord and his community, a community of warriors. The so-called "retrospective poems" (*Ruckblicksgedicht*) of the *Eddica Minora*, Norse poems dating from the tenth to twelfth centuries, record similar instances of heroes being caught between unresolvably conflicting loyalties. In *Vikarsbalkr*, from *Gautrekssaga*, Starkathr is granted a lifespan three times the normal lifespan but in return must sacrifice King Vikar, his lord and friend, thereby causing his own exile from a comitatus:

Skylda ek Vìkar	I had to sacrifice Vikarr
í viði hávum,	to the Gods,
Geirpiófsbana,	Geirthiofr's slayer,
goðum of signa;	in the high tree;
lagða ek geiri	I pierced the prince to the
gram til hiarta,	heart with a spear: that
þat er mér harmast	is to me the most grievous
handaverka.	of my hand-works.
Þaðan vappaðak	From there I wandered
villtar brautir,	aimlessly,
Hǫrðum leiðr,	hated by the Horthar,
með huga illan,	in bad spirits,
hringa vanr	without rings
ok hróðrkvæða,	and songs of praise,
dróttinlauss,	kingless,
dapr allz hugar	sad in all thoughts.[3]

Hrokr in *Hrokslied* from *Halfssaga* laments his inability to avenge his King Halfr, who was betrayed in a truce (stanzas 21–22). In stanza 26, Hrokr describes himself as helpless and without a community:

Hér þykkik nú	Here in Haki's
í Haka veldi	kingdom I now seem

2. The comitatus was in Germanic culture a band of retainers who owed allegiance and military service to a lord and in exchange received protection and treasure [*Editor*].
3. Andreas Heusler and Wilhelm Ranish, eds., *Eddica Minora* (Dortmund: F. Wilh. Rufhus, 1903), stanzas 19–20. Translation of poems from from the *Eddica Minora* are taken from Daniel G. Calder et al., eds. and trans., *Sources and Analogues of Old English Poetry II. The Major Germanic and Celtic Texts in Translation* (Totowa: Barnes and Noble, 1983).

hornungr vera	to be the outcast
hverrar þióðar;	of every nation;
allir eigu	they have all gone
innar at sitia,	to sit farther in,
hallar gumnar,	the men of the hall
en Hálfs rekkar.	and Halfr's warriors.

But the elegies also involve histories of the speakers' own exploits as a way for each speaker to identify himself,[4] and so, like Beowulf's speech before meeting the dragon (lines 2510 ff.), serve to contrast former glory and power to present doom or helplessness.

The female lament tradition is seen as coming out of greater weakness, since women were never part of the system and could never act to determine their fate or to achieve glory.[5] Elaine Tuttle Hansen sees the "use of the suffering female as a voice for human pain and weakness," and she cites as examples *The Fortunes of Men* 13b–14a, *Wulf and Eadwacer*, *The Wife's Lament*, and the female characters in *Beowulf*: Hildeburh is "the helpless and innocent victim of human passion and fate"; Freawaru is a passive pawn; and even Grendel's mother is a symbol of "weakness and limitation." For Hansen, the female mourner combines the functions of mourning and foretelling doom, but these two functions emphasize the woman's helplessness:

> these two activities are the last and fitting steps left to woman when life has taken away her men, her court, her treasure, and her strength.[6]

In *God's Handiwork: Images of Women in Early Germanic Literature*, Richard Schrader presents a similar view: "Nearly every woman in *Beowulf* is presented as a victim."[7] Their political and moral power is useless against brute force, and all the females, including Grendel's mother, depend for survival on male protectors (41). Schrader sees the poet using "the plight of an individual woman to mirror the troubles of society at large" (37). This tendency culminates in the figure of the female mourner who combines personal loss with the doom of her race:

> Without the protection of the best of the world's kings, the *meowle* must endure war and captivity, becoming, with this first of many laments, the commonplace victimized woman of the elegies. (45)

4. Joseph Harris, "Hadubrand's Lament: On the Origin and Age of Elegy in Germanic," *Heldensage und Heldendichtung in Germanischen* (New York: de Gruyter, 1988), 90–91; *Eddica Minora*, xxxi.
5. In Plato's *Republic* III 387e–388a, Socrates says (cited by Irigaray in *Speculum*, 156):

Then we shall be right in getting rid of the lamentations of famous men, and making them over to women (and not even to those women who are good for anything), or to men of a baser sort, that those who are educated by us to be the defenders of their country may scorn to do the like.

6. "Women in Old English Poetry Reconsidered," *The Michigan Academician* 9 (1976): 113–6.
7. Richard Schrader, *God's Handiwork: Images of Women in Early Germanic Literature* (Westport: Greenwood Press, 1983), 36.

However, for female elegists, lamentation constitutes their way into or around a system that excludes them.[8] Absent from the field of action, women surround the action with their words: urging before and officially mourning after.[9] Arguing that incitement and lamentation are two aspects of the same function, Carol Clover says that, just as it was a man's duty to take revenge for a relative's murder,

> it was no less the duty of women to remember and remind. . . . In the feud situation, women's . . . words are the equivalent of men's deeds; it is as incumbent on a woman to urge vengeance as it is incumbent on a man to take it.[1]

Unlike men, women in Germanic tradition were properly allowed to express grief. According to Tacitus (*Germania* 27), "A woman may decently express her grief in public; a man should nurse his in his heart."[2] More-

---

8. In Greek society, women's mourning functions at funerals gave them a voice in decisions about property rights, and Icelandic women's affinity for inciting blood revenge was a likely result of their exclusion from legal recourse (Clover, "Hildigunnr's Lament," 165, 174–5).

9. The tradition of female speech most powerful in determining the outcome of action is that of the female wise woman/prophesier. Of the view held by Germanic men concerning women's wisdom, Tacitus says: "They even believe that there is in woman a certain holiness and power of prophecy, and they do not neglect to seek their advice, nor do they disregard their replies" (*Germania*, Chap. 8, trans. Fred C. Robinson, in "The Prescient Woman in Old English Literature," *Philologia Anglica: Essays Presented to Professor Yoshio Terasawa on the Occasion of his Sixtieth Birthday* [Tokyo: Ken Kyusha, 1988], 241). Jacob Grimm traces examples of women priestesses and prophets from ancient times, women who possess both wisdom and supernatural powers (*Teutonic Mythology* [New York: Dover Publications, 1966], 1:400). These wise women included Norns and Valkyries, who determine the future and know magic (John Arnott MacCulloch, *The Mythology of All Races* [New York: Cooper Square Publishers, Inc., 1964], 2:248–57; H. R. Ellis-Davidson, *Gods and Myths of Northern Europe* [Baltimore: Penguin Books, 1964], 61–66). Valkyries' most widespread role is as "arrangers of destinies" (Helen Damico, *Beowulf's Wealhtheow and the Valkyrie Tradition* [Madison: University of Wisconsin Press, 1984], 38; "The Valkyrie Reflex in Old English Literature," *Allegorica* 5 [1980]: 149): "As Odinn's maids, they determine the outcome of the central issues that concern Germanic warrior society—battle and warriors' afterlife" ("The Valkyrie Reflex," 155). Thus, while they control the outcome of the battle, most often they do not actually participate. The valkyrie tradition is, then, a tradition of powerful speaking about the future. Fred Robinson sees a positive prescient-woman image of this valkyrie tradition in Wealhtheow, Hygd, and the female mourner. He traces the presence of the "woman prophesying (accurately) the doom of the people" as it recurs in Germanic literature, the culmination being the seeress in *Voluspà*, who foresees the final doom of the gods ("Prescient Woman," 245); and Robinson argues that the woman's prediction is "the climactic and ultimate corroboration that doom is at hand" ("Prescient Woman," 244–45).

1. Clover cites Bjargey in *Harvarðar saga*: "It is manly for those unfit for vigorous deeds to be unsparing in their use of the tongue in saying those things that may avail" ("Hildigunnr's Lament," 144–45).

2. H. Mattingly's translation in Schrader, 46. This double standard regarding lamentation lies behind the contrast in *The Wife's Lament* between the female speaker who describes her position:

> þær ic wepan mæg   mine wræcsiþas,
> earfoþa fela, (38–39a)

> there may I mourn my miseries, many hardships,

in opposition to the male prescription for behavior:

> A scyle geong mon   wesan geomormod,
> heard heortan geþoht,   swylce habban sceal
> bliþe gebæro,   eac þon breostceare,
> sinsorgna gedreag. (42–45a)

> Always should the young man be sad in mind,
> hard the thoughts of his heart; likewise
> shall he have a blithe bearing, and also

over, when female elegists contrast former joy to present grief, their words form a critique of the patriarchal heroic ethic, by which women are not bound. In *Atlamál in groenlenzco*, from the *Poetic Edda*, Guthrun tries to warn her brothers against coming to Atli's court. She sends runes which are deciphered by Kostbera, Hogni's wife. The women both warn against the journey, but the men believe only in deeds:

> Allar ro illúðgar (qvað Hǫgni),   áca ec þess kynni,
> vilca ec þess leita,   nema launa eigim.   *Atlamál* 13: 1–4

"All women are mistrustful," said Hǫgni; "I retreat from this attitude. I will look for this [i.e. betrayal], only if we are obliged to requite it [to act]."[3]

No amount of talk or prophetic dreams can prevent the encounter. After her brothers have been slain, Guthrun says to Atli:

> Kostom drepr qvenna   karla ofríki.   *Atlamál* 73: 1–2

Women's choice is destroyed by the tyranny of men.

Earlier in the same poem, Guthrun actually fights and kills warriors in defense of her brothers (stanzas 50–51), and later she kills her and Atli's children as revenge for her brothers' death (*Atlamál* 82–84). Yet, when the poem is over and Guthrun has carried out revenge, she does not die:

> urðo dvǫl doegra,   dó hon í sinn annað.   *Atlamál* 104: 7–8

her days were delayed, she died at another time.

In *Guðrúnarhvǫt*, which follows in the *Edda* and in Guthrun's life chronologically, Guthrun uses lamentation in two powerful ways. First, she uses the recounting of her grief to encourage her sons to avenge their sister, Svanhild (stanzas 1–3). Weeping, she tells her story "in many a way" (*á margan veg*, stanza 9: 8). She tells of all her losses and her attempt to end her own life (stanza 13), to preempt the decree of the Norns. At the end of the poem, she says:

> Iǫrlom ǫllom   óðal batni,
> snótom ǫllom   sorg at minni,
> at þetta tregróf   um talið væri.   *Guðrúnarhvǫt* 21

For all noblemen, may their lot improve,
For all gentlewomen, may sorrow be diminished,
by this tale of woe being spoken.

---

breast-care, a multitude of perpetual grief.

For a thorough analysis of the power in the wife's speech, see Barrie Ruth Straus, "Women's Words as Weapons: Speech as Action in 'The Wife's Lament'," *TSLL* 23 (1981): 268–85.
3. Eddic passages are taken from Gustav Neckel and Hans Kuhn, eds., *Edda: Die Lieder des Codex Regius Nebst Verwandten Denkmalern* (Heidelberg: Carl Winter Universitatsverlag, 1962). All translations of Eddic poetry are mine.

There is, then, a second kind of strengthening purpose for lamentation, a catharsis associated with the expression of grief.[4]

In her preeminence as lamenter, Guthrun stands as contrast to Brynhild within several of the eddic poems. While in *Helreið Brynhildar*, the valkyrie is presented sympathetically, as doomed for sorrow and lovelessness, in *Sigurðarkviða in scamma* and in *Guðrúnarkviða in fyrsta*, Brynhild is cold-hearted, vindictive, and prophetic, rather than mournful. In *Sigurðarkviða* (stanzas 24–25 and 29), Guthrun mourns as Brynhild laughs:

> Hló þá Brynhildr,   Buðla dóttir,
> eino sinni   af ǫllom hug,
> er hon til hvílo   heyra knátti
> giallan grát   Giúca dóttur.   *Sigurðarqviða* 30

> Laughed then Brynhild, Buthli's daughter,
> one time only, out of inmost heart,
> on her couch, when came to her ears
> the grievous wailing of Giuki's daughter.[5]

After inflicting the death-stroke, but before her death, Brynhild has a lot to say, but it is masculine in subject (a review of her history) and prophetic in tone (she predicts Gunnar's and Guthrun's sorrows); it is not mournful.

Guðrúnarkviða in fyrsta traces Guthrun's inability to grieve for Sigurthr. To encourage her, companions tell of their sorrows—loss of kinsmen and women, captivity, bondage. Finally, after Gullond uncovers Sigurth's body, Guthrun is able to cry and mourn (stanzas 18–22). She contrasts her former high status to her present destitution due to Sigurth's death (stanza 19); she laments the loss of him in bed and at the table (stanza 20); and she curses Gunnar (stanza 21). Not only can Brynhild not grieve in this situation, but she curses the woman who enabled Guthrun to grieve, to give voice to her sorrow (stanza 23). Lacking that outlet, Brynhild kills herself. It is almost as if Guthrun's ability to speak gives her the

---

4. This cathartic effect is noted by Clover, "Hildigunnr's Lament," 160, in connection with *Guðrúnarhvǫt* and *Egils saga.* Clover's examples involve both male and female speakers. Clover cites Margaret Alexiou. *The Ritual Lament in Greek Tradition* (Cambridge: Cambridge University Press, 1974), 125, on the Trojan women's advice to Hekabe: "grief, finding expression, is relieved and lightened, hence the ritual lament is just as necessary for the mourner as it is for the dead."

In modern psychoanalysis, the cartharatic effect of verbalization constitutes Freud's "talking cure" for (hysterical female) patients, whereby "the putting into words of the [traumatic] event (in the patient's 'stories') determined the lifting of the symptom" (Jacques Lacan, *Écrits: A Selection*, trans. Alan Sheridan [New York: W. W. Norton & Company, 1977], 46).

5. Clover notes the laughing and crying motif in *Hamðismal*, where Guthrun laughs (anticipating revenge) and cries (grieving) at the same time, and in *Guðrúnarhvǫt* where Guthrun laughs first and later cries. Clover's point is that "whetting and lamenting are two sides of the same coin" ("Hildigunnr's Lament," 158). But in *Sigurðarqviða*, the two actions serve to contrast the two women.

power to live, to endure. Brynhild's "masculine" ethic necessitates her death.

In *Beowulf*, too, the female mourner and the character with whom she is most often associated, Hildeburh, are both survivors of male conflicts, left to mourn their dead and to go on living. After the violence, the women still stand, next to the funeral pyres, committing their beloved lords and kinsmen to the flames, watching and singing sad songs as the patriarchal world "goes up in smoke." They will both be subject to a new patriarchal order, the mourner as captive, but they are empowered by their endurance and their speech. Excluded from the world of action, woman becomes the reader of its text, author of its record. Appropriately, male elegists who do not speak heroic elegies are poets (*Deor* and *Widsith*), who share with women the custody of history.

But whose history is it? Is the so-called "female" voice really her own? Whose language is she speaking? After all, the mourner is in the text only as the long line of male editors have defined her, speaking words put into her mouth. Using traditional research and methodology, one can establish the female mourner as a figure of strength, but according to whose rules? Even if she survives to speak, she is still the inverted image of the male hero, deriving her power from being *not man*. Whatever role is assigned her incorporates her into the patriarchal symbolic order; whatever emendation is accepted, the patriarchal desire for a visible, completed text is fulfilled. According to Luce Irigaray,

> the "masculine" is not prepared to share the initiative of discourse. It prefers to experiment with speaking, writing, enjoying "woman" rather than leaving to the other any right to intervene, to "act," in her own interests.[6]

Can woman speak as woman? Jacques Lacan sees woman as having been excluded from the symbolic order of language which defines being human: "Man speaks, . . . but it is because the symbol has made him man";[7] "in man and through man *it* [the signifier] speaks (*ça parle*)."[8] For humans, "the world of words . . . creates the world of things—the things originally confused in the *hic et nunc* [here and now] of the all in the process of coming-into-being."[9] Rather than simply expressing the self, the speaking subject must construct a self out of the preexisting language. Within this language, however, woman is acknowledged only by

---

6. *This Sex Which Is Not One*, trans. Catherine Porter with Carolyn Burke (Ithaca: Cornell University Press, 1985), 157. In *Speculum* (13), Irigaray cites Freud's introductory remarks to his lecture "Femininity":

> Throughout history people have knocked their heads against the riddle of the nature of femininity. . . . Nor will *you* have escaped worrying over this problem—those of you who are men; to those of you who are woman this will not apply—you are yourselves the problem.

7. *Écrits*, 65.
8. Ibid., 284.
9. Ibid., 65.

negation, by being *not man:* "There is no such thing as *the* woman since of her essence . . . she is not all. . . . There is woman only as excluded by the nature of things which is the nature of words."[1] Women complain about this exclusion, but "they don't know what they are saying."[2] Feminist theorists attribute the fault to the language, not to women. To have any voice, to be understood at all, woman must mimic masculine language, expressing the male concept of femininity which gives back to man an image of himself.[3] This speech masks her lack of identity in the patriarchal economy.[4]

Lacan associates woman with what exceeds language:

> By her being in the sexual relation radically Other, in relation to what can be said of the unconscious, the woman is that which relates to this Other.[5]

Although Lacan contends that the unconscious is structured like a language, we get glimpses of that structure only indirectly, as disruptions of conscious speech and order.[6] Similarly, when woman tries to speak as herself, her incomprehensible speech is termed hysterical or mystical.[7] Both the hysteric and the mystic transgress the linear syntax and logic governing the established symbolic order. Transgressions and disruptions of order are deemed undesirable because they do not "fit." What is open and unfinished, what does not have clear divisions between inside and outside, beginning and ending is considered grotesque and abject.[8]

This disruptive ambiguity defines the mourner. Her namelessness puts her outside the patriarchal symbolic order, beyond the reach of the Name-of-the-Father; hence, the previously cited "general tendency in heroic poetry [and in patriarchal critics] . . . to prefer . . . [named] individuals . . . to nameless types." Pope's statement is itself paradoxi-

1. Jacques Lacan, *Feminine Sexuality: Jacques Lacan and the École Freudienne*, eds. Juliet Mitchell and Jacqueline Rose, trans. Jacqueline Rose (New York: W. W. Norton & Company, 1985), 144.
2. Ibid.
3. Irigaray, *This Sex*, 76.
4. Mary Russo, "Feminine Grotesques: Carnival and Theory," in *Feminist Studies/Critical Studies*, ed. Teresa de Lauretis (Bloomington: Indiana University Press, 1986), 223–4.
5. *Écrits*, 151.
6. Ibid., 49–50.
7. In *Feminine Sexuality*, Lacan describes the mystical experience as an ex-static *jouissance* [inexpressible pleasure] which the mystic "experiences and knows nothing of" (147), and therefore cannot express. Irigaray (*Speculum*, 193) explains more fully this inability of the mystic to speak of a loss of self that brings self-unity:

   she cannot specify exactly what she wants. Words begin to fail her. She senses something *remains to be said* that resists all speech, that can at best be stammered out. All the words are weak, worn out, unfit to translate anything sensibly. For it is no longer a matter of longing for some determinable attribute, some mode of essence, some face of presence. What is expected is neither a *this* nor a *that*, not a *here* anymore than a *there*. No being, no places are designated. So the best plan is to abstain from all discourse, to keep quiet, or else utter only a sound so inarticulate that it barely forms a *song*.

   Irigaray also discusses how the hysteric is misrepresented in *Speculum*, 60, and *This Sex*, 136.
8. Julia Kristeva, *The Powers of Horror: An Essay in Abjection*, trans. Leon S. Rudiez (New York: Columbia University Press, 1982). 102–3.

cal since one cannot designate a type without naming it. The real point is the preference for namable objects with predefined identities that will fit the system. But she (the text, woman) is never quite satisfied; she never quite becomes what the critic wants, never quite settles into one super-imposed identity.

The way to let the mourner "be herself" by *not* being comes from fem-inist theorists whose language, in contrast to phallocentric discourse, privileges rather than marginalizes the significance of silence and non-linearity.[9] Jessica Benjamin suggests a departure from the symbolic mode privileging a single (masculine) subjectivity in the spatial rather than symbolic *intersubjective* mode:

> inner space should be understood as part of a continuum that in-cludes the space between the I and the you, as well as the space within me; and, further, the space within should be understood as a receptacle only insofar as it refers to the receptivity of the subject.[1]

This *inner space* would allow the lacunae in the text to stand as repre-sentative of the intersubjectivity of any interpretation. Just as Lacan and Irigaray argue for a cross-transference between analyst and analysand dur-ing psychoanalysis,[2] for a completion through another, and against the analyst as "the subject presumed to know,"[3] so this model can be applied to literary analysis. The result coming from the space between reader and text (inter-subjectively), there would be no question of mastery (appro-priation) of the text, in which the text (and the woman caught in it) serves the critic. Relinquishing the desire for a complete, authorized text allows the reader to see *Beowulf*'s mourner as lamenting lost structure, social and symbolic. But, of course, the end of existing structures does not nec-essarily herald an end to meaning; it also represents liberation, especially for women. As Tania Modleski says of feminist criticism in general:

> By working on a variety of fronts for the survival and empowerment of women, feminist criticism performs an escape act dedicated to freeing women from *all* captivity narratives, whether these be found in literature, criticism, or theory.[4]

9. Calling for an examination of the "grammar" for figures of discourse, Irigaray includes "what it does not articulate at the level of utterance: *its silences*" (*This Sex*, 75). Julia Kristeva challenges exclusive validity of linear syntax (*The Kristeva Reader*, ed. Toril Moi [New York: Columbia Uni-versity Press, 1986], 190–93).
1. "A Desire of One's Own," in *Feminist Studies/Critical Studies*, 95. This feminist advocacy for inner space as not passive appears in Edith Whitehurst Williams' solution to riddle 91 ("What's So New About the Sexual Revolution? Some Comments on Anglo-Saxon Attitudes towards Sex-uality in Women Based on Four Exeter Book Riddles," *Texas Quarterly* 18 [1975]: 46–55). For the widely accepted "key," Williams suggests "keyhole":

   > instead of forcing certain distorted meanings to apply rather doubtfully to a male in-strument, I suggest accepting the very obvious allusion to a female receptacle, active though it might be.

2. *Écrits*, 42; *This Sex*, 148.
3. *Écrits*, 35.
4. "Feminism and the Power of Interpretation: Some Critical Readings," in *Feminist Studies/Crit-ical Studies*, 136.

NICHOLAS HOWE

The Uses of Uncertainty: On the Dating of *Beowulf*[†]

> This trivial trope reveals a way of truth.
> —Wallace Stevens, 'Le Monocle de Mon Oncle,' 1918

Reading letters by nineteenth- and twentieth-century poets can be very disturbing to Anglo-Saxonists, for they are filled with exactly the information we long to know—and despair of ever discovering—about Old English poems: who wrote them, and when, and where, and even perhaps, why they did so. Take, for example, something as banal as the short letter and accompanying list sent by Wallace Stevens to his publisher Alfred A. Knopf on 16 October 1930 from Hartford, Connecticut. The letter reads in full: 'You wrote to me in the spring about re-printing Harmonium. I hand you such new material as I have, with a suggestion or two.'[1] In the attached list, Stevens names three poems to be dropped from the second edition of *Harmonium* and fourteen to be added in a precisely specified order. Stevens's letter and list can seem almost heartbreaking to the Anglo-Saxonist because, in their exquisite brevity, they provide more information about the dating and circulation of poems than do all the surviving records of pre-Conquest England.

The dating of *Beowulf*, the question of how to set a year and perhaps with it a local habitation for the longest, most widely read poem in the language, can be taken as an emblematic critical issue for Old English studies.[2] Worrying about when Beowulf was composed is, as a problem, closely akin to asking if Cynewulf is the only poet who can reasonably be described as the author of more than one Old English poem, or to wondering about the political allegiance and literary taste of the poet who composed *The Battle of Maldon*.[3] Anglo-Saxonists must accept

---

[†] From *The Dating of Beowulf*, ed. Colin Chase (Toronto: U of Toronto P, 1997) 213–20. Howe's references to "this volume" and "this collection of essays" are to the volume in which this piece was originally published, *The Dating of Beowulf*.

1. *The Letters of Wallace Stevens*, ed. Holly Stevens (New York 1981), pp. 259–60.

2. This afterword does not survey the debate that has flourished since the publication of *The Dating of Beowulf*. It would be foolish to attempt such a survey after the searching essay by Roy Michael Liuzza, 'On the Dating of Beowulf,' in *Beowulf: Basic Readings*, ed. Peter S. Baker (New York 1995), 281–302. My debt to Liuzza's essay will be apparent to anyone who has read it. That arguments about dating *Beowulf* remain lively is abundantly clear from items summarized in the most recent issue (as I write) of the *The Year's Work in Old English Studies*; see the *Old English Newsletter* 28 (1995), pp. 22–3; 42–4. I should also acknowledge my debt to John Dagenais, *The Ethics of Reading in Manuscript Culture: Glossing the Libro de buen amor* (Princeton: 1994). My thanks as well to Roberta Frank, first for inviting me to write this afterword, and then for engaging in a sustained conversation on what it means to do Old English studies today.

3. This point is nicely illustrated by the fact that a recent collection of essays on Cynewulf offers only two previously unpublished pieces, both of which center on questions of dating. See Robert E. Bjork, ed., *Cynewulf: Basic Readings* (New York 1996), pp. 3–55, for pieces by R.D. Fulk and Patrick W. Conner. See, similarly, Jonathon Wilcox. 'The Battle of Maldon and The Anglo-Saxon Chronicle, 979–1016: A Winning Combination,' *Proceedings of the Medieval Association of the Midwest* 3 (1995), pp. 31–50.

a burden of ignorance about matters of authorship and chronology that would be, I think, intolerable to those who work in most other periods of literary history. Yet our predicament rests not simply on our ignorance about such matters. It is also that Anglo-Saxonists have been trained as literary and historical scholars to work in disciplines that treat such knowledge as basic to all serious study. Yet, by ironic contrast, even literary theorists who celebrate the death of the author, or historians who resist the temptations of vulgar biography, can still rely on knowing basic chronological facts about authors and texts. Whatever they might do with this knowledge, these readers can be certain that the poems in *Harmonium* come at the start of Steven's career and those in *The Auroras of Autumn* come towards its end. About Old English poets, we will probably never know even these trivial facts.

Our uncertainty about the shape of an Old English literary career stands on a small scale for our uncertainties about the shape of Old English literary history. We have firm dates for some of the prose, many conjectures about the poetry, and an unspoken habit of pretending to more certainty about such matters than the evidence warrants. Or, perhaps more accurately, we have a tacit agreement not to worry in public about the chronological premises of our scholarly work. That is, the discipline argues freely and vociferously about when *Beowulf* might be dated, but it tends to evade the underlying questions about whether *Beowulf* can be dated within the state of our current knowledge. We evade these questions, naturally enough, because they threaten to induce a critical paralysis that is, if not unthinkable, then certainly unproductive. The dating of *Beowulf* is in this regard simply the most visible form of a larger disciplinary problem. To put it more historically, the controversies that have animated Old English studies over that last century or so have always swirled around *Beowulf,* and the question of dating is no exception. Indeed, arguments about how and when to date *Beowulf* are never merely about chronology but extend to the ways in which we read other Old English poems both in themselves and as forming a larger context for *Beowulf.*

Attempts to date *Beowulf* almost always carry with them some implicit, often unacknowledged, sense about the way the poem came into being. In the nineteenth century, to speak broadly, scholars emphasized the oral development and transmission of *Beowulf* from generation to generation so that they could establish a very early date for the original composition of the poem, as distinct from the date of its transcription in the manuscript. The poem was not the work of a single author, according to this argument, but the result of a long folk evolution by which anecdotes gradually cohered into episodes and then into an extended narrative as the matter of the poem was told and retold by anonymous bards. The slow growth of the poem through popular circulation was for such scholars essential to its greatness as folk-epic; it mattered as a cultural monument precisely because it was early and could not be assigned to a single author or precise moment of composition. That *Beowulf* had no set date proved that it had always been traditional, that is, it proved that the poem was not and had never been 'modern' within its own culture because it was not created through the new technology of literacy.[4] Indeed, much nineteenth-century writing on *Beowulf* is more comprehensible as the manifestation of nationalistic and ethnic desires than as literary scholarship. *Beowulf* mattered because it was epic, Germanic, originary, that is, because it was not at root Christian, Latin, derivative. If it seemed Christian, that was merely the thin glaze of piety left by monks who, through the very act of writing it down, consciously betrayed its authentic genius as a poem of the folk.

The obvious analogy for this vision of *Beowulf* would seem to be the *Iliad* and the *Odyssey*, but it is partial at best—and then quite misleadingly so—because these two poems occupy a position of radical earliness in Greek literature. Classicists may disagree about their dates but none would argue, as do reputable Anglo-Saxonists for *Beowulf*, that the *Iliad* and the *Odyssey* close out the last moments of a poetic tradition. None would make their Homers into Alexandrians. Classicists have this great advantage over Anglo-Saxonists: they know that these two long poems, whatever their dates, appear early in Greek poetry and are originary for much that follows. The dating of the *Iliad* and the *Odyssey* depends at least partly on the references to and retellings of them that appear in later works. Indeed, if we lacked these poems we could reconstruct their narratives and much of their verbal texture from this commentary tradition. Above all, we could posit their existence and argue their cultural significance.

By contrast, if BL MS. Cotton Vitellius A.xv (also known as the *Beowulf* manuscript) had been lost, as it might easily have been, no trace of the poem we call *Beowulf* would remain and Anglo-Saxonists would have little if any reason to imagine its existence. For *Beowulf* is unusual not simply in being the longest poem in Old English. It is also in its historical, ethical, and political concerns quite different from Old English poems that run to longer than lyric length. The absence of references to *Beowulf* elsewhere in Old English or Anglo-Latin works means that there is no external cultural evidence to help us date the poem or at least set some plausible boundaries for it. If late in the eighth century Alcuin had alluded to *Beowulf* in one of his letters bemoaning the Viking ravages in northern England—'Why aren't they like the peaceable Danes whom Beowulf befriended at Heorot?'—there would be much less need for this collection of essays, for we would be able to narrow the poem's date to the relatively

---

4. For the oral formulaicists' resistance to literacy as a form of 'ethnographic pastoral,' see James L. Clifford, 'On Ethnographic Allegory' in *Writing Culture: The Poetics and Politics of Ethnography*, ed. James L. Clifford and George Marcus (Berkeley and Los Angeles 1986), pp. 98–121.

acceptable term of a century. That there is no commentary tradition for *Beowulf* obviously frustrates attempts at dating the poem, but also should chasten those who argue that it thrived for a long time as an epic in Anglo-Saxon England.

The impetus to date *Beowulf* early had its origin at least in part in the position of Homer's works early in the Greek tradition. If *Beowulf* were to be the epic of Anglo-Saxon England, and achieve literary parity with the *Iliad* and the *Odyssey*, it required a comparably early date. If it did achieve such parity, then Germanic philology could enjoy a status comparable to that of classical philology.[5] Call it Homer-envy, or, the beginnings of English studies as a discipline. When Anglo-Saxonists became less willing, in the wake of J.R.R. Tolkien's 'Beowulf: The Monsters and the Critics,' to identify the poem as an epic, some of the impetus for an early date was lost.[6]

Yet one feature of oral composition did survive this critical shift away from reading *Beowulf* as an epic. Scholars who wished to maintain an early date for *Beowulf* found it useful to assume a long interval of circulation for the poem between the time it was composed and the time it was written down in manuscript. Like the people they study, Anglo-Saxonists have tended to relate the value of a text to its antiquity: wisdom comes with age, as the meanings of the Old English word *frod* instruct us. No one surveying this debate should discount what Roberta Frank identifies as the 'emotional commitment' of past scholars to an early date.[7] More recently, especially through the work of Kevin S. Kiernan, the orthodoxy of an early date for the poem has been challenged much as was the orthodoxy of its oral-formulaic origin.[8] In ways that would have been unimaginable as recently as the 1970s, none of the contributors to this volume explores the dating of *Beowulf* through the machinery of oral-formulaic theory. On the contrary, the undercurrent in these essays is that *Beowulf* as we know it is a written text with, quite probably, an identifiable moment of composition.

Arguing the written status of *Beowulf* is not, however, at all the same as demonstrating that it had a set meaning throughout the Anglo-Saxon period. Textuality does not fix meaning in an overdetermined or deadening manner, despite what some idealizers of oral composition would have us believe. Instead we must recognize that any inscription of *Beowulf* in a manuscript creates a new context for the poem and thus shifts the grounds for its interpretation. As a result, the poem's status in a

5. Colin Chase addresses this matter in his 'Opinions on the Date of *Beowulf*, 1815–1980' pp. 3–4 of this volume.
6. J.R.R. Tolkien, 'Beowulf: The Monsters and the Critics,' PBA 22 (1936), pp. 245–95.
7. Roberta Frank, 'Skaldic Verse and the Date of *Beowulf*,' p. 123 of this volume.
8. Kevin S. Kiernan, 'The Eleventh-Century Origin of *Beowulf* and the *Beowulf* Manuscripts,' pp. 9–21 of this volume; see also his *Beowulf and the Beowulf Manuscript* (New Brunswick, N.J. 1981; rprt. with Foreword by Katherine O'Brien O'Keeffe, Ann Arbor 1996); and 'The Legacy of Wiglaf: Saving a Wounded *Beowulf*,' in *Beowulf: Basic Readings*, ed. Baker, pp. 195–218.

manuscript as textuality rather than orality must be recognized as decisive by the interpreter. This new position in Old English studies is well articulated by Carol Braun Pasternack, who closes her *The Textuality of Old English Poetry* by arguing that the manuscript version of a poem is not merely a mechanical transcription of a previously composed work: 'we should consider the extant texts of Old English poetry as treating issues of concern contemporary to the era of their manuscript production.'[9]

It may well be a healthy corrective to the excess of oral-formulaic theory that none of the contributors in *The Dating of Beowulf* articulates a gradualist creation for the poem: that is, none suggests that its text grew through a slow process of accretion as it passed orally from one generation to the next until it achieved a form something like that recorded in Cotton Vitellius A.XV. In 'The Eleventh-Century Origin of *Beowulf* and the *Beowulf* Manuscript,' Kiernan argues for the joining of two distinct poems about a figure known as Beowulf sometime after c. 1016, but he does so without recourse to oral-formulaic theory: 'Palaeography and codicology, in any case, do not support the theory that the *Beowulf* manuscript is a late copy of an early poem. On the contrary, they support the view that *Beowulf* is an eleventh-century composite poem, and that the *Beowulf* manuscript is a draft, the archetype of the epic as we now have it.'[1] His claim that *Beowulf* was written at or very close to the time when it was written down in the manuscript, in the years after Knut came to the English throne in 1016, brings us much closer to our own literary climate in which poets like Stevens publish their poems shortly after writing them. It would thus follow in Kiernan's argument that *Beowulf*, with its evocation of a Danish past, had a precise political and poetic function to play in a Danish-ruled England that it would not have had in an earlier period when lines of political and cultural allegiance were drawn less starkly or at least with less insistent reference to the overseas connection.

Arguments about the date of *Beowulf* are thus also arguments about the circulation the poem may have enjoyed in Anglo-Saxon England. The closer a date to Cotton Vitellius A.XV that one offers for the composition of the poem, the less time it would have had to circulate, and thus, arguably, the less cultural work it could have accomplished in the interval. Conversely, the more compelling a case one wishes to argue for the poem's epic centrality, the earlier a date one would presumably be likely to offer. Remembering these competing visions for the function of poetry in Anglo-Saxon England, one can understand why reputable scholars have dated *Beowulf* anywhere from (roughly) 675 to 1025, a span of some 350 years. The embarrassment, even the scandal of Old English scholarship is not merely that we have no accepted date for *Beowulf* but that we

---

9. Carol Braun Pasternack, *The Textuality of Old English Poetry* (Cambridge 1995), p. 200.
1. Kiernan, 'The Eleventh-Century Origin,' p. 20 of this volume.

cannot even agree on a century. Roy Michael Liuzza offers a disturbing comparison for our critical uncertainty:

> Without a doubt, the date of *Beowulf* matters; imagine the confusion that would result if some critics placed *Paradise Lost* in the late seventeenth century, others in the early sixteenth, still others in the middle of the nineteenth, and viewed Milton variously as a contemporary of Wyatt, Pope, or Tennyson.[2]

Perhaps all that saves us from the interpretive anarchy envisioned by Liuzza is that Anglo-Saxonists have not only no date for our *Paradise Lost* (*Beowulf*) but also no dates for, as it were, our Wyatts, Popes, or Tennysons (e.g., the poets of *Deor, The Seafarer,* or *Exodus*). In this larger context, the problem of unknown dates becomes less of a source of confusion than in Liuzza's scenario about a *Paradise Lost* stranded undatably within the ineluctable chronological march of English poetry.

Liuzza's telling observation also prompts one to speculate that our desire to date *Beowulf* precisely has been shaped, as well as preserved, by our practice of reading it within the otherwise chronologically secure tradition of English literature. We may argue about which of Chaucer's *Canterbury Tales* were written in the late 1380s or the early 1390s, or about which of Shakespeare's plays were written early rather than late in the 1590s, but these are uncertainties of a relatively few years and do not seem as disconcerting as the uncertainty of centuries we face with *Beowulf*. Indeed, the problem of its date might seem less troublesome to us as readers if we were to remove *Beowulf* from the chronological frame of this tradition, especially as it has been maintained by undergraduate anthologies.

A reader, especially one who learned to love *Beowulf* after reading it in a standard survey course, might well ask if there is any reason for scholars to date *Beowulf* so variously. Is the nature of the evidence so malleable that it can yield such widely divergent results? For not only is the period from 675 to 1025 a very long stretch of time, it also constitutes about three-quarters of the period traditionally labelled Anglo-Saxon (600–1100). One might answer this question by quoting Emerson's aphorism: 'If I know your sect I anticipate your argument.' That is, from the type of evidence offered, one can predict a scholar's dating of *Beowulf*. In general terms, the more closely one works with the language and meter, the more likely one is to date the poem early. Conversely, the more closely one works with the manuscript, the more likely one is to date the poem late.[3]

---

2. Liuzza, 'On the Dating of *Beowulf*,' p. 283.
3. For a recent study that works with language and meter to argue an early date for *Beowulf*, see R.D. Fulk, *A History of Old English Meter* (Philadelphia 1992), especially pp. 348–92. For the relation between manuscript study and a late date for *Beowulf*, see the studies cited in n. 8 above. See also Angus Cameron et al., 'A Reconsideration of the Language of *Beowulf*,' pp. 33–75 of

Perhaps the only generalization about the dating of *Beowulf* I would hazard is that the evidence one chooses will shape, even predetermine, one's findings. The situation of those who argue from historical evidence may seem rather different because they have offered a very wide range of dates for the poem. Yet one can still observe that the type of historical evidence adduced will usually determine the date offered for the poem. If one reads the poem through other depictions of Germanic tribes before the conversion to Christianity, one will probably date it early. If one reads it as a treatise on rulership, one will probably relate it to some exemplary Anglo-Saxon king, such as Offa or Alfred the Great.[4] If one seizes on the poem's flattering (or at least not overtly hostile) depiction of the Danes, then one might well argue it was written very late in the period.

These generalizations can, of course, be complicated or refuted by other examples. What seems less open to contradiction is the further claim that almost every scholar who has pursued the date of *Beowulf* has chosen to do so largely from a single perspective: that of language, or social institutions, or manuscript (to cite only the three most common). While *Beowulf* scholars are usually scrupulous about admitting counter-examples from within their own type of evidence, they have been less willing to consider opposing or complicating factors from other types of evidence. Those who pursue the linguistic approach rarely engage with those who pursue the manuscript approach, and vice-versa. And those who pursue the historical approach, broadly defined, are usually reluctant to engage the technical aspects of language and manuscript study. If there is to be a persuasive case for the poem's date, it will of necessity draw from and synthesize these various kinds of evidence. As the current debate demonstrates to anyone who can maintain even a minimal distance, any monocausal argument for the date of *Beowulf* is inevitably weakened because it does not refute or otherwise accommodate arguments based on different but equally legitimate types of evidence. Only if we believe a priori that one category of evidence is more compelling than all others can we accept a monocausal argument. If that turns out to be the case, then there is further evidence for my claim that most debates about *Beowulf* are arguments in shadow about how we are to do Old English studies.

Rereading the essays brought together in *The Dating of Beowulf* some fifteen years after their original publication has the great value of reminding us that the central monument of this poetic corpus—on which rests most critical claims for the value of the language and its poetry and thus for the place of the discipline within the scholarly and academic world—

---

this volume; and Thomas Cable, 'Metrical Style as Evidence for the Date of *Beowulf*,' pp. 77–82 of this volume.

4. On these issues, see further Alexander Callander Murray, '*Beowulf*, the Danish Invasions, and Royal Genealogy,' pp. 101–11 of this volume.

has no fixed basis in time or place. The most immediate contribution that *The Dating of Beowulf* made to Old English studies was to destroy the illusion that there was substantial evidence for the then-current consensus about the poem's date. That this collection has effected a deep change in our way of thinking as a discipline is vividly signalled by the differences between the first and second editions of the standard history of Old English literature. Writing in 1965, Stanley B. Greenfield rehearsed the critical consensus of the time: 'Whether the *Beowulf* as we have it was orally composed or not—and I incline to the latter view—a written text in the Anglian or Mercian dialect probably existed by the middle of the eighth century.' Some twenty-one years later, and after the influence of the Chase collection had been registered, Greenfield and his co-author, Daniel G. Calder, could only make this observation: 'The early consensus on dating, that *Beowulf*, a poem of Mercian or Northumbrian origin, was fixed in its present form by the eighth century and then transmitted through one or more scribal copies to its present manuscript, has crumbled. Various linguistic, historical and esthetic arguments suggest dates of composition from the late eighth through the early eleventh century.[5]

Ten years after Greenfield and Calder spoke with a hint of despair about a consensus that had crumbled, we can speak more persuasively about the uses of uncertainty. The most profound contribution made by *The Dating of Beowulf* to Old English studies in general has been to introduce a vital and stringent uncertainty into a discipline that for too long proceeded comfortably in the belief that certainty was itself a marker of critical value. Yet with this sense of uncertainty comes as well the recognition that it makes for a difficult and potentially self-contradictory critical practice. If, as I argue elsewhere, the dominant and persistent critical method in Old English studies has been historicist in one variety or another, how then can one work on a poetry that has no accepted chronology or even sequence?[6] To put it bluntly, how can one be a historicist if one cannot conclusively date *Beowulf* within the span of three centuries?

One answer to this question, though not a very happy one, is to follow those general handbooks on the subject that imply Anglo-Saxon England enjoyed a degree of cultural consistency during these centuries sufficient to allow one to date the poem at any moment within that duration.[7] A stasis of 300 years is, however, a very long claim to make, even if one believes Anglo-Saxon England to have been a dark age. Another answer, more complicated and perhaps more satisfying, is to suggest there is a his-

---

5. Stanley B. Greenfield, *A Critical History of Old English Literature* (New York 1965), p. 82; Stanley B. Greenfield and Daniel G. Calder, *A New Critical History of Old English Literature* (New York 1986), p. 136. At the conclusion of this quotation, Greenfield and Calder add a note citing *The Dating of Beowulf.* I follow Liuzza in making this comparison.
6. Nicholas Howe, 'Historicist Approaches' in *Reading Old English Texts*, ed. Katherine O'Brien O'Keeffe (Cambridge 1997), pp. 79–100.
7. For a valuable counter-argument to this assumption, see Colin Chase, 'Saints' Lives, Royal Lives, and the Date of *Beowulf*,' pp. 161–71 of this volume, especially p. 168.

toricism that can accomodate this problem because it is not completely invested in locating and dating a work, but instead defines its critical method by articulating the relation between its object of study and its own moment. In other words, one might envision a historicism that takes as its central issue this matter of historical understanding. Liuzza has noted that this situation makes our critical practice formalist despite our historicist allegiances; as he puts it with epigrammatic force: 'any approach to *Beowulf* is of necessity not documentary but monumental.'[8]

This claim that we search for meaning in forms of expression, in the text itself, because we remain in such uncertainty about the context of the work is compelling, and damaging to a strict historicist position. Yet there can be in the techniques of formalism, in its struggle with language and figuration, ways to apprehend a text's cultural and historical position. Formalism can become something more than a description of the text as verbal artefact; it can also be an interpretive method to engage historical questions. The insight offered by the art historian Michael Baxandall that 'the *style* of pictures is a proper material of social history'[9] can be translated to a poetic canon, especially one that has certain set forms of metrical, verbal, and figural expression. The traditional moves of formalist practice can, when revived by a theoretically informed historicism, yield evidence about the thematics and thus the historical situation of Old English poems. The danger, of course, is that the critic will employ style as others employ historical context: not as the material of history but as the key that alone will unlock the chronology of all Old English poetry.[1]

There is perhaps only one critical assumption shared by all parties to this debate about dating, though it remains largely implicit: that once we fix the date of *Beowulf* with reasonable exactness. our interpretive difficulties will resolve themselves. This claim seems most immediately evident of the late-daters: if the poem's composition in its current form should be dated after 1016 then its function as pro-Danish propaganda seems to impose a self-evident reading on the poem. Yet one must resist the assumption that a firm date for *Beowulf* will settle any or all of our interpretive difficulties. To belabour the obvious, there are many texts in English about which critics disagree in every particular—except their dates of publication. *Moll Flanders* (1722), *The Rime of the Ancient*

---

8. Liuzza, 'On the Dating of *Beowulf*,' p. 295. For fundamental discussions on the relations between formalism and historicism, see Hayden White, *Tropics of Discourse: Essays in Cultural Criticism* (Baltimore 1978), especially chapter 4; and Dominick LaCapra, *Soundings in Critical Theory* (Ithaca 1989).
9. Michael Baxandall, *Painting and Experience in Fifteenth-Century Italy*, 2nd ed. (Oxford and New York 1988), p. v.
1. In this regard, it is salutary to reread Ashley Crandall Amos, *Linguistic Means of Determining the Dates of Old English Literary Texts* (Cambridge, Mass. 1980) for its cautionary tales about scholars who claimed to have found the key to dating Old English poetic texts. For a recent news report on such a scholar, see John Dugdale, 'Who's Afraid of Beowulf?' *The New Yorker*, 23 & 30 December 1996, pp. 50–2. This account of David Howlett's dating of *Beowulf* in the Alfredian period appears in a special issue of *The New Yorker* devoted to fiction.

Mariner (1798), *The Adventures of Huckleberry Finn* (1884), *Heart of Darkness* (1902), and *Ulysses* (1922) are just a few works of known date that have yielded radically divergent interpretations. To have the date of *Beowulf* would be useful in itself and also as a corrective to its misuse as historical evidence; but in the absence of such knowledge we must not overestimate its value. Having the date of *Beowulf* would not in itself resolve any of our interpretive problems because they must be traced as much to our own cultural moment as to the historical milieu of the poem. In fact, this quest for the date of *Beowulf* shows at times a touch of the interpretive error that has flawed much historicist criticism of Old English poetry: namely, the belief that we know enough about Anglo-Saxon England to know how our interpretation of the poem would be affected by the fact that it was datable to 725 or 895 or 1025. And, to press this claim harder, we must resist attributing to Anglo-Saxon England at any given date—725 or 895 or 1025—a cultural homogeneity that would make our work easier but which is otherwise unwarranted. To know the date of a poem is not the same as to know the contexts that date might provide.

At the risk of seeming merely paradoxical, one can suggest that our interpretive work with *Beowulf* would become more difficult the more exactly we could date it. Thus, for example, if it is late and written in an England under Danish occupation, is it an encomium of the continental Danes and thus flattery of their descendants, the occupiers of the island? Or, more problematically, is it meant to chasten the occupying Danes into some recognition of their shared ancestry and thus commonality with the Anglo-Saxon English they have conquered and oppressed? Or, if the poem was written as a primer for princes in Alfredian England, what was its lesson? That a young Anglo-Saxon prince should follow Hrothgar's injunctions to the young Beowulf? Or that the young Christian prince should understand that Beowulf's pagan virtues as manifested by the crisis at Hrothgar's court are admirable but fatally limited? Chronology, no matter how precisely measured, never yields only a single context.

All this said, where do we stand today in 1997 with the dating of *Beowulf*? The reader can choose a date for the poem from among the possibilities argued in these essays as well as in other sources. To decide on a date for *Beowulf* is certainly possible, especially as it allows one to recognize that any date is also implicitly a theory about the poem's composition, circulation, and meaning. Alternatively, one might decide that all one can do is adopt, as I once did, the engaging (though somewhat obscurantist) scepticism of Alain Renoir: 'I readily confess that I should be at a loss to tell when, where, by whom, and under what circumstances, this greatest of all early-Germanic epics was composed.'[2] Or one might

2. Alain Renoir, 'Old English Formulas and Themes as Tools for Contextual Interpretation,' in Phyllis Rugg Brown, et al., ed., *Modes of Interpretation in Old English Literature: Essays in Honour of Stanley B. Greenfield* (Toronto 1986), 65–79, at p. 68. One might note, somewhat scep-

end by suggesting that while we may never know the date of *Beowulf* we should keep asking the question because it has been for generations, and seems likely to remain so, a powerful means for thinking about the poem. If we hold to this position, then it follows we should also entertain the possibility that there was never a single, commonly accepted reading in Anglo-Saxon England of this poem we call *Beowulf*. Instead, as is typical of complex texts, we should accept the likelihood that for as long as people knew the poem in Old English there may have been different, possibly contradictory readings of the poem—even among those who lived at the same time and in the same place. Our anxiety as scholars who work in a time of interpretive multiplicity should not lead us to imagine nostalgically that Anglo-Saxon England was a haven of certainty for readers. To quote Stevens one last time, from 'The Poems of our Climate' (1938), his meditation on the 'flawed words and stubborn sounds' of poetry: 'the imperfect is our paradise.' Our sense of the past and its poetry should honor the same possibilities for subtlety, contingency, and contradiction we admit in our time.

To have a date for *Beowulf* would simply allow us to begin in another way our work of interpretation.

---

tically, that Renoir's critical approach in this essay certainly sits better with an early than a late date for *Beowulf*. In that sense, his claim to not know the date of the poem should not be taken as meaning that he had no opinion (implicit, in this case, I would suggest) about the matter. For my use of Renoir as a defensive maneouver, see *Migration and Mythmaking in Anglo-Saxon England* (New Haven 1989), p. 177, n. 38. If I were writing that note today, I would be more hesitant to quote Renoir though I would still refrain from offering a date for *Beowulf*.

Glossary of Proper Names

Parenthetical page references are to the Donaldson translation, used in this Norton Critical Edition.

Abel. Son of Adam and Eve, murdered by his brother, Cain (5). See Genesis 4:1–8.

Aelfhere. Probably a Scylfing; kinsman of Wiglaf (44).

Aeschere. A Dane, Yrmenlaf's elder brother (24); favored retainer, battle-companion, and counselor of Hrothgar; Grendel's mother kills him and leaves his head near the mere for Beowulf and the Danes to find (23–25, 36).

Battle-Bright. Sword of Hunlaf the Half-Dane, who like his lord, Hnaef, is killed in battle by the Frisians (21, note 6).

Beanstan. A Bronding, father of the young Beowulf's swimming rival, Breca (11).

Beow. Successful Danish king, son of Scyld Scefing, father of Healfdene, and Hrothgar's grandfather (3–4).

Beowulf. His father was Ecgtheow, his mother daughter of the Geatish king, Hrethel, and sister of Hygelac; hero of the poem.

Breca. A Bronding, son of Beanstan; he competes with the young Beowulf in a swimming match (11).

Brondings. The tribe of Breca and his father, Beanstan (11).

Brosings. Perhaps the fire-dwarfs of Norse mythology, they made a famous necklace worn by the goddess Freya, which Hama later stole from the Gothic king, Eormenric (22).

Cain. Son of Adam and Eve; murderer of his brother, Abel; and in our poem, evil ancestor of trolls, elves, and monsters such as Grendel and his mother (5, 23). See Genesis 4:1–17.

Daeghrefn. Beowulf kills this standard-bearer of the Hugas tribe in the same battle in which Hygelac dies (42).

Danes. Tribe of Hrothgar; also called Bright-, East-, North-, Ring-, Spear-, and West-Danes; or Scyldings ("sons or followers of Scyld"), Victor-Scyldings; genealogy (3–4); Heremod's Danish followers are called South-Danes, Honor-Scyldings, or sons of Ecgwela (17, 30); Hnaef's men are called Half-Danes or War-Scyldings; the phrase "Ing's friends" (24) seems to apply only to Hrothgar's tribe.

Eadgils. Son of Ohthere, he is a Scylfing (Swedish) prince and brother of Eanmund; Beowulf helps him win the Swedish throne from his uncle, the usurper Onela, whom Eadgils kills (40).

Eanmund. Scylfing (Swedish) prince, son of Ohthere and brother of Eadgils; he is killed by order of his uncle, the usurper Onela, together with the Geatish king Heardred (Hygelac's son), who had given him refuge (40, note 7); Weohstan, Onela's follower, actually kills Eanmund, and his son, Wiglaf, later uses Eanmund's sword to help Beowulf kill the dragon (44).

Earnaness. "Cape of the Eagles," the headland near where Beowulf fights the dragon (50).

Ecglaf. A Dane, father of Hrothgar's court spokesman, Unferth (11).

Ecgtheow. Beowulf's father, husband of the sister of the Geatish king Hygelac (7); after Ecgtheow kills the Wylfing Heatholaf, Hrothgar gives him refuge and pays the *wergild* (6, note 7) to the Wylfings in his behalf (10); Ecgtheow's exact tribal descent is uncertain; he seems to be a Geat more by marriage and other affiliations than by birth.

Ecgwela. An early Danish king, ancestor of Heremod's South-Danes or Honor-Scyldings (30).

Eofor. A Geat, son of Wonred; he is part of Hygelac's force that arrives too late to prevent Haethcyn's defeat and death in the battle with the Swedes at Ravenswood; Hygelac's army pursues the Swedish king Ongentheow to his citadel; after Ongentheow wounds Eofor's brother, Wulf, Eofor kills Ongentheow and Hygelac rewards him with his daughter's hand (42, 49).

Eomer. Son of the fourth-century continental Angle king, Offa; kinsman of Hemming; and grandson of Garmund (33).

Eormenric. Gothic king from whom Hama stole the legendary Brosing necklace (22); Eormenric lived in the late fourth century and figures greatly in Germanic heroic legend.

Finn. Son of Folcwalda; Frisian (Jutish) king; and husband of Hildeburh, sister of the Half-Dane king Hnaef; Finn and his men kill Hnaef at Finnesburg, and Finn is later defeated and killed there by Hnaef's follower, Hengest (19–22).

Finnesburg. The stronghold of Finn, king of the Frisians (Jutes) (19–22).

Fitela. Nephew of Sigemund, the dragon-killer (17); probably the Sinfjötli of Norse mythology.

Folcwalda. Father of the Frisian (Jutish) king Finn (20).

Franks. A powerful West German people living near the Rhine River who conquered Gaul about 500 C.E.; they included the Hugas and Hetwares, who with their Frisian (Jutish) allies defeated the Geatish king Hygelac about 520 C.E. (22, 42, 48).

Freawaru. Danish princess, daughter of Hrothgar; she will be married to Ingeld, the Heatho-Bard king, in what Beowulf describes to Hygelac as an abortive attempt to abate the bloody feud between the two tribes (34–35).

Friesland. Land of the Frisians (Jutes) (21).

Frisians (Jutes). Finn's tribe (19–22); allies of the Franks who defeat and kill Hygelac (22, 40).

Froda. Heatho-Bard king, Ingeld's father (34); he was probably killed early in the Danish–Heatho-Bard feud.

Garmund. Father of King Offa the Angle (33).

Geats (War-, Weather-, Sea-). Tribe dwelling in southern Sweden, ruled successively by Hrethel, Haethcyn, Hygelac, Heardred, and Beowulf; the Scylfings (Swedes), who lived to their north, were their deadly enemies.

Gifthas. An East Germanic tribe mentioned by Beowulf as a usual source of mercenaries (42).

Grendel. A cannibalistic monster who ravages Heorot and Hrothgar's Danes by night for twelve years; his name perhaps means "grinder"; an evil descendant of the murderer Cain (5), he is killed by Beowulf (14–16), who later cuts off his head after disposing of his mother (28–29).

Guthlaf. A Half-Dane, he and his brother Oslaf, desiring revenge for their brother, Hunlaf, urge Hengest to turn on Finn (21, note 6).

Haereth. Father of Hygd, Hygelac's queen (33).

Haethcyn. Geatish prince, son of Hrethel; and elder brother of Hygelac; he accidentally kills his brother Herebeald and becomes king after their father, Hrethel, dies of grief; he is later killed in battle by the Scylfings (Swedes) at Ravenswood, and Hygelac then becomes king of the Geats (41–42).

Halga. Danish prince, son of Healfdene elder brother of Hrothgar, and father of Hrothulf (4).

Hama. Perhaps a Dane, he stole the precious Brosing necklace from the Gothic king Eormenric (22).

Healfdene. Danish king; son of Beow; and father of Heorogar, Halga, Hrothgar, and an unnamed daughter who marries Onela the Swede (4).

Heardred. Geatish king, son of Hygelac and Hygd, and nephew of Hereric (perhaps Hygd's brother); after Hygelac's death he becomes king (40) and is later killed in battle by the Scylfing (Swedish) usurper, Onela, whereupon Beowulf succeeds him (37–38).

Heatho-Bards. Germanic tribe dwelling probably on the South Baltic coast; ruled by Froda and later by his son, Ingeld, to whom Hrothgar will marry his daughter, Freawaru, in an attempt to abate the deadly feud that results in the destruction of Heorot (35–36; 4, note 3).

Heatholaf. A Wylfing killed by Beowulf's father, Ecgtheow; Hrothgar pays the Wylfings Heatholaf's *wergild* (6, note 7) on Ecgtheow's behalf (10).

Heathoraemas. Tribe dwelling where Breca swims ashore after his swimming match with the young Beowulf (11).

Helmings. Tribe of Wealhtheow, Hrothgar's queen (13).

Hemming. Kin or forebear of the fourth-century continental Angle king Offa (33).

Hengest. A Half-Dane who succeeds Hnaef, whom he later revenges by killing Finn (20–21); he may be the same Hengest who traditionally was among the first Germanic mercenaries to arrive in England ca. 449 C.E.

Heorogar. Hrothgar's elder brother whom he succeeds as king of the Danes; the grateful Hrothgar gives his armor to Beowulf, who gives it to Hygelac (4, 10, 37).

Heorot. Means "hart"; elaborate Danish hall built by Hrothgar; construction, foreshadowing of its destruction by Ingeld (4–5); Grendel's first attack (5); Beowulf's arrival (8); Beowulf's fight with Grendel (14–16); Grendel's mother's attack (23–24); for the significance of the hart or stag, see William A. Chaney, *The Cult of Kingship in Anglo-Saxon England* (Berkeley: U of California P, 1970),130–32.

Heoroweard. Danish prince, son of Hrothgar's elder brother, Heorogar (37); it is not mentioned in *Beowulf*, but Heoroweard will defeat Hrothulf and become king after Hrothulf kills Hrothgar's son and heir, Hrethric.

Herebeald. Son of King Hrethel the Geat and brother of Hygelac; accidentally killed by his other brother, Haethcyn, in an archery match (41) a contrasted version of the Cain-Abel story.

Heremod. Early ruler of the South-Danes (Honor-Scyldings); a prototype of the evil king, he kills rather than rewards his companions (30) and then seeks refuge among the Jutes, who kill him (17).

Hereric. A Geat perhaps; Hygd's brother possibly; uncle of Hygelac's son, Heardred (37).

Hetware. Frankish tribe allied with the Hugas and Frisians when they defeat Hygelac and his Geats (40, 48).

Hildeburh. Daughter of the early Danish king Hoc and sister of Hnaef; her husband, Finn, king of the Frisians (Jutes), is killed by Hnaef's follower, Hengest (19–21).

Hnaef. King of the Half-Danes, son of Hoc and brother of Hildeburh; killed by Finn and his Frisians (Jutes) (20–21).

Hoc. Early Danish king, father of Hnaef and Hildeburh (20–21).

Hondscioh. One of fourteen Geats who accompany Beowulf to Hrothgar's court; killed by Grendel (14, 35).

Hreosnabeorh. Geatish area raided by the Swedish king Ongentheow and his sons prior to their defeat at Ravenswood (42).

Hrethel. Geatish king; son of Swerting; father of Herebeald, Haethcyn, Hygelac, and Beowulf's mother; grandfather and guardian of Beowulf, whom he raises from age 7 (9, 41); dies of grief after his son Haethcyn accidentally kills his own brother Herebeald (41–42).

Hrethric. Danish prince, son of Hrothgar and Wealtheow, and brother of Hrothmund (22, 32).

Hronesness. "Cape of the Whale," the site of Beowulf's funeral pyre (52).

Hrothgar. Danish king; son of Healfdene; brother of Heorogar, Halga, and the wife of Onela the Swede; father of Hrethric, Hrothmund, and Freawaru; builds Heorot (4); rewards Beowulf (19, 32); gives Beowulf advice ("Hrothgar's Sermon") (29–31); plans to betroth his daughter, Freawaru, to Ingeld, the Heatho-Bard (34–36).

Hrothmund. Danish prince, son of Hrothgar and Wealhtheow, and younger brother of Hrethric (22).

Hrothulf. A Dane, son of Hrothgar's brother Halga (22); the cousin of Hrothgar's sons, Hrethric and Hrothmund, he will later kill Hrethric after Hrothgar's death and be defeated and slain in turn by Heoroweard, his cousin, son of Hrothgar's elder brother, Heorogar (37).

Hrunting. Sword Unferth lends Beowulf for use against Grendel's mother; despite its heroic pedigree it, like Unferth, is little help against monster (26–29), but the characteristically magnanimous Beowulf later thanks Unferth for its use (31).

Hugas. Frankish tribe; in alliance with the Hetware and Frisians they defeat and kill Hygelac; Beowulf kills their hero, Daeghrefn (42, 48).

Hunlaf. Danish warrior, brother of Guthlaf and Oslaf, killed in Hnaef's fight with the Frisians (21).

Hygd. Geatish queen, daughter of Haereth, wife of Hygelac, and mother of Heardred (33); Beowulf gives her the necklace Hrothgar gave him (37); she offers Beowulf the kingdom after Hygelac dies (40).

Hygelac. Grandson of Swerting (22), son of Hrethel, and king of the Geats; Beowulf's uncle and lord and husband of Hygd (33), he dies in defeat at the hands of the Franks and others during an aggressive expedition (22, 40); gives Beowulf Hrethel's sword (37) and dies wearing the necklace Beowulf got from Hrothgar (22).

Ing. Legendary Danish king (19).

Ingeld. Son of Froda and king of the Heatho-Bards (34); Hrothgar will attempt to abate the deadly feud between Danes and Heatho-Bards by giving Ingeld his daughter, Freawaru, in marriage; Beowulf predicts that the plan will fail (34–35), and the *Beowulf* poet also alludes to this (4, note 3).

Jutes. Or Frisians, ruled by Finn (19–20); they and their allies, long after Finn's death, defeat and kill Hygelac (22, 40); the evil Danish king, Heremod, dies among them, perhaps in exile (17).

Merewioing. Merovingian, or Frankish (48).

Modthryth. A queen contrasted with Hygd (33); probably the wife of Offa the Angle, famed fourth-century continental king.

Naegling. Sword used by Beowulf to kill the Hugas hero, Daeghrefn, at Hygelac's defeat (42); it is useless, however, against the dragon (45).

Offa. Fourth-century continental Angle king, son of Garmund, father of Eomer, and husband of Modthryth (33). A theory is that *Beowulf* was composed at the court of the famous Anglo-Saxon king Offa of Mercia (reigned 757–96 C.E.), a descendant of the Offa praised here.

Ohthere. Scylfing (Swedish) king, son of Ongentheow, and brother of Onela, who usurps the throne from Ohthere's sons, Eanmund and Eadgils (40).

Onela. Swedish (Scylfing) king, husband of Hrothgar's sister (4); he usurps the throne from Eanmund and Eadgils, sons and heirs of, his elder brother, Ohthere, and slays Heardred, whereupon Beowulf becomes king of the Geats; he is later defeated and slain by Beowulf and Ohthere's son Eadgils (40).

Ongentheow. Swedish (Scylfing) king, father of Ohthere and Onela (34); he defeats and kills Haethcyn near Ravenswood (49) and is shortly afterward defeated by Hygelac and killed by Eofor (49).

Oslaf. A Half-Dane and brother of Hunlaf and Guthlaf (21, note 6).

Ravenswood. Stronghold of the Swedish king Ongentheow; site of the famous battle between Geats and Swedes wherein first Haethcyn and then Ongentheow are slain (42, 49–50).

Scyldings. The Danes, descendants of Scyld (3); also called Honor-Scyldings (i.e., Heremod's tribe, the South-Danes), Victor-Scyldings, and War-Scyldings (Hnaef's tribe, the Half-Danes).

Scyld Scefing. Legendary founder of the Danish (Scylding) royal line, great-grandfather of Hrothgar (3–4).

Scylfings. The Swedes, possibly descendants of Scylf (Battle-Scylfing, 4; Heatho-Scylfings, War-Scylfings, 49).

Sigemund. A legendary hero and dragon-killer, son of Waels (16–17).

Swedes. Also called Scylfings; traditional enemies of the Geats.

Swerting. Early Geatish king, grandfather of Hygelac (22).

Unferth. A Dane, son of Ecglaf and retainer of Hrothgar; taunts Beowulf (11); lends his sword, Hrunting, to Beowulf (26).

Waegmundings. Geatish family to which both Wiglaf (44, 47) and Beowulf (47) belong.

Waels. Father of Sigemund, the hero and dragon-killer (16).

Wealhtheow. A Helming; Danish queen, wife of Hrothgar and mother of Hrethric and Hrothmund (12–13); asks Beowulf's support for her sons if Hrothgar dies (21–22).

Weland. Norse god of the forge, an artificer, and maker of the mail-shirt Beowulf receives from his grandfather, King Hrethel (10).

Wendels. Tribe of Wulfgar, Hrothgar's officer and herald (9); probably the Vandals of Sweden or Jutland.

Weohstan. A Scylfing (Swede), retainer of Onela, slayer of Eanmund, and father of Wiglaf (44).

Wiglaf. Like Beowulf, a Waegmunding, he helps his lord slay the dragon (44–52); son of the Scylfing Weohstan.

Withergeld. A Heatho-Bard leader, follower of King Froda, he is slain early in the feud with the Danes (35).

Wonred. A Geat, father of Wulf and Eofor, heroes of the Battle of Ravenswood (49).

Wulf. A Geat, son of Wonred and brother of Eofor; he is wounded by Ongentheow at Ravenswood (49).

Wulfgar. Herald and officer of the Danish king Hrothgar (9–10); he is not a Dane, but a Wendel (Vandal).

Wylfings. The tribe of Heatholaf, whom Beowulf's father, Ecgtheow, kills (10).

Yrmenlaf. Younger brother of Hrothgar's beloved counselor, Aeschere, the Dane killed by Grendel's mother (24).

Selected Bibliography

The number of studies published each year on *Beowulf* has grown remarkably during the last two or three decades. As a result, the bibliography offered here can point to only a few of the most useful and important works. The bibliographies cited in the first section below will lead to additional studies on all aspects of the poem. For guidance in working through the mass of available materials, I strongly suggest that readers consult the excellent *Beowulf Handbook*, edited by Robert E. Bjork and John D. Niles (listed below under "Handbooks and Guides"), where they will find lucid survey essays written by leading scholars.

• indicates works included or excerpted in this Norton Critical Edition.

Bibliographies

Anglo-Saxon England. Cambridge: Cambridge UP, 1972–. This annual contains full bibliographies for the previous year's work on all aspects of Old English literature.

Modern Language Association Annual Bibliography. New York: Modern Language Association, 1921–. This bibliography is available for electronic searches on CD-ROM.

Old English Newsletter. Kalamazoo, MI: Medieval Institute Publications, 1968–. This periodical publishes a complete bibliography of the previous year's work in Old English as well as an invaluable series of evaluative essays on "The Year's Work in Old English Studies."

Greenfield, Stanley, and Fred C. Robinson. *A Bibliography of Publications on Old English Literature from the Beginnings through 1972.* Toronto: U of Toronto P, 1980.

Hasenfratz, Robert J. *Beowulf Scholarship: An Annotated Bibliography, 1979–1990.* New York: Garland, 1993.

———. *A Bibliography of Beowulf Criticism, 1979–94.* Available at www.georgetown.edu /labyrinth/labyrinth-home.html.

Dictionaries

Amos, Ashley Crandell, et al. *The Dictionary of Old English.* Toronto: Pontifical Institute of Medieval Studies, 1989–. This dictionary is being published letter by letter in microform. For letters completed, this is the dictionary to use; for other words, see the entry below. The database for this dictionary is available through site licenses from the University of Michigan Press: www.press.umich.edu.

Bosworth, Joseph, and T. Northcote Toller. *An Anglo-Saxon Dictionary.* Oxford: Oxford UP, 1898. *Supplement* by T. Northcote Toller (1921); *Supplement* by A. Campbell (1972). Although each of the three volumes must be consulted for any given word not yet covered by *The Dictionary of Old English,* this remains the standard dictionary of Old English.

Clark-Hall, John R. *A Concise Anglo-Saxon Dictionary.* 4th ed. With a supplement by Herbert Dean Meritt. 1960 Reprint, Toronto: U of Toronto P, 1984.

Grammars

Campbell, A. *An Old English Grammar.* Oxford: Oxford UP, 1959.

Hogg, Richard M. *A Grammar of Old English, Volume I: Phonology.* Oxford: Blackwell, 1992.

Mitchell, Bruce. *Old English Syntax.* 2 vols. Oxford: Oxford UP, 1985.

Mitchell, Bruce, and Fred C. Robinson. *A Guide to Old English.* 5th ed. Oxford: Blackwell, 1992.

Moore, Samuel, and Thomas A. Knott. *The Elements of Old English*. 10th ed., rev. by James Hulbert. Ann Arbor: Wahr, 1972.

Concordances

Bessinger, Jess B., ed. *A Concordance to the Anglo-Saxon Poetic Records*. Ithaca: Cornell UP, 1978.
Healey, Antonette diPaolo, and Richard Venezky. *A Microfiche Concordance to Old English*. Toronto: Dictionary of Old English, 1980.

Editions

Chickering, Howell D. *Beowulf: A Dual-Language Edition*. New York: Anchor, 1977.
Dobbie, E. V. K. *Beowulf and Judith*. Anglo-Saxon Poetic Records, vol. 4. New York: Columbia UP, 1953.
Jack, George. *Beowulf: A Student Edition*. Oxford: Clarendon, 1994.
Kiernan, Kevin. *The Electronic Beowulf*. A continually evolving electronic edition and resource. Available at www.uky.edu/~kiernan/BL/kportico.html.
Klaeber, Fr. *Beowulf and the Fight at Finnsburg* 3rd ed. Boston: Heath, 1950.
Mitchell, Bruce, and Fred C. Robinson. *Beowulf: An Edition*. Oxford: Blackwell, 1998.
Wrenn, C. L. ed. *Beowulf*. Rev. by W. Bolton. New York: St. Martin's, 1973.
Zupitza, Julius, ed. *Beowulf: Reproduced in Facsimile*. 2nd ed., rev. by N. Davis. Early English Text Society, o.s., 245. London: Oxford UP, 1959

Sources and Analogues

Garmonsway, G. N., et al., eds. *Beowulf and Its Analogues*. New York: Dutton, 1971.

Meter and Versification

Bliss, Alan J. *An Introduction to Old English Metre*. Oxford: Blackwell, 1962.
Fulk, R. D. *A History of Old English Meter*. Philadelphia: U of Pennsylvania P, 1992.
Kendall, Calvin. *The Metrical Grammar of Beowulf*. Cambridge: Cambridge UP, 1991.
Lewis, C. S. "The Alliterative Metre." *Rehabilitations and Other Essays*. London: Oxford UP, 1939. 117–32.
Pope, John C. *The Rhythm of Beowulf*. 2nd ed. New Haven: Yale UP, 1966. Summarized in his *Seven Old English Poems*. New York: Norton, 1984. 97–138.
Russom, Geoffrey. *Old English Meter and Linguistic Theory*. Cambridge: Cambridge UP, 1987.

Translations

Alexander, Michael. *Beowulf*. New York: Penguin, 1973.
Bradley, S. A. J. *Anglo-Saxon Poetry*. London: Everyman, 1982.
Crossley-Holland, Kevin. *The Anglo-Saxon World*. Oxford: Oxford UP, 1984.
Greenfield, Stanley. *A Readable Beowulf*. Carbondale: Southern Illinois UP, 1982.
Heaney, Seamus. *Beowulf: A New Verse Translation*. New York: Farrar, Straus and Giroux, 2000. Also in *The Norton Anthology of English Literature*, 7th ed.
Liuzza, R. M. *Beowulf: A New Verse Translation*. Peterborough: Broadview Press, 2000.
Osborn, Marijane. *Beowulf: A Verse Translation with Treasures of the Ancient North*. Berkeley: U of California P, 1984.
Raffel, Burton. *Beowulf*. New York: Mentor, 1963.
Rebsamen, Frederick. *Beowulf: A Verse Translation*. New York: HarperCollins, 1991.

Handbooks and Guides

Bjork, Robert E., and John D. Niles, eds. *A Beowulf Handbook*. Lincoln: U of Nebraska P, 1997.
Godden, Malcolm, and Michael Lapidge, eds. *The Cambridge Companion to Old English Literature*. Cambridge: Cambridge UP, 1991.
Lapidge, Michael, et al., eds. *The Blackwell Encyclopedia of Anglo-Saxon England*. Oxford: Blackwell, 1999.
Mitchell, Bruce. *An Invitation to Old English and Anglo-Saxon England*. Oxford: Blackwell, 1995.
O'Brien O'Keeffe, Katherine, ed. *Reading Old English Texts*. Cambridge: Cambridge UP, 1997.

Critical Anthologies

Baker, Peter S., ed. *Beowulf: Basic Readings.* New York: Garland, 1995.
Bessinger, Jess B., and Robert F. Yeager, eds., *Approaches to Teaching Beowulf.* New York: Modern Language Association, 1984.
Bloom, Harold, ed. *Beowulf.* New York: Chelsea House, 1987.
Fry, Donald K., ed. *The Beowulf Poet: A Collection of Critical Essays.* Englewood Cliffs, N.J.: Prentice-Hall, 1968.
Fulk, R. D., ed. *Interpretations of Beowulf: A Critical Anthology.* Bloomington: Indiana UP, 1991.
Nicholson, Lewis E., ed. *An Anthology of Beowulf Criticism.* Notre Dame: U of Notre Dame P, 1963.
Shippey, T. A., and Andreas Haarder, eds., *Beowulf: The Critical Heritage.* London: Routledge, 1998.

Critical and Literary Studies, Books

Bonjour, Adrien. *The Digressions in Beowulf.* Oxford: Blackwell, 1965.
Brodeur, Arthur. *The Art of Beowulf.* Berkeley: U of California P, 1959.
Chambers, R. W. *Beowulf: An Introduction to the Study of the Poem.* 3rd ed. Cambridge: Cambridge UP, 1959.
Chance, Jane. *Woman as Hero in Old English Literature.* Syracuse: Syracuse UP, 1986.
Chase, Colin, ed. *The Dating of Beowulf.* 1981. Reprint, Toronto: U of Toronto P, 1997.
Damico, Helen. *Beowulf's Wealhtheow and the Valkyrie Tradition.* Madison: U of Wisconsin P, 1984.
―――, and Alexandra H. Olsen, eds., *New Readings on Women in Old English Literature.* Bloomington: Indiana UP, 1990.
Earl, James. *Thinking About Beowulf.* Stanford: Stanford UP, 1994.
Frantzen, Allen J. *Desire for Origins: New Language, Old English, and Teaching the Tradition.* New Brunswick: Rutgers UP, 1990.
―――. *Before the Closet: Same-Sex Love from Beowulf to Angels in America.* Chicago: U of Chicago P, 1998.
Goldsmith, Margaret. *The Mode and Meaning of Beowulf.* London: Athlone, 1970.
Greenfield, Stanley B., and Daniel G. Calder. *A Critical History of Old English Literature.* New York: New York UP, 1986.
Hill, John M. *The Cultural World in Beowulf.* Toronto: U of Toronto P, 1995.
Howe, Nicholas. *Migration and Mythmaking in Anglo-Saxon England.* New Haven: Yale UP, 1989.
Irving, Edward B. *A Reading of Beowulf.* New Haven: Yale UP, 1968.
―――. *Rereading Beowulf.* Philadelphia: U of Pennsylvania P, 1989.
Jones, Gwyn. *Kings, Beasts and Heroes.* London: Oxford UP, 1972.
Kiernan, Kevin S. *Beowulf and the Beowulf Manuscript.* 1981. Reprint, Ann Arbor: U of Michigan P, 1996.
Lee, Alvin A. *Gold-Hall and Earth-Dragon: Beowulf as Metaphor.* Toronto: U of Toronto P, 1998.
Lerer, Seth. *Literacy and Power in Anglo-Saxon Literature.* Lincoln: U of Nebraska P., 1991.
Magennis, Hugh. *Images of Community in Old English Poetry.* Cambridge: Cambridge UP, 1996.
Niles, John D. *Beowulf: The Poem and Its Traditions.* Cambridge: Harvard UP, 1983.
Orchard, Andy. *Pride and Prodigies: Studies in the Monsters of the Beowulf Manuscript.* Woodbridge: Brewer, 1995.
Overing, Gillian R. *Language, Sign, and Gender in Beowulf.* Carbondale: Southern Illinois UP, 1990.
Pasternack, Carol Braun. *The Textuality of Old English Poetry.* Cambridge: Cambridge UP, 1995.
• Robinson, Fred C. *Beowulf and the Appositive Style.* Knoxville: U of Tennessee P, 1985.
―――. *The Tomb of Beowulf and Other Essays on Old English.* Oxford: Blackwell, 1993.
Shippey, T. A. *Beowulf.* London: Edwin Arnold, 1978.

Critical and Literary Studies, Articles

Andersson, Theodore M. "The Thief in Beowulf." *Speculum* 59 (1984): 493–508.
Baker, Peter S. "Beowulf the Orator." *Journal of English Linguistics* 21 (1988): 3–23.
• Bennett, Helen. "The Female Mourner at Beowulf's Funeral: Filling in the Blanks/Hearing the Spaces." *Exemplaria* 4.1 (1992): 35–50.
Benson, Larry D. "The Pagan Coloring of Beowulf." *Old English Poetry: Fifteen Essays.* Ed. Robert P. Creed. Providence: Brown UP, 1967. 193–213.
Bjork, Robert E. "Speech as Gift in Beowulf." *Speculum* 69 (1994): 993–1022.
Bloomfield, Morton. "Understanding Old English Poetry." *Annuale Mediaevale* 9 (1968): 5–25.
Clover, Carol J. "The Germanic Context of the Unferth Episode." *Speculum* 55 (1980): 444–68.
Desmond, Marilynn. "*Beowulf*: The Monsters and the Tradition." *Oral Tradition* 7 (1992): 258–83.
Donahue, Charles. "*Beowulf* and Christian Tradition: A Reconsideration from a Celtic Stance." *Traditio* 21 (1965): 55–116.

• Frank, Roberta. "The *Beowulf* Poet's Sense of History." *The Wisdom of Poetry: Essays in Early English Literature in Honor of Morton W. Bloomfield*. Ed. Larry D. Benson and Siegfried Wenzel. Kalamazoo, MI: Medieval Institute Publications, 1982. 53–65, 271–77.

Frantzen, Allen J. "Writing the Unreadable *Beowulf*: 'Writan' and 'Forwritan,' The Pen and the Sword," *Exemplaria* 3 (1991): 327–57.

Galloway, Andrew. "*Beowulf* and the Varieties of Choice." *PMLA* 105 (1990): 197–208.

Georgianna, Linda. "King Hrethel's Sorrow and the Limits of Heroic Action in *Beowulf*." *Speculum* 62 (1987): 829–50.

Greenfield, Stanley B. "The Authenticating Voice in *Beowulf*." *Anglo-Saxon England* 5 (1976): 51–62.

Hanning, Robert W. "*Beowulf* as Heroic History." *Medievalia et Humanistica* 5 (1974): 77–102.

Harris, Joseph "Beowulf's Last Words." *Speculum* 67 (1992): 1–32.

• Hill, Joyce. "'Þæt Wæs Geomuru Ides!' A Female Stereotype Examined." *New Readings on Women in Old English Literature*. Ed. Helen Damico and Alexandra Hennessey Olsen. Bloomington: Indiana UP, 1990. 235–47.

• Howe, Nicholas. "The Uses of Uncertainty: On the Dating of *Beowulf*." *The Dating of Beowulf*. Ed. Colin Chase. Toronto: U of Toronto P, 1997. 213–20.

John, Eric. "*Beowulf* and the Margins of Literacy." *Bulletin of the John Rylands Library* 56 (1974): 388–422.

Kaske, R. E. "*Sapientia et Fortitudo* as the Controlling Theme of *Beowulf*." *Studies in Philology* 55 (1958): 423–56.

Kinney, Clare. "The Needs of the Moment: Poetic Foregrounding as a Narrative Device in *Beowulf*." *Studies in Philology* (1985): 295–314.

Lapidge, Michael. "*Beowulf*, Aldhelm, the *Liber Monstrorum* and Wessex." *Studi Medievali*, 3rd ser., 23 (1982): 151–92.

• ———. "*Beowulf* and the Psychology of Terror." *Heroic Poetry in the Anglo-Saxon Period in Honor of Jess B. Besslinger, Jr.* Ed. Helen Damico and John Leyerle. Kalamazoo, MI: Medieval Institute Publications, 1993. 373–402.

Lerer, Seth. "Grendel's Glove." *English Literary History* 61 (1994): 721–51.

Leyerle, John. "The Interlace Structure of *Beowulf*." *University of Toronto Quarterly* 37 (1967): 1–17.

Lionarons, Joyce Tally. "*Beowulf*: Myth and Monsters." *English Studies* 77 (1996): 1–14.

McNamee, M. B. "*Beowulf*: An Allegory of Salvation?" *Journal of English and Germanic Philology* 59 (1960): 190–207.

Near, Michael, R. "Anticipating Alienation: *Beowulf* and the Intrusion of Literacy." *PMLA* 108 (1993): 320–32.

• Niles, John D. "Locating *Beowulf* in Literary History." *Exemplaria* 5 (1993): 79–109.

———. "Reconceiving *Beowulf*: Poetry as Social Praxis." *College English* 61.2 (1998): 143–66.

Osborn, Marijane. "The Great Feud: Scriptural History and Strife in *Beowulf*." *PMLA* 93 (1978): 973–81.

Scowcraft, R. Mark "The Irish Analogues to *Beowulf*." *Speculum* 74 (1999): 22–64.

Stanley, Eric. "*Beowulf*." *Continuations and Beginnings*. Ed. E. G. Stanley. London: Thomas Nelson, 1966, 104–41.

Tolkien, J. R. R. "*Beowulf*: The Monsters and the Critics." *Proceedings of the British Academy* 22 (1936): 245–95.

Welsh, Andrew. "Branwen, *Beowulf*, and the Tragic Peaceweaver Tale." *Viator* 22 (1991): 1–13.

Wormald, Patrick. "Bede, *Beowulf* and the Conversion of the Anglo-Saxon Aristocracy." *Bede and Anglo-Saxon England*. Ed. Robert T. Farrell. Oxford: British Archaeological Reports. 1978 32–95.

Historical and Cultural Studies

Campbell, James, ed. *The Anglo-Saxons*. Ithaca: Cornell UP, 1982.

Carver, Martin. *Sutton Hoo: Burial Ground of Kings?* London: British Museum, 1998.

Dodwell, C. R. *Anglo-Saxon Art*. Ithaca: Cornell UP, 1982.

Fell, Christine. *Women in Anglo-Saxon England*. Oxford: Blackwell, 1984.

Hill, David. *An Atlas of Anglo-Saxon England*. Toronto: U of Toronto P, 1981.

Hunter Blair, Peter. *An Introduction to Anglo-Saxon England*. 2nd ed. Cambridge: Cambridge UP 1977.

Mayr-Harting, Henry. *The Coming of Christianity to England*. University Park: Penn State UP, 1991.

Stenton, Sir Frank M. *Anglo-Saxon England*. 3rd ed. Oxford: Oxford UP, 1971.

Webster, Leslie, and Janet Backhouse. *The Making of England: Anglo-Saxon Art and Culture, AD 600–900*. Toronto: U of Toronto P, 1991.

Whitelock, Dorothy. *The Beginnings of English Society*. New York: Penguin, 1968.

———, ed. *English Historical Documents, c. 500–1042*. 2nd ed. London: Eyre Methuen, 1979.